THE
FEATHER
MEN

Also by Ranulph Fiennes

A Talent for Trouble
Icefall in Norway
Headless Valley
Where Soldiers Fear to Tread
Hell on Ice
To the Ends of the Earth
Bothie, the Polar Dog
Living Dangerously

THE
FEATHER
MEN

RANULPH FIENNES

BLOOMSBURY

First published in Great Britain 1991
Bloomsbury Publishing Limited, 2 Soho Square, London W1V 5DE

Copyright © 1991 by Ranulph Fiennes

The moral right of the author has been asserted

Map on page 274: Artbar

A CIP catalogue record for this book
is available from the British Library

ISBN 0–7475–1049–0

10 9 8 7 6 5 4 3 2 1

Typeset by Butler and Tanner Ltd, Frome and London
Printed by Richard Clay, St Ives plc

To four brave men –
John, Mike, Michael and Mac

I am not of that feather to shake off
My friend, when he must need me.
Shakespeare, *Timon of Athens*

Acknowledgements

I would like to thank the thirty-two individuals who helped me to research the events described in this book and to check the accuracy of my account. For reasons that will be apparent, I cannot name them, but they will know who they are and be assured of my sincere gratitude.

I am especially grateful to the close relatives of John Milling, Mike Kealy, Michael Marman and Mac.

To Bridgie, who, on 7 May 1977, gave birth to Patrick John Milling, who today bears a striking resemblance to his late father.

To Pauline and Lucia, at whose request I have withheld Mac's full name for security reasons.

To Maggi and to Nancy, widow and mother, respectively, of Mike Kealy.

To Rose May and the parents of Michael Marman.

All have been more than helpful and patient with their advice.

My thanks also to Jan Milne for her patience and support, and to Frances Pajouic for her good humour and efficiency.

I am grateful to Hodder & Stoughton for allowing me to reproduce three pages from one of their titles.

Ranulph Fiennes

CONTENTS

Author's Note

For the reader's benefit I would like to quote the following lines from page 271 of this book:

'In the spring and summer of 1991 I described these events with complete attention to accuracy. Some of the dialogue and the emotions, the inner thoughts and the assumptions are, of course, mine. In fiction there is always a villain. But real life does not fit into neat themes.'

Part 1

1

Daniel had never left home before. Vancouver in the clean, crisp summer of 1945 was full of wonder to this prospector's son from a remote village on the Arctic coast of Alaska. The reason for this happy visit was the end of the war in Europe and the return of his father by troopship that day.

Amid whirling bunting and the cheering of proud relatives, the veterans clambered off the Canadian Pacific steam train, some to renew their previous lives and loves, many to face the bitter realization of unattainable dreams or unexpected betrayals.

Daniel did not notice that his father was thin and gaunt, for he was still a great bear of a man and he bore gift-wrapped parcels of exciting shapes.

A taxi-cab took the family to their cheap lodgings close to Lion's Gate bridge. After tea and once the first waves of excitement were spent, Father made his long-planned pronouncement.

'We have six days before the steamer takes us home, my hidjies.' Nobody knew why he called them that — only that it had a good, warm meaning. 'And we will never forget these days, because the Hun are smashed for ever and we are together.'

The deep, flaky bilberry pie did the rounds again and everyone slept well despite their excitement, all five to the single bedroom.

The days flickered by in a kaleidoscope of happiness. They watched folk skiing on the lower slopes of Mount Grouse, on long planks of wood that looked impossible to control. Many skiers came to grief and Dan and his family laughed till the tears came.

They took a horse and cab to the wharves, bought toffee-apples and walked hand in hand to watch the tradesmen at the sugar factory, and the trawlers with their brawny crews. Thousands more soldiers and sailors returned on giant troopships and the family joined the welcoming crowds. They saw the zoo and a pantomime, gazed at the sleaze of Gas Town and sang with gusto on the Sunday, for

1

Mother and Father were keen Presbyterians, he with his Dutch Reform Church upbringing and she with a background of Wyoming and pioneer stock.

The Sunday before they were to take the steamer north, Father sprang his big surprise ... There was a travelling circus in town and, dammit, they would check it out that very night.

Before the great event they squeezed into a packed church and joined in the songs of praise and the prayers of thanksgiving of the Vancouver people for the deliverance of their loved ones.

Then to the circus.

Clowns, elephants that could count, a giraffe, bears in kilts, dwarves, a sasquatch monster from the forests of the Rocky Mountain Trench, black fuzzy men, balloon shoots for prizes and coconuts from the South Pacific propped on posts.

Even at five, brought up among Esquimaux children, Daniel could throw the wooden ball straight and true. And he could shoot a light gun with fair accuracy providing he could take his time. He glowed with pride at his armful of coconuts and wooden teddies.

They cried with delight inside the sparkling waterways of the Canal of Love; they ooh'd and aah'd with delicious horror in the House of Screams as ghouls of sacking and animal bones swished by on unseen pulleys.

Everyone but seven-year-old Naomi, who hated heights, was awed when Father pointed to the monstrous Roller-Wheel with its eighteen swinging gondolas. Daniel sat on his narrow seat, filled with curiosity and sticky-lipped with candy floss. An Indian and a grinning China-man, both in top hats, checked that the family were all strapped in. Because he was so little he was jammed in beside eleven-year-old Ruth, his eldest sister. In front of him sat Naomi, his mother's hands clenched about her and, at the prow of the gaily painted craft, just behind the carved redskin figurehead with its fearsome features, sat their father, beaming with pride and forever glancing over his shoulder to check that his brood were 'having the finest time of their lives', especially his dear wife, to whom he had sworn that very morning, as he held her close, that he would never, never leave her again ... not for the Commonwealth nor yet for the King himself.

As other families took their seats, the great twinkling wheel rotated in fits and starts until all the gondolas were filled with laughing, or gaping, passengers.

Then a whistle blew, the Chinaman waved a flag and two gates

of steel clanged shut below them. Daniel smelled hot oil and roast chestnuts. The cool air lifted Naomi's golden hair. Dad shouted, 'Hold on, my love. Hold tight, my little darlings ... try to kiss the stars.'

The wheel spun ever faster and Daniel loved the speed, the height, the newness of it all. Only when Naomi screamed did the intense wonder that he felt begin to fade. And as his other sisters started to moan, even big Ruth, he knew that he too should be sensing fear. But he felt only more aware, more able to observe and consider. The giddy, lurching passage of the gondola was not as before. Something had changed. They were out of kilter with the mother wheel. He saw sparks in growing streams and a broken spar. Their cockleshell had come away from its housing on one side and as they swung over the top of the great arc and began the downward rush, so the remaining hinge-spar split and they were free, cartwheeling through space.

Nobody heard their screaming as they fell, for the carousels and the brass bands, the loudspeakers and sideshow criers produced a cacophony of sound that would have drowned out the knell of doom. And nobody saw the lace bonnet of young Anna, who clung by herself to the rearmost seat, glide and dip away like a falling kite.

The gondola crashed through the canvas of a small marquee. Ruth's body and the whim of chance saved Daniel's life. He was thrown against a pile of clothing. The wind was knocked out of him and his legs were broken but he remained fully conscious.

He saw the wrecked and green-painted prow, the head of a warrior, deeply impaled in the bowels of a fat gypsy lady. He saw that his mother and Naomi had landed, tightly embracing, on the gypsy's table. Their heads had come together with such force that the grey hair and the golden hair seemed to sprout from a single pulp. They were mercifully still but for their stockinged legs, which jerked in time with the billowing canvas of the ruined tent. Of sister Anna he could see no trace: perhaps an angel had caught her in the air and she was saved, as he was. He could feel no pain, only a desperate need to gulp for more air.

He thought he heard his name whispered aloud. Father was staring down at him, attached by one arm to the shattered upper end of the main tent pole. But now he was foreshortened, like the circus dwarves, for his torso had been severed at the waist. Daniel could see this all so clearly for his father's remains were close above him and the

mouth, agape beneath the thick moustache, did indeed seem to pout with the shape of Daniel's name.

From that moment until the present day, whenever de Villiers felt the images of that night hover at the fringes of his mind, he clenched his fists and forced them away.

With the passage of years, the warmer human emotions, with which he had been genetically blessed, remained in place on the far side of his self-imposed shutter. By excluding his sensitivities, de Villiers had retained his sanity. He was, but for his chosen profession as a contract killer, a pleasant enough human being...

2

Dhofar is the southern province of Oman, sharing desert borders with Saudi Arabia and South Yemen. In the 1960s a band of Dhofari nationalists, aiming to rid their country of an oppressive Omani Sultan, visited the USSR in search of support. Their nationalist and Muslim aspirations were soon redirected by the Soviets into a new guerrilla unit called the Popular Front for the Liberation of Oman (PFLO). The unit's Marxist fighters, operating on their own home ground, were frighteningly efficient, and for a while invincible. Fortunately, in 1970, Qaboos bin Said exiled his reactionary father, became the new Sultan and proclaimed an amnesty. Many terrorists responded and were formed into armed *firqat* groups to fight against their former comrades, often from the same tribe or family.

Amr bin Issa, Sheikh of the Bait Jarboat tribe in Dhofar, was not a happy man. At forty-seven he was envied by many of his fellow *jebalis*, mountain tribesmen, for he was rich – richer than most *jebalis* could imagine.

As a seventeen-year-old Amr had left home with an uncle and sailed the Gulf waters in sardine dhows. For a while he worked as a gardener in Bahrain and as a delivery courier around town using a Lambretta moped. He had a keen eye for business and took advantage of the new-found wealth of the United Arab Emirates to set up a grocery and hardware shop in Dubai. A retail chain of Woolworth's

lookalikes then evolved, second only to Khimji Ramdas in size and profitability.

Amr had married young, for he had a strong sexual appetite. His first wife was a great disappointment to him. She was an orphan girl who, like the majority of Dhofari women, had been brutally circumcised soon after birth. Her clitoris had been removed and, with it, most of her sensuality. Two sons were born who remained with their mother when Amr divorced her and went abroad. She remarried a man from the Bait Antaash and Amr rarely saw the two boys. None the less they remained the blood of his blood.

His second marriage was altogether different. At the age of twenty-four he stopped off at an island on a fishing voyage and fell in love with a fourteen-year-old Shahra girl, Shamsa. Even before he discovered that her sexuality was intact he had determined to marry her, for to him she seemed the most alluring creature on earth.

The Shahra ranked low in the strict tribal hierarchy of Dhofar. Once the most powerful tribe in the land, they had borne the brunt of a century's fighting against Portuguese invaders. Greatly weakened, the Shahra gradually became subjugated to the Qara tribes until they were 'non-tribe', losing the right to carry weapons and working only as serfs to the Qara in return for security. Shahra men could not take wives from the master tribes although the women, lighter-skinned than most Dhofaris, were available to all as brides at especially low prices.

Out of a powerful sexual bond grew a friendship and trust that was rare in Dhofari marriages. Shamsa bore Amr four sons over the next seven years. Amr was a proud husband and father, a successful businessman and popular within the Bait Jarboat tribe when, in 1970, their sheikh died without a hereditary successor. The dead leader had spent much of his life avenging the tribe's honour following a series of raids which had decimated and impoverished them in the 1940s. There was great contention among the Bait Jarboat about who should succeed him. Those of the tribe associated with the hard-core communists of the PFLO had their champion, while the non-atheistic majority favoured Amr, whose great wealth, personal wisdom and family connections were held in high esteem. Amr won and became sheikh.

Like most of his countrymen, from sheikh to humble wood-collector, Amr and his sons fought with the PFLO for the freedom of Dhofar. One of his sons was killed in 1969, a second in 1972 and

yet another in January 1975, all at the hands of the government forces. In accordance with the tribal tradition of *thaa'r*, or revenge, it was Amr's duty to avenge himself for the killing of his sons.

For three years, with the war at its height, the newly appointed Sheikh Amr did his best for the tribe, leaving his business concerns to his managers in the Gulf. In Dubai he was an extremely wealthy man, but on the *jebel* he lived much the same sort of life as other *jebalis*.

In 1974 Shamsa had conceived unexpectedly and, following a fall while she was driving their goats over the hill pastures, had died in childbirth. Amr was stunned. His tribal duties lost their importance to him. His popularity slowly waned and the machinations of his opponents stirred accordingly. A cousin named Hamoud, envious of Amr's position, used Amr's failure to fulfil the *thaa'r* and avenge the deaths of his three sons as fuel to rouse tribal sentiments against him.

Fundamentalist Islamic law embraces various rules, or *sharia*, but by far the most binding for a Dhofari are those of *thaa'r*. The aggrieved relative is expected by law to insist on an eye for an eye. In return for murder, execution. For manslaughter, blood-money. No time limit is set on the deed of vengeance. It can take place forty years on, but the executor must show his intention clearly and act as circumstances allow.

There are many different applications of the *thaa'r* even within a single Islamic country, because the dictates of the Koran simply reflect, in a modified form, the principles of pre-Islamic tribal behaviour. If among the elders of a tribe there is dissension as to how the *hadiyth*, the Prophet's sayings, should be applied, then a consensus of opinion, *ijma'*, can produce any solution. Over the years the differences in the severity with which Koranic punishments are applied in different lands have increased greatly. Sunni, Shi'ite and, in Oman, Ibadi Muslims apply further differences as a result of their own considerable divergences within the body of Islam.

Sudan is a Muslim country but the *thaa'r* there has become all but non-existent. In 1988 five Palestinian terrorists murdered two Sudanese and five British peace workers in a Khartoum hotel. They were arrested and the Sudanese government contacted the parents of the dead Britons through the Foreign Office. A middle-aged suburban couple in Britain were suddenly faced with the choice of whether they wished their child's murderers to be executed, fined or pardoned. They were unable to make up their minds, and all five

terrorists were released from jail in January 1991. In Dhofar Sultan Qaboos has had enormous success in subduing the *thaa'r*, to the extent that there were more tit-for-tat killings in Northern Ireland in 1990 than there were *thaa'r* murders in Dhofar. But the hard-core believers merely bide their time.

In July 1990 a *jebali* civil servant, a long-since pardoned member of the PFLO, was commuting to his air-conditioned office in Salalah in his air-conditioned Mercedes. He stopped at a zebra crossing to allow a pedestrian to pass. Over the past twelve years the two men had often passed each other in the street. That morning something snapped in the mind of the civil servant and he rammed the pedestrian against a wall, seriously injuring him. He was sent to jail, having readily admitted his intention to kill the man, who had murdered his brother back in 1973.

In 1976 a Dhofari lieutenant revealed to Tony Jeapes, SAS (Special Air Service) commanding officer, that he expected to be killed according to *thaa'r* for the chance shooting, two years previously, of his *firqat* sergeant-major. The lieutenant often encountered the man asked by the late sergeant-major's family to kill him. This man was always friendly and they shook hands whenever they met, but both knew that one day, when the time was ripe, one would try to kill the other. The lieutenant had not actually shot the sergeant-major, and no one thought that he had, but the real murderer had escaped to the Yemen and the lieutenant, as picket lieutenant and therefore the man locally in charge on that fateful night, was held responsible.

The *thaa'r* system was to cause Sheikh Amr a great deal of trouble.

On 7 April 1975, Amr was seventy miles to the north-west of his home, at the oasis of Shisr. A message reached him that day that was to change, or end, many lives over the next fifteen years.

Arabia's central feature, the Empty Quarter, is the greatest sand desert in the world. Six-hundred-foot-high dunes, constantly on the move, make up much of the sweltering landmass of Oman and Saudi Arabia. The dunes tail away a day's journey by camel to the north of Shisr and the oasis is, to many desert nomads, the most wonderful place on earth. To the few urban Omanis or Europeans who reach it, Shisr is a fly-blown outpost on the edge of nowhere.

The remains of an old fort, fashioned from stone and mud, guard a well at the base of a cliff. In the shade of the low rock face that abuts the water, Sheikh Amr and his son Bakhait listened to three

Bait Sha'asha' nomads, the true desert bedouin, *bedu-ar-ruhhal*, who wished to purchase rice in exchange for camels.

To the south the dust trail of a vehicle was visible, stirred by the dry blast of the *shimaal*. Soon a land-cruiser appeared beneath the scrawny palm trees of Shisr and a short man in a khaki shirt and checked *wizaar* (a skirt-like wraparound garment) approached. While the man was still a silhouette Amr logged him as a Qara *jebali* from his hair-style. Then he recognized the man and felt both pleased and uneasy.

After the traditional greetings and much gossip of little consequence, Amr and his son took leave of the nomads and followed the newcomer to his vehicle. 'What is your news, Baaqi? Why should you come to Shisr where you have no business with man or God?'

Baaqi was kin and the closest of friends to Amr. 'They have convened a conference of the tribe in two days' time. Your cousin Hamoud is behind it. He has stirred up the others against you, using your failure to fulfil the *thaa'r* as a sign of your disgrace. Those are his words.'

'But why a tribal conference this year? It is not due for sixteen months. If Hamoud wishes to depose me, he will have to wait. The tribe will be on the move now. Spring is over and everyone will need to move the herds to the summer grazing.'

When the PFLO attempted to force Marxism and atheism on to the *jebalis* in the early 1970s, it was the older folk who bore the brunt of the killings and torture. They proved steadfast in their devotion to Islam and forced a retrenchment of the hard-core communist *adoo* (enemy), including the likes of Hamoud. By 1975 the coercion had ceased but the older folk faced a new threat to their traditional ways. The Omani Sultan wished to break up the more tribal, regressive customs and to encourage trade and progress. However, many conservatives, seeing that the *adoo* were no longer all-powerful, began to exhort a return to the *thaa'r*. Thus encouraged, revenge murderers set to work and by early 1975 a great many feuds had been pursued to their ends.

Baaqi placed his arm, sinewed by a life of physical effort and a subsistence diet, on his friend's shoulders. 'Hamoud has argued his case with the elders. Soon, he says, the war will be over. The government are daily strengthening their hold on the mountains. Soon *jebali* life will change for ever. *Insh'Allah*. There will be great new opportunities and the tribe must have a strong, respected leader

to take advantage of such times. He says you are weak and your disgrace is a blemish on our tribal name. By the *sharia*, he maintains, you should be exiled because you have failed to avenge your own blood not once but three times.'

Baaqi held a forefinger to alternate nostrils and cleared his nose into the dirt.

'He has suggested the conference take advantage of the cattle drives by convening in the great cave at Qum. Enough of the families have already agreed.' He paused, looking skywards, as a Hawker Hunter of the Sultan's Air Force, one of a squadron donated by Jordan, streaked overhead. 'Amr, my friend, you must go to the conference. Indeed you must chair the meeting as though nothing was in the wind. Then seize the initiative ... promise that you will avenge the death of your sons.'

Baaqi saw the hesitancy in Amr's eyes, the lack of set to his shoulders and the aimless movements of his hands. He sighed.

'For many months now you are a different man to the Amr bin Issa I helped elect as our sheikh. Your heart is gone away.' Baaqi looked into the eyes of his cousin. 'Is that so? Do you wish to give in? Do you wish Hamoud to plant one of his murdering atheist friends as our leader?' He shook his head and grasped Amr by the elbows. 'Remember, there are many of us who will suffer if you go. Your family and your friends. We, who risked much to speak out in harder times to have you as *tamimah* [head of the local tribal grouping] and to keep out Hamoud's faction.'

Amr nodded wearily at Baaqi and looked down at his son. Bakhait, a handsome fifteen-year-old, was clever beyond his years. He said little and missed even less. He loved his father as corn loves the sun. 'We will go, Father,' Bakhait said with an intonation neither interrogative nor decisive, but merely encouraging.

Amr's Land Rover, laden with sacks of rice, Korean combs and boxes of German knives, followed Baaqi's vehicle just beyond the reach of his dust cloud.

In two hours they came to Midway camp for fuel. An isolated oil-company base of six wooden huts erected in the 1960s, the place now sprawled over a square mile of military installations and a modern airstrip used by the sultan's fighters. A thousand tracks, of camels and vehicles, radiate out through the moon country that surrounds Midway. Muscat, capital of all Oman, lies six hundred miles to the north-east, the South Yemen border a hundred miles to

the west and the Qara mountains a mere hour by vehicle to the south.

They passed no sign of life but camels, grazing the dry scrub of the wadi beds. Only ghaf, acacia and gnarled *mughir* trees can tolerate this arid region. As the outline of the mountains skittered about in the heat shimmer ahead, they sped by the ruins of Hanun. Potsherds and the detritus of neolithic flint factories lay scattered over the gypsum wastes. Here, two thousand years ago, was a frankincense storage centre and, at Andhur to the east, a main entrepôt for the *laqat* incense gum that sold throughout the Roman empire at a price often higher than gold.

When the Queen of Sheba, from neighbouring Yemen, ruled this land, the tribes were animist, worshipping the Moon god, Sin, and were slaves to myriad fearful superstitions. Their lives were also ruled by the *ghazu*, the inter-tribal raid, and the interminable blood feuds that could last for a hundred years. Wahhabi Islam and its religious reforms swept the old beliefs from much of Arabia but never reached the dark recesses of the Qara hills, where the old ways continued alive and well into the latter half of the twentieth century.

As early as the 1960s the old sultan, from his Dhofar palace at coastal Salalah, had attempted to outlaw the blood feud. He might as well have spat at the devil, for the *thaa'r* was not merely a custom; it was the law and a deeply ingrained way of life. In 1975 Sultan Qaboos, alarmed by a fresh surge of feud killings resulting from the war, appeared on Omani television and threatened the death sentence to any perpetrator of the *thaa'r*.

Baaqi's land-cruiser slowed at the approach to the steep ramp of Aqbat al Hatab and began the climb from the barren *nejd* to the mountain-top grasslands of the Qara.

For three months of the year monsoon clouds from the Indian Ocean cover the mountains in a cloud of mist several hundred yards thick. The drizzle falls without ceasing onto the *jebel*, turning it into a magical paradise as green as South Virginia and bursting with life. Hummingbirds, venomous cobras, hyenas and every creepy-crawly on God's earth are to be found here. Along with some thirty thousand *jebalis*.

The two vehicles snaked up the Aqbat al Hatab and accelerated as the cliffs and the desert fell away behind and the dry mountain zone, the *gatn*, stretched moon-like on either side. After a mile or so the slopes showed a threadbare covering of grass, tinder-dry from

the long post-monsoon drought. Outcrops of bush and thorny scrub increased until the road ran over the top of the world and there were rolling prairies, herds of cattle and valleys, hidden by jungle-like vegetation, cutting between the grasslands like the veins of a leaf.

More than sixty adult males of the Bait Jarboat tribe from fourteen family groupings were present in the Ghar of Qum. Millennia of erosion and flash-floods had cut deep fissures into the limestone cliffs of the Qum valley. Continued roof falls had opened up a cave as big as a school gymnasium. For three hours either side of noon this south-facing amphitheatre was irradiated by the sun. The floor, deep in goat dung, sloped gently upwards to meet the innermost limestone walls. Several groups of *jebalis* sat, squatted or leant on their rifles. One or two wore army-issue trousers and cotton shirts, and many mixed *jebali* shawls and *wizaars* with Western clothing. To a man they carried weapons, mostly Belgian FN rifles donated by the government to ex-communists but here and there was an AK47 or a Kalashnikov assault rifle as used by the PFLO.

Amr's younger brothers and their teenage sons were grouped about a wood fire within the cave. All rose to greet the new arrivals. Tea was taken and news exchanged. Everyone knew why they were there but for a while the topic was avoided.

Baaqi's eyes were active. He categorized each visitor to the cave. All were interrelated. He knew who hated whom, which man had killed and tortured for PFLO's Idaaraat execution squads in the early seventies, who had committed adultery and, more important, who might support Amr to continue as the tribal sheikh at this vital time. The fighting was coming to a head and the new Sultan would, if victorious, offer great riches to the tribes – especially to the sheikhs whose loyalty he wished to woo.

'Amr, you must assert yourself now.' Baaqi's words were loud enough within the little group for all to hear and every man nodded his assent. Amr merely smiled and murmured, 'I will think about it. Nothing need be said as yet, for the judgement will start tomorrow after midday.'

Some miles to the north-west of the Ghar of Qum, as the shadows lengthened over the *jebel*, a lone Dodge water truck trundled west between two government outposts. It belonged to the government's

Civil Aid Department, which had been set up to help *jebalis* in areas supposedly freed by the army from PFLO control.

A PFLO killer unit ambushed the defenceless Pakistanis in their Dodge. Their first missile, an RPG7 rocket, missed the target but a bullet killed the driver and the Dodge slewed to a halt.

The *adoo*, as sultanate soldiers referred to all members of the PFLO, were members of the Lenin Regiment. Their leader, a Masheiki, walked down to the road. The Pakistanis were speechless with fear. One ran away but his legs were shot away from under him and his life was ended with a bullet through the back of the neck.

The survivors were prodded into a line beside the ditch and dispatched one by one.

Satisfied with the success of their evening's work the *adoo* separated to return to their various villages. Two headed east towards the Ghar of Qum.

Amr lay awake, unable to sleep. He should be working out a plan for his survival at the conference on the morrow. Politicking had once been a skill he had enjoyed, and perhaps if he tried hard enough he could find a way around this immediate problem. But his thoughts returned inevitably to his dear lost Shamsa, to her supple warmth and her elfin smile. She had been so proud when he became sheikh of the Bait Jarboat and likely *tamimah*. But ever since her death, the chess game that was tribal mediation had held no pleasure for him.

If it were a straightforward matter of demotion, loss of his number-one rank, Amr would have felt little or no unease. But Hamoud and his group of erstwhile Marxists, Amr knew, would wish him permanently out of the way. His crime was simple. His three dead sons, both the children of his first marriage and his first child with Shamsa, had been killed during the past six years in the fighting against the government forces, and he was bound by the *sharia* of the tribe to fulfil their *thaa'r*. There were a number of reasons why he had not done so, despite the accumulating disgrace caused by his inaction. All his life, like every other *jebali*, Amr had listened to the tribal history of bravery and honour, of horrific *ghazu* raids and blood feuds lasting generations, for such was the very heart and history of tribal existence. Yet he felt no urge for vengeance.

The brilliant stars above Amr seemed close. He lay and listened to the outbreaks of *jebali* chatter, birdlike and brittle, from the white *khayma* tents of a nearby Bait Antaash village. Nobody slept in the

caves for fear of the ticks. These emerged, in response to body warmth, from the goat dung. There were giant *muesebeckis* that caused raging irritation and fever for a week, Latreille bat-ticks whose victims suffered chancre-like lesions and diabetes symptoms, and rhipistomas, hosted by leopards and foxes, that caused deep, poisonous ulcers.

Echoes of feline screams from the wooded depths of the Arzat valley reached Amr's ears. There were wild cats and lynx in plenty as well as the larger predators, wolves, hyenas and the occasional leopard, to threaten the tribe's goats. So, at night, the animals were corralled into caves behind stockades of thorn.

Amr loved the *jebel* but half his soul lay in the Gulf, where the hustle and bustle of commerce had always made his blood run fast. Perhaps it was only fair that Hamoud should become sheikh, for *his* whole life was wrapped up within the confines of the *jebel* and its age-old ways. Without Shamsa, the magic of the *jebel* had lost much of its hold on Amr. The place held too many memories of their time together. In Dubai, amid the scramble of business, Amr might find happiness again. He would take Bakhait and his younger son too. He felt no inner compulsion to fend off the ambitious Hamoud.

With sunrise, came the call to prayers. Amr had slept little. Four times the ululation 'Allahu Akhbar.' (God is the greatest) rang out. Then 'La ilaha illa Allah.' (There is no God but Allah).

The young Jarboati women, driving the cattle to new pastures, had long since left the village and the valley of the cave when the adult males of the Bait Jarboat tribe met to sit in judgement over their sheikh. Every man knew that if the decision went against Amr, it would go further than a change of leader. His life could even be at stake. Hamoud would see to it.

Amr did not attempt to force his chairmanship on the day's proceedings. Baaqi had warned him at dawn of Hamoud's schemings. 'He has been clever. He has paid a judge to settle the problem. A *qadhi* of the Ashraf tribe to whom all the older folk will listen.' The Ashraf claim ancestry from Al Hashim, the house of the Prophet, and all the tribes respect their judgement.

Woven *ghadaf* mats had been unrolled on the dung floor of the cave for the Ashrafi's comfort. His grey hair was plaited into a two-foot pigtail, his upper body, racked by tuberculosis, was bare and he smoked a short clay pipe. Both eyes were opaque with glaucoma but he sat straight and commanded the respect of his superstition-ridden

audience. Beside the Ashrafi squatted the tribe's *rashiyd*, a wise man whose views all respected. Along the front of the limestone slope within the cave were some fourteen older men; the elder and therefore the senior Jarboatis. These men were the key to the consensus decision that would be needed to determine the future of Amr and his family.

Hamoud was invited by the Ashrafi to speak his mind. He was a small, thickset man with an impressive bullet exit wound in one bicep. He clutched an AK47 rifle as he spoke.

'I do not wish to complain about our sheikh, Amr bin Issa, behind his back but much less do I wish our tribe to be disgraced by his continued presence as our leader.' He paused to wipe sweat from his nose. Far away to the west the dull crump of heavy artillery sounded like tropical thunder and a faint chirruping chorused from the dark dome of the cave, home to a thousand bats. 'So I have asked our families to meet at this time, a time riven by change and threats to our way of life and to the law of the Prophet.'

Hamoud, like many of the former hard-core communists who had joined the government force, found no dichotomy in reverting to Islam; at least on the surface. He was adept at retaining his options. As he spoke his eyes roved between the elders and the Ashraf. No one else mattered; these men alone would decide.

Hamoud continued. 'The Prophet spoke words that clearly indicate Amr must go: "Those who do not command obediences should not issue orders." The sheikh of the Bait Jarboat has always been neither more nor less than the strength of his personal reputation. He is merely the first among equals. That is our way.'

Hamoud ground the butt of his rifle into the goat dung to emphasize his words. 'Amr bin Issa has disgraced us all. He is *ayeb*, one who neglects the obligations of blood relationship. An *ayeb* has no position and even his cousins may kill him. Six years ago his son Salim was killed here in this very village.' He shook his free fist in the direction of the cave mouth. 'Three years later his first-born child was killed at Mirbat and earlier this year another son was killed at the caves of Sherishitti. You will remember how at first he swore vengeance. For three years we believed him. Then the fire went out of him and, despite the urging of our respected *rashiyd*, he continued to neglect his duty. To me the matter reached the end of the camel when this man, our sheikh, was heard in Salalah to pronounce that the *thaa'r* was no longer a religious requirement.'

14

Hamoud paused for effect and was plainly successful. There was a murmur of shock and disapproval from the body of the audience. The elders looked at one another. White beards shook with dismay.

'This is no case for *qithit*, blood-money, since those responsible for the murder of Amr's sons will clearly not admit their guilt. It is for him to identify each guilty party, confront them and execute them. Only then can he redeem himself and avoid further disgrace. O Ashrafi, I request that you, as our *qadhi*, order Sheikh Amr bin Issa to state his intentions unequivocally here and now in front of Allah and our people.'

Hamoud returned to his family grouping. A hooded woman of the tribe called out: the morning meal was ready. The gathering moved out of the cave and down to the clearing.

Three cows, short, stringy beasts with stubby horns, munched a mixture of dried sardine, coconut pulp and hashish. One beast was selected by a powerfully built black man, a *khadim*, or ex-slave, of the late Sultan. Two boys emerged from a nearby wattle hut and, at the slave's bidding, squatted together in the dirt. With four men immobilizing the cow, the slave slit its jugular. Blood splattered the shaven heads, backs and shoulders of the boys. They were lucky, for cows were not often killed and this was a powerful cure for all sicknesses.

A woven bowl containing the cow's warm entrails was passed around as an hors-d'oeuvre. Then the lightly-boiled intestines were cut up and mixed with rice. This was served on four great tin platters around which the Bait Jarboatis sat.

A youngster cradling a six-foot-long flintlock rifle, a useless relic, switched on a Sony ghetto-blaster that blared the Voice of Aden. But the *qadhi* waved in irritation and the noise ceased. Amr listened half-heartedly to the conversations going on around him. His thoughts were far away. Baaqi listened but overheard little, for the Qara language, *jebbali*, is spoken in staccato bursts and to miss a single word can be to miss a complete sentence. For instance, *fdr* means to shiver with fear, *ikof* to pick off scabs and *stol* to brandish a dagger. *Ged* means to drift ashore after a shipwreck. All useful phrases.

The Ashrafi and the elders had separated from the rest. During and immediately after the meal they would come to their decision. Two armed men in the dark-brown fatigues favoured by many *adoo* entered the clearing. There were reserved greetings but a marked

lack of the spontaneous warmth that normally marks the arrival of a visitor.

The two men ignored the coolness of their reception. Then, spotting Hamoud, they expressed friendly greetings. Here was an old friend. They sat beside him. The eating continued.

'We have been active between Zeak and Jibjat.' The man who spoke was obviously the leader of the two, a wiry *jebali* in his thirties with black, curly hair, high cheekbones and narrow, almost slit eyes — a caricature of the Devil. He ate with his AK47 across his thighs.

'The Army think we are finished in this region. They are wrong. Yesterday we destroyed a Civil Aid team on the main road only five hours from here. Where were the Army then? We can still move and do as we please.'

'Why do you attack the Civil Aid people?' The Ashrafi asked the question that was in everyone's minds. 'They are not the Army. Their only work is to help us by building wells and schools. They have good animal doctors for our cattle.'

There was no answer to this. The PFLO's stated intention was to bring progress to the Qara. Now that Sultan Qaboos was, through Civil Aid, doing just that, the *adoo* were only alienating the population by such acts as their murder of the Pakistani Civil Aid workers.

'Do not be taken in by the *hindee* [Indian] puppets of the government.' The *adoo* then began a peroration of Marxist invective that he had learned at the PFLO school in Hauf, South Yemen. He probably understood no more of what he preached than did his audience.

The Ashrafi and the elders were silent. They more than anyone had learned to detest the strident bluster of the PFLO bully-boys. The Ashrafi's family had been tortured and killed by men like these just two years before. His only surviving daughter, badly hurt at the time, had since lost her mind and the power of speech.

The elders were caught between two stools. They wished to make an example of Amr in order to stop the rot that might otherwise set in. The open failure of a tribal sheikh to respect the age-old law of the blood feud, especially when three of his own sons were to be avenged, might lead to a general collapse of the system and this, as conservatives who knew no other way, they greatly feared. Amr must obey the *sharia* or else be seen to be punished. On the other hand the elders knew that Hamoud and his large clan had prepared the ground with care. If Amr were to go, there could be little doubt

that Hamoud would become sheikh, a prospect they feared, for they associated him with the worst of the PFLO bully-boys, the blackshirts of Dhofar, and their anti-Islamic atrocities. It was a matter of choosing the lesser of two evils.

Back in the cave the elders found they were unable to reach a unanimous decision and formally invited the Ashrafi to settle the matter on behalf of the tribe. The Ashrafi had decided to pronounce not for the good of the Jarboatis but in memory of his once garrulous, life-loving daughter. 'The *sharia*,' he said, as the marble glare of his near-sightless eyes traversed his expectant audience, 'divides human activities into five groups, the first of which, the *fardh*, are strictly enforced. Such is the law of justice for the killing of kin.'

The Ashrafi stared at Amr. 'By flouting the *thaa'r*, Sheikh Amr bin Issa appears to believe that he can disregard the *sharia*. I say to you all, especially to your sheikh, that nobody is above the law. Others today have said that Amr bin Issa is *ayeb*, and has disgraced himself and his clan. I agree that this is so.'

The old man snorted within his throat and spat bile.

'As your selected *qadhi* I submit that Amr bin Issa be given six months in which to avenge any one of his dead sons. Failing this, that he and his family be exiled from the country that lies between the Hadhramaut, the Rhubh al Khali and the sea. This exile to be until such time as he avenges each and every one of his dead children. Thanks be to Allah, the gracious.'

The Ashrafi sat down. To Baaqi, no one's fool, this judgement was a clear reprieve, or at least a second chance for Amr and as such a better deal than he had dared hope for. He had seen the Ashrafi's black looks at the Lenin Regiment men and their open comradeship with Hamoud. He thanked God for sending these thugs at such a timely moment.

Baaqi's relief was short-lived. Events overtook, or at least modified, the Ashrafi's pronouncement when, five months later, Amr's favourite son Tama'an, a fighter with the Bin Dhahaib unit, was killed in the western war zone. Amr was sad at his latest bereavement but not bitter. He knew that the scandal of his inaction had spread beyond the hearths of the Bait Jarboat and he suspected correctly that Tama'an's death would bring matters to a head.

Amr still felt no inner desire for vengeance. The day set by the Ashrafi passed and he had still avenged none of his sons. The elders

came to him and asked if he knew of any reason why the edict of the conference should not be carried out. There being none, as far as he could see, he bowed to the inevitable. Failure to comply would mean death for his family so, in the autumn of 1975, he said farewell to Baaqi and his remaining supporters and left Dhofar for ever, taking with him his closest kin.

3

De Villiers immersed himself in the demi-monde of Paris night-life. He needed a honey-pot trap, but with a difference. Davies meanwhile watched the judge, sought out his 'pattern', meticulously logged his every move. It was early October 1976. In two or three weeks the pair would meet and put together a schedule for the judge's death. The lady client had specifically ordered that the target's posthumous reputation be disgraced. So de Villiers concentrated on the sordid. He ignored the obvious tourist traps of Pigalle, Montparnasse, St Germain des Prés and the Champs-Elysées. All expensive froth and no action; or, as Davies put it, 'All mouth and no trousers.'

The hostess masseuses offering gentlemen 'the ultimate body massage', the pseudo-Thai girls with their body-body bathrooms and the quick hand or blow-jobs of the parks − all these lacked the extreme denigration de Villiers sought. Zoophilia was available; indeed the Paris *Milieu* interfered only 'if the animals suffer'. The most commonplace were canine seances but there were also studios with donkeys, horses, pigs and monkeys. Most of these dens of iniquity made their profit through selling videos of the action.

De Villiers considered the possibilities of paedophilia, rampant in Paris with paedophiliac rings and films featuring two- to twelve-year-olds of both sexes, but decided against it. Not with a member of the judiciary. It lacked the ring of truth and he was a perfectionist. In his experience most paedophiles had one thing in common: they were men whose careers put them in close contact with children. Social workers, vicars, schoolteachers, but not judges.

He looked into the closed world of sado-masochism. There were only four women in Paris who specialized in flagellation and 'tortures'.

Their clients, who averaged one or two visits per month, were forbidden to touch them and yet paid 1,000 francs per hour. Not the sort of scene de Villiers was seeking. Too parochial; a strange face would stand out a mile.

By the end of his first week in Paris, having made short work of the private-subscription orgy clubs and the exhibitionists of the rue de Roland-Garros, de Villiers was concentrating on the gay scene and in particular the graveyard where his old favourite, Edith Piaf, resided. In the late seventeenth century a Jesuit named Père Lachaise was Confessor to Louis XIV. The graveyard that is named after him is a dismal, rambling place with many dingy corners, gothic tombs and derelict chapels. After the war the cemetery served as a perfect spot for DIY prostitutes with no rooms of their own. Homosexuals took over in the sixties. De Villiers counted seventy-nine young men, between eighteen and twenty-five years of age, who operated in the graveyard between 1 p.m. and 6 p.m. Their customers, numbering hundreds at certain times of the week, were usually middle-aged or elderly pederasts. Uniformed inspectors of the Brigade des Parcs et Jardins patrolled between the rows of chrysanthemums but had little authority and seldom intervened. On the approach of an inspector, or one of the mainly Soviet tourists who came to see Piaf's tomb, the young man and his client, sitting on a gravestone, would simply cover their laps with a tourist map or a copy of Le Figaro.

De Villiers decided the Père-Lachaise cemetery was a distinct possibility but, wishing to explore every lead, he took a cab to the frenetic roundabout of the Porte Dauphine, on the edge of the city near the Bois de Boulogne. Every evening of the week, their work done, a host of Parisians descend by car on the Porte. Each driver circles until he or she makes eye contact with a fellow joy-seeker. Hand signals are exchanged and the two parties leave the concourse to seek intimacy elsewhere. This custom, de Villiers discovered, was a favourite with wife-swapping couples, and so again lacked sufficient degradation for his purposes. His dilemma was resolved by good fortune. Davies confirmed on the twelfth day of his judge-watching that on two Tuesday evenings in succession the judge had driven his Citroën ID19 to the Bois de Boulogne. Davies called de Villiers at his hotel and the method was agreed.

To Parisians the Bois has always meant romance, the mythical forest

of the fairy temptress Mélusine, a place of moonlit fauns and summer idyll.

In 1970 a handful of the entrepreneurial freelance prostitutes known as *tapineuses* tried their luck with motorists either in the back seat of the car or in the bushes. Harmless fun that bothers nobody, the chief of the Brigade decided. Then, in 1973, the *travelos* came.

Veroushka was the first. In São Paulo, where she learnt to '*faire la nuit*', she met a Madame who sold her a package deal for twelve thousand francs including air tickets, identity papers and a three-month tourist visa for France. At first, tolerated by the established Bois whores as an oddity, Veroushka made up to two thousands francs a night. But by 1976 a further two hundred Brazilian transvestites had followed her route to the forest and thrown out all but half a dozen of the 'genuine' prostitutes. Competition was fierce.

Minister Poniatowski tried that year to oust the *travelos*. He failed and the police continued to turn a blind eye. Every three months, each of these androgynous workers took a day-trip to Belgium to receive a passport stamp enabling him/her to apply for a further three-month visa. This was no great trouble in return for a job paying an untaxed fortune compared with likely takings back in Rio or Bahia.

Pia was twenty-four and about as sexy a *travelo* as the Bois regulars could remember. She was blonde, tall and sad: exactly what de Villiers was after except that her specific beat was in the wrong part of the forest. The best spots, on the roads most used by motorists, were jealously guarded by the older and richer bisexuals. Davies, given the job of changing Pia's beat, drove out to the Bois around midnight. Most of the 'girls' worked between 11 p.m. and dawn, for daylight was their enemy, revealing hair growth and highlighting other remnants of masculinity.

The *travelos* were heavily outnumbered, Davies discovered, by voyeurs who parked their cars, left the headlights on and mooched around the business sites staring at the weirdos and their customers. Vendors of hamburgers and beer did good business in the most popular areas. Their trade, Davies noticed, was with the girls and the voyeurs, never with the clients, many of whom slunk away when sated, their eyes averted from the light − a fact that pleased Davies. The *travelos* mostly displayed their breasts, and those with more feminine thighs wore miniskirts or just a G-string. In winter, Davies mused, this sort of business conducted al fresco must leave a lot to be desired. What clothes the girls did wear were gaudy in the extreme:

leopard-skin leotards, polka dot T-shirts, plumes reminiscent of Rio samba queens and glittering sequins tacked on everything from high-heeled shoes to hairbands. Davies cruised the roads of the Bois for an hour or more until he was satisfied he knew its layout and the location of all the girls.

Pia was indeed a good-looker. Davies warmed to the idea of his job. Initially he had felt disgusted. As he watched the voyeurs he realized many were affluent. They had only to visit river banks or sandy beaches anywhere in summertime France to enjoy the sight of countless real breasts and bare bodies. Davies shrugged. It takes all types, he thought, unaware of any irony, since he saw himself and his work as perfectly mundane.

The *Milieu* has completed studies of the *travelos'* clients. Over half go only once in their lives to 'see what it is like' and are put off for good. The majority of the rest are 'normal' citizens – plumbers, professors and office workers – happily married with happy children. They appear merely to be pursuing their hidden fantasies despite the knowledge that they are entering the body of a man who, high on drugs and unwashed, has just received many other clients among the discarded condoms and beer cans of the same copse. Why they thrill to the false, pumped-up breasts, the body odour and the baritone voice with its heavily accented Portuguese, remains a mystery to the *Milieu*. How to explain the non-stop supply of clients and the ever-increasing attractions of this outside theatre of sodomy is not the job of the local police, the Brigade Mondaine.

Davies parked at the kerb behind two other cars and right beside the waste bin that marked Pia's habitual site. He had not long to wait. A small man, a town clerk Davies decided, in a rumpled brown suit and thick spectacles, emerged from the bushes and made for his car, fumbling with the key. Pia followed, wearing a black mini-petticoat that concealed little. Her blond hair was cropped urchin-style and Davies felt himself roused despite the dictates of common sense.

Pia leant against the waste bin. Davies's window was down. He could clearly see Pia's maleness and smell the mix of sweat, cheap aftershave and the after-odour of previous clients. She had a pretty smile.

'How much?' Davies asked.

'It's a hundred francs.'

'But if I . . .'

She cut him off. 'Anything extra is fifty more francs.' Davies nodded. He locked the car and followed her into the bushes.

Afterwards he told her, truthfully, it was the first time for him. Her French was only a little better than his, so he kept his sentences short and spoke slowly.

'You are very beautiful,' he said.

She seemed to like his flattery, but already she was showing signs of impatience. Perhaps she was losing a customer. He took the plunge. 'Here is an extra two thousand francs, Pia. You're unlikely to have another twenty clients tonight, so let's go to a nightclub of your choice for an hour or two. I have a special proposition to make you. Good money is possible.'

Pia was of course interested. She fetched a chic mackintosh and calf boots from a holdall in the shrubbery.

'Where are you living?' she asked.

'In a motel in town,' Davies told her.

'We go there. I do not like nightclubs.'

This suited Davies. He stopped off at a bar to buy whisky and cheese biscuits.

In the car Pia unwound a bit. She was, Davies soon realized, a desperately unhappy person. Every Sunday she prayed at the church in Pigalle dedicated to Saint Rita, who, in Brazil, is the Patron Saint of the Hopeless. She was homesick for her parents in a shanty town in São Paulo. Much of her savings was spent each winter on a two-month trip back to Brazil.

'I like to buy myself pretty clothes,' she laughed; a quick, masculine noise.

Vice in the Bois, thought Davies, must be a hideous, tortured misery for these people. Why do they do it, he wondered. It can't be for money. To alleviate her black moods Pia took alcohol, cocaine and marijuana. She craved the love of a real relationship, but she knew men never fall in love with *travelos*. Some of her Bois friends had committed suicide from despair. All professional *travelos* have the regular hormone treatment, silicone operations and expensive weekly hair removal necessary to prevent reversion to visible masculinity. Life consists of the taunts of voyeurs, the fear of murder by weirdos or mugging by one of the many Bois predators, the dubious pleasure of twenty or more possibly diseased clients per night in all weathers, and the never-ending cost of unnatural medical inputs. Since there is no way of saving money the only apparent gain is the

ability to remain a trans-sexual.

They chatted together in the tiny motel room for three hours. Pia understood that Davies wanted her to entertain an important customer in the Bois the following Tuesday night. If the man failed to turn up, she would still be paid by Davies and they would try again on successive Tuesdays. She looked at a photograph of the judge until she was certain she would recognize him. She also memorized the details of his Citroën. She accepted Davies's assurances that she would be able to ply her trade on the agreed night or nights at the prime Bois site that he had described to her, for the normal occupants would be well paid to accept her temporary presence there.

Davies took Pia back to her lodgings not long before dawn but first he drove her to the chosen site and together they walked into the forest to a section of loose undergrowth unlittered by the ubiquitous condoms of the well-used patches.

Excited at the prospect of major earnings in the near future and grasping the half-empty whisky bottle, Pia waved fondly at the departing Davies.

The judge slipped into his astrakhan overcoat and looked about his office close to the Ile de la Cité. He was a careful man and cheated on his wife with the same attention to detail as he handled his cases. Nothing was left to chance. From time to time he did work for the security service and not all of it was savoury. For many reasons it was wise to be circumspect.

In the underground car park he selected the keys to the old Citroën ID19. Only the attendant knew about the Citroën and he was tipped to the eyebrows. The world in general, and certainly his family, associated the judge only with his black Alfa-Romeo. But he still felt a sliver of unease. Despite the many threats he had received over the years he was never able to ignore open hostility and the woman last month had been especially venomous. He had put the three brothers from Marseilles away for life for murder and conspiracy to blackmail. Quite which one the woman belonged to was uncertain, but he remembered her beetle-black eyes above the mink coat and the intensity of her brittle scream: 'You bastard. You destroy his life. Now I destroy yours.' He made an effort to forget her, to concentrate on the sharp pleasures of the immediate future.

Two years ago, driving home through the Bois de Boulogne in

the early morning, the judge had chanced to pass a teenage transvestite named Zita. Whether it was his mood at the time, the flux of
the moon, or merely the effect of his head-lights on her cheekbones
and thighs, he did not bother to ponder. She possessed a magnificent
body, pert little breasts and ash-blond, shoulder-length hair. He later
discovered that Zita alternated a wardrobe of ten wigs, but by then
he was hooked.

His table of Rotarian colleagues met on Tuesday evenings for nine
months of the year and since the judge had never looked at another
woman his wife in their well-appointed flat in La Muette was not
suspicious. He developed a routine. Once away from the office he
exchanged his astrakhan for the scruffy flasher's mac and cloth
cap that lived in the Citroën. Thus transformed, he felt safe from
recognition in the Bois and titillated by the touch of the bizarre, the
forbidden, that enhanced the whole procedure.

He ceased to be bothered by middle-aged feelings of rusting away.
Life was no longer a mundane groove. Should he be discovered in
pursuit of his perversion, his career and his marriage would not
survive the shock. He savoured, indeed nurtured, the risk in much
the same way as a climber relishes a dizzy void.

Fearing the darker, less accessible parts of the Bois, the judge
habitually cruised the main thoroughfares, especially the northern
end of the Avenue du Mahatma Gandhi. He invariably chose tall,
fair transvestites, a hangover perhaps from Zita, who had killed
herself in a public lavatory not long after introducing him to the
dubious pleasures of the Bois. He grew to love the alien smell of the
earth and the sounds of the forest as he pounded away in the scrub.
To the judge, sex without the Bois soon became like strawberries
without cream.

Three weeks passed before the judge spotted Pia. He parked the
Citroën and listened to her argue with a pock-faced Moroccan.

'You are not busy,' he whinged. 'Three times I come by here and
always you are free. Maybe you don't like Arabs. Huh? Come on, I
pay you double.' Pia's response was negative.

'Va te faire sauter ailleurs, conasse,' shouted the frustrated Arab,
moving on to a buxom brunette.

The judge edged the car forward as soon as Pia was alone on the
verge.

He spoke gently. 'A hundred and fifty for an hour?'

She responded at once. She was not absolutely sure about him

because the cap shadowed his features. But the car was enough.

'I'm all yours, darling ... let's go.'

She led him by the hand to a tiny clearing in a thicket.

'How do you like it, m'sieu?'

He explained and was quoted an extra fifty francs. This was normal and he agreed. When both were naked but for the judge's black socks, Pia lay on her back on a prepositioned tartan rug. She spread her legs and smiled up at her client.

Davies rehoused the CB radio. 'De Villiers says the judge has taken the bait.' He closed the boot quietly and handed Meier one of two iron bars. These he had purchased together with other farm implements from a hardware store in Dieppe a week previously.

Both men, clad in baggy, grey cotton tracksuits over slacks and shirts, entered the forest. Davies led without a torch: he knew the path well. Only that afternoon he had walked along its winding length and removed twigs for the last hundred yards and right up to the thicket. Twice he hissed at his companion. He never liked this sort of work with Meier.

De Villiers himself was quiet as a cat and quick as an adder but Meier, short-sighted and unfit, verged on being a liability. He was, however, undeniably brilliant with technical matters: no electronic or mechanical challenge was too great. Davies had often wondered why Meier had left the Mercedes factory in Wolfsburg where he had worked as a senior research scientist for nine years. Meier had, over the years, refined various electronic and mechanical methods of untraceable murder. He was an invaluable asset to the team and could be forgiven his nocturnal clumsiness.

After five minutes Davies stopped by a solitary birch tree and raised his hand in the gloom of the forest. Both men could hear clearly the low grunts of pleasure and the ritual endearments of the *travelo*. Meier followed Davies closely. As always they had rehearsed the kill.

The first blow of Davies's iron bar split open the judge's skull. Pia's legs were clasped together around the judge's back and the sudden shock of her terror seemed to lock them there. Davies dragged the corpse sideways so that Meier had access to Pia's head and chest. She recognized Davies. Her voice rasped with fear.

'Do not hurt me. Please. I have done exactly what you asked. You wanted a photograph. So take as many as you like, but I beg you,

do not hit me.' Her long, white arms, already wet with the judge's blood, stretched out in supplication.

Meier brought his iron bar straight down on Pia's temple. She relaxed. The rest was for show: a dozen wicked blows to her silicone-filled breasts and finally – the Manson touch as stipulated by de Villiers – the writing in blood across the judge's back.

They stood back and surveyed the scene. The corpses were still entwined. 'We have done the poor girl a favour,' Davies muttered. 'She had a miserable life and no future.'

He removed the judge's wallet, keys and credit-card holder. These and the iron bars he threw into the scrub after pocketing the banknotes and credit cards. A few minutes later they were driving back to Paris to rejoin de Villiers.

The bodies were found by a lorry-driver, or, more precisely, by his travelling companion, a wire-haired terrier, the following afternoon.

Patrol cars from the police districts of the eighth, sixteenth and seventeenth *arrondissements* converged on the scene within minutes. The crime was classified as murder by youths in search of money for cocaine or, because of the word 'COCHONS' crudely etched into the skin of the judge, the random work of crazed moralists. Either way an unhappy epitaph for the deceased. A government department blocked all media enquiries, perhaps because of past activities by the judge on their behalf. This was a move welcomed by the police, for the crime coincided with a good deal of criticism of moral laxity. It was yet another disgrace to the good name of France.

Some months later Minister Poniatowski launched a 'clean up the Bois' operation, the effects of which lasted for a few months, and in August 1983 the head of the Paris police, Monsieur Fougère, conducted Operation Salubrité with great élan and amid much publicity. Its effects were initially severe on the *travelos*, but in 1991 their business was still going strong and, like royalty in London, or the girls in Bangkok, was considered no bad thing by the relevant French authorities.

4

James Mason, an Englishman, was born on 24 June 1824; where and of whom is not well documented. He gained a degree in geology from Paris University and participated in France's bloody revolution in 1848. He became manager of the Bilbao iron mines and made a fortune from copper extraction in São Domingos, southern Portugal, where he owned vast estates. The King of Portugal, alarmed at Mason's increasing influence, sent an army to re-establish royal authority. Mason's private security force defeated the soldiers, so the King, changing tack, ennobled the Briton with the title Conde de Pomarao, a hereditary title, held to this day by his great grandson.

Mason sank his fortune into the four-thousand-acre estate of Eynsham Park, five miles west of Oxford. His only son had an affair with the King of Portugal's daughter, married the Earl of Crawford's daughter, was director of the Great Western Railway and in due course handed Eynsham Park to *his* only son, Michael.

After Eton and Sandhurst, Michael became Army Boxing Champion in 1918 and travelled to Canada for three years as a prizefighter, bootlegger and hunter. In 1938 he was recruited by the Director of Naval Intelligence and spent much of the Second World War on clandestine assignments in Europe. A great sailor and traveller, he wrote many books and became High Sheriff of Oxfordshire in 1951. He died thirty years later, leaving Eynsham Park to his eldest son, David.

Perhaps this unusual pedigree explains why David Mason was born without fear.

On Sunday 31 October 1976, a week after the killing of Pia and the judge in Paris, Captain David Mason's alarm clock woke him from a deep sleep in his bedroom on the first floor of Buckingham Palace. He dressed as quickly as his uniform allowed and left the palace.

Straightening his back, he walked over the gravel of the front courtyard. Above, in the cold autumn breeze, the Royal Standard fluttered to confirm that the Queen was in official residence. In fact,

David knew, she had been away for some time. A gust caught at his bearskin as he emerged past the police sentry-box. Instinctively he braced his lower jaw against the chinstrap and cursed the fact that it did not lie below his chin at all, but sat just below his lower lip. The bearskin itself was hollow, with plenty of room for carrying loose items. The previous week one of David's guardsmen had been caught on sentry duty with a transistor radio tuned to Radio Caroline on his head. When approached by the ensign he had come smartly to attention and jogged the volume control. He got eight days' detention.

Such temptations had been unknown in the less boring days when the sentry-boxes were outside the palace railings. Sadly the tourists had grown more and more familiar when posing for photos — sometimes girls would strip off — and even steal items of uniform. The young guardsmen could only grin and bear the indignities, so they had been brought inside the railings. Many regretted this and various lost perks. It had not been unknown for American tourists to part with good money when prompted by a veteran, speaking out of the side of his mouth, 'That will be twenty dollars for the photo, sir. Just roll it up and stuff it down my rifle barrel ... Thank you very much, sir. Anyone else? How about you, madam?'

Underneath his greatcoat David wore his dark-blue 'Number One Dress tunic'. The trousers sport a broad red band and are worn outside 'Wellingtons', footwear that looks like cowboy boots minus the high Cuban heels. Since the tunic jacket is often too warm when worn beneath a greatcoat, many officers dispense with it except in very cold weather. One lieutenant was badly caught out when summoned into the royal presence and invited to make himself comfortable. He wore only a Snoopy T-shirt under his greatcoat and HM was not amused.

At 8 a.m. sharp David crossed from the palace to the 'Birthday Cake', as Guards officers describe the Victoria Memorial, and then across to the far side of the busy roundabout. Many officers, frightened of being run over, take the slower route to St James's Palace, by using the pedestrian crossing at the Buckingham Palace end of Constitution Hill, but David regarded this as a waste of time. He carried his sword menacingly free of its polished steel scabbard and, since his bearskin appeared to perch on his nose, obscuring his vision, the traffic invariably screeched to a standstill and let him pass.

On arriving at St James's Palace, he acknowledged the shouldered

rifles and salutes of the sentries and entered to eat a full cooked breakfast in sumptuous surroundings. In the officers' sitting room on the first floor, he paused to look at *The Times* headlines. In a revenge raid following the murder of white farmers, Rhodesian commandos had penetrated deep into Mozambique. During the night, at midnight, 3 a.m. and 6 a.m., while his Ensign, the young and rather green Second Lieutenant James Manningham-Buller, had inspected the St James's Palace Guard, he had inspected the Buckingham Palace Guard. Now he wrote up his Guard Report and signed for his mess bill.

David paused in front of a large mirror inside the door of the officers' guardroom and adjusted his calf-length, blue-grey greatcoat and the brass-link chinstrap of his bearskin with its six-inch green and white plume. He emerged from the guardroom without bending. In his bearskin David was almost eight feet tall, but the doorway had been designed with just such problems in mind. He returned to Buckingham Palace, causing *en route* a motorcyclist to collide with a taxi.

At 10.30 a.m. Major Charles Stephens, Captain of the Queen's Guard, handed over to the New Guard to the camera-clicking delight of the tourists.

As the majority of the New Guard marched off down the Mall with the Corps of Drums, the Old Guard, including David and his men, headed for the nearby Wellington Barracks to the tune of 'Liberty Belle'. As well as being good marching music this was also the signature tune of the television comedy series *Monty Python's Flying Circus*. David had nobbled the Band Sergeant-Major, who substituted the correct final note with a huge, discordant fart from the tuba as in the Python version. This was enjoyed by the troops and tourists alike.

David gave his orderly his uniform for cleaning back at the Guards Barracks in Caterham, south of London. Then, in slacks and a tweed jacket, he located his R-registration Porsche 911 Targa convertible and drove through near-empty streets to his flat in South Kensington.

Letting himself in, he noticed a white, two-inch-square card with the rest of his mail. The card was blank. He felt a surge of anticipation, for this was no ordinary caller.

David, a great believer in priorities, went into the kitchen, switched on the kettle and put hot water in the teapot. Then, without removing the brown paper band that circled its butt, he lit up a Montecristo

Number 5 cigar. He smoked half a dozen a day and especially relished his first post-palace-duty puff.

Spike Allen was standing by the bookshelf and greeted David with a creasing of the skin at the corners of his eyes. David disguised his pleasure. 'You break in here on a Sunday morning when I am knackered by forty-eight hours of ensuring the Queen's personal safety.' He gestured at the copy of *The Times* that lay beside a green cardboard file. 'I had assumed you were in Mozambique leading the attack.'

Spike grimaced. 'I hope you're not sardonic with Her Majesty. Sarcasm ill becomes an officer of the Welsh Guards.'

David had been on a sniper's course in West Germany when one of Spike's talent-trawlers had spotted him and, a year later, Spike had made the approach while David was on a demolition and explosives course with the Royal Engineers. The Committee had specifically instructed Spike never to recruit from the Armed Forces and, in the case of ex-soldiers, no one who had ever served with the regular (22nd) Special Air Service Regiment. Spike had adhered rigidly to this rule until 1971, when a specialist job in Edinburgh had proved beyond the expertise of his two dozen operatives, his 'Locals' as he called them, in Britain. He had needed a man with up-to-date military contacts and skills.

He managed on that occasion by himself but decided then and there to recruit a suitable person from Her Majesty's Forces. Since he and he alone knew the identities of the Founder, the Committee members *and* the Locals and since the Committee entrusted the work of running the Locals entirely to Spike, no one objected to the recruitment of an active soldier because no one except one or two of the other Locals knew about it. Ignorance was bliss, decided Spike, who was a realist.

David had worked for the Feather Men for four years and Spike had every cause to congratulate himself on his choice. He knew the details of Captain Mason's file, as he knew those of every one of his Locals. Spike was married with two children, but the Locals were his extended family and Mason, Local 31, was a star performer. His file read:

Born Oxford 13.08.51.
Arrogant but fiercely loyal. Old-fashioned but quick, confident and decisive.
Eynsham Park, Witney, Oxon.; 97a Onslow Square, South Kensington.

Eton. Mons Officer Cadet School. 1st Bn. Welsh Guards.
Skills/Abilities: Cross-country runner BAOR Championship '71, ski, marksman.
Instructor – Sniper's Course BAOR '72.
Northern Ireland '71–'72.
O.C. IS/CRW weapons trials '72/'73
Demolitions/Explosives courses '72.
Best Regimental handgun shot '73.
Military adviser to BBC for Internal Security Programme '73.
Sultan's Bravery Medal '75 (Oman active service '74–'76).
London District duties '76.
Height 6'4". Weight 200 lbs. Hair brown. Eyes grey.
Languages: Arabic, French, German.

One of Spike's practices before selecting a Local was to discover his views on a number of topics, some apparently immaterial. Mason's responses were also filed:

Abortion: 'I think Parliament has got it about right. I don't think a woman should be forced to give birth to an unwanted child, especially if it is diagnosed early on to be disfigured. Many handicaps can now be diagnosed by twenty-two weeks into pregnancy and a termination should be at this early stage or not at all.'

Racism: 'A whole industry has sprung up around this issue. Ostensibly to prevent racism, it has the opposite effect by noisily drawing undue attention to the subject. People should be treated the same and, if black or brown, they should neither be penalized nor rewarded. Positive discrimination is counter-productive.'

Arming the Police: 'This would be a dreadful mistake. The police on the whole know very little about firearms. The training given to those officers who are occasionally authorized to carry firearms is inadequate.'

Sounds: 'Dislike: Radio 1, Radio 2, airport announcements, in-flight announce-ments, women gossiping, telephones ringing, BBC reporters' voices, children whingeing, traffic.'
'Like: clocks ticking, birds singing, stags roaring, children laughing, huge explosions, wind in trees, foghorns.'

Smells: 'Dislike: gangrene, B.O., fast food, car exhaust, wet sleeping bags, hospitals, nylon socks, dog shit, instant coffee, government offices.'
'Like: the sea, sawn timber, mown grass, heather, cordite, woodsmoke, Harrods Food Hall, clean children, cigar smoke, the African bush.'

People: 'Impossible to categorize. Every time I have tried to do so I have found an exception to the rule. But if I had to paint a stereotype of the sort of character for whom I reserve particular derision ... chin sticking in rather than

out, watery eyes, runny nose, wispy red beard, CND amulet around the neck, plays guitar in modern church services, goes to ante-natal classes with the wife after she has been made pregnant by the milkman, lives in Hampstead, faints when a car backfires, vegetarian, no sense of humour, follows trends, reads the *Guardian*, feet smell despite (or because of) sandals, uses words like "totally", "at the end of the day", "up and down the country", "ongoing struggle", etc.'

Germaine Greer: 'An intelligent and interesting woman. Unfortunately a horde of shrill harpies have taken over the feminist issue in much the same way as strident black activists have the race industry. If someone applied to me for a job I would appoint the person most suited to it, regardless of sex.'

Politics: 'In a nutshell I am a right-winger, but there has been almost as much interference with personal freedom under the Conservatives, even if they have been more subtle about it. Government should be kept to a minimum. People should be able to get on with their lives unimpeded by bureaucracy, nannying, hectoring and meddling by ignorant politicians anxious to make their names.

'Socialism is a religion espoused by fools, crooks or liars or, as in the case of many people at the BBC, people who are all three. It has failed miserably, but the more dim-witted of its adherents have still not realised this.

'Liberalism is not much better. There are just fewer crooks and more fools. There are some honourable exceptions but not many.'

Coming from the majority of people, these responses would have put Spike off right away. A fascist bigot, a narrow-minded élitist, were descriptions that sprang to mind. But he decided, and the recruit-trawler agreed, that Mason simply liked to appear bluff and autocratic.

The passage of time and a number of testing jobs at home and abroad had confirmed Mason to be a fair-minded man, a friend to anyone regardless of background, once he had decided they were genuine.

Like the rest of the Locals, David Mason operated for Spike without remuneration and often without payment even of his expenses. He knew only that the Committee of the Feather Men commanded Spike's loyalty and stood for freedom and democracy. They aimed to operate within the law to protect individuals or to prevent crimes, where the official arm of the law was powerless or too undermanned to be effective. For the most part Spike worked the Locals within their home areas, where they were likely to be streetwise. This also saved travel expenses. Few of the Locals knew one another since Spike kept them apart as far as possible.

David studied the scanty contents of the file Spike handed him. It

contained street maps of Bristol and the personal details of one Patrice Symins, drug dealer. When David laid the file down and stubbed out his cigar, Spike told him the background.

'Two weeks ago the only daughter of a Chippenham accountant, once a squaddie with C Squadron in Hitchin, died of drug abuse. She was supplied by the same group who organized her introduction to heroin when she was a student at Bristol University last year. The police know all about the dealer, Symins, but can prove nothing. There is a local Hungarian who has helped us in the past. He knows the city like the back of his one good hand. He will be your guide. Symins is well protected, which is why I want you to back up our Local, a Welshman called Darrell Hallett.'

They talked for an hour. Then Spike Allen handed over some equipment and left. David sighed. He had asked for a day to recover from palace duties, but Spike's hit was planned for that Monday night.

5

A great deal of redevelopment took place in Bristol during the mid-seventies, but Pennywell Road, though only a mile from the city centre, remained a shoddy backwater skirting the fringes of St Paul's and joining Easton with the old market district.

A number of self-contained housing estates and small industrial units lined both sides of this long, ill-lit road, as well as a smattering of derelict and vandalized lock-ups. In one such unit a kangaroo court took place on the evening of Monday 1 November 1976. The functions of judge and jury were assumed by Patrice Symins. His five colleagues, uniform in their bulk and ugliness, stood around a sixth man whose hands were secured behind him to the plumbing of a disused wash-basin.

Symins wore an ermine-collared overcoat and leather driving gloves. He grinned a good deal as he spoke, either because he admired his own teeth or because he had been told his smile made him look charming. He was a tall, rangy man of about fifty who enjoyed the considerable influence he wielded within his particular sphere of the Bristol drugs scene.

Jason had been seen twice with 'snouts' operated by Lionel Hawkins of the local drug squad. Both times he had loudly proclaimed his innocence. The men were old friends of his and he had not the faintest idea that either was a snout. Symins knew he should have acted the first time but he had a soft spot for Jason, who had worked for him since his arrival in Bristol. Twice was not just suspicious, it was downright incriminating; and Jason must now serve as a memorable example to others.

'You can sweat it out a bit, Jason. Think about yourself, mate, and you'll be the first to admit you done bad wrong. We will be lenient this time. You squeal again – so much as get seen in spitting distance of those bastards – and next time it'll be terminal.'

Symins ran his hand over his bald head, donned a cloth cap with a loud check and turned to the Cockney black girl, his secretary and mistress since she was fifteen.

'Get the cars up, Di. I don't want you here when Jason gets the surgery. Your stomach's flat and firm, OK, but is it strong enough? A masonry drill grinding through our friend here's kneecaps will not be a beautiful thing, my love. Not to see and not to hear. So we'll go back to the office for an hour or two, leave you there, then come back with the Bosch.'

The cars, parked four hundred yards up the street, responded to Di's phone and arrived at the lock-up.

'Harry, be a good lad and wait here with Jason,' Symins ordered. 'Any trouble, you fix him any way you please, but leave him *compos mentis* for the joy to come.'

Darrell Hallett drove south from his parents' smallholding in Tenby. He always felt at ease with the world after visiting them. The Avenger car headed east over the Severn Bridge, then south down the M5. Rowntree, the chocolate manufacturers, owned it and the sample boxes of Yorkie bars in the rear. Darrell was star salesman for his district and he knew it. He had worked for Rowntree for seven years since leaving the Forces.

He was at heart a country boy and most weekends he returned home to grab his rod or twelve-bore. From the age of five Darrell, with his three brothers, had spent every spare moment in the woods and fields, poaching, egg collecting, destroying wasps' nests by hand and jumping from tree tops. By the age of ten Darrell could paunch and skin a rabbit in under sixty seconds, then sell it for two bob to the local butcher. He knew the separate signs and the smells of the fox, the stoat and many other woodland creatures.

Born the year the Second World War ended, Darrell was a natural fighter. From kindergarten onwards he punched his way through half a dozen school playgrounds and, when still a youngster, became Air Training Corps Welsh Boxing Champion. In 1962 he joined the RAF Regiment and became Middleweight Champion of the RAF and the Combined Services. Trained by Dave James, he was asked by the great Al Philips to turn pro. He was a streetfighter with gloves on, but he loved Forces life too much and missed his chance for the international ring.

Darrell spoke with a gentle Welsh accent. Honesty was a religion to him and, despite his air of latent aggression, his temper was slow to rouse and his reputation for honesty and fairness had seen him reach the rank of sergeant with his regiment. He worked in the sixties

in Cyprus, Singapore, Malaya, Zambia and South Yemen, as part of the rearguard to the Empire's mostly honourable retreat from the colonies.

In 1970, two years before Darrell became a salesman for Rowntree, he was accepted into the ranks of 21 SAS Regiment (Territorials) and, four years later, was recruited into the Feather Men by Spike Allen, who needed a highly mobile Local in the South-West.

Darrell eased the Avenger off the M5 at Junction 18 and down the Portway to Hotwell Road. Bristol was not his sales area but there were few towns in the South-West he did not know reasonably well. He parked by the side of the Iceland Freezer Centre in Easton Road and crossed the street to the Pit Pony pub.

Rows of Victorian terraced houses and ill-lit streets abounded in Easton, an area of ethnic hotch-potch. There were dozens of small, shabby pubs, but the Pit Pony was different. It had recently been redecorated, and the management had kept the original atmosphere of a local working-class haunt where you could safely take your wife so long as her dictionary was wide. The walls sported brass Davy lamps, pit-pony harnesses, shovels and other coal-mining accessories, ranged above wooden booths in which stood tables and benches.

Darrell ordered two pints of Guinness and took them straight to the corner booth where Jo was waiting for him.

'Good to see you, my friend.' Jo's East European accent clashed with his checked Viyella shirt, tartan tie and immaculately pressed tweed suit. At 6.15 p.m. the pub was still fairly empty but, after greeting Josef Hongozo, Darrell fed the nearby jukebox with enough coins to keep their conversation drowned for a while.

'It's been a while, Jo,' he said, shaking the Hungarian's left hand. A Soviet tank had torn off Jo's right hand during the 1956 Budapest uprising but now, at forty-nine, he could still beat all contenders at arm wrestling.

Darrell gave Hongozo Spike's file on Symins. He felt it was unlikely to contain information that Jo did not already know, since, for a week now, he had shadowed the drug dealer's every move. The little Hungarian looked up sharply and said, 'This man is evil, you know, a bastard! He is killing our city's young people, even little children.' Jo disliked drugs in any form, even medicines when he was ill. Drug pushers he loathed.

Only Darrell and Spike knew of Hongozo's help for the Feather Men. Darrell had recruited him two years earlier after a meeting in

The Ravers transport café in Bristol's Stapleton Road. Darrell had spent three hours there awaiting darkness with interminable cups of espresso. Jo, the café's owner, had time on his hands and, being a gregarious sort, pounced on his lone clients for a friendly chat. One thing had led to another.

Jo's early life, like that of millions of Europeans, reflected the human miseries of the mid-twentieth century. Born near the Yugoslav-Hungarian border, in the farming village of Keleshalom, he had been haunted throughout his childhood by the pervasive shadow of Hitler. Local Nazis would mark village trees with the names of non-Nazi folk. 'When Hitler comes,' they would leer, 'you will dangle there.' The Stormtroopers came and many villagers died, were raped or starved. Then, in 1945, the Soviets arrived and the horrors continued.

Jo had joined the freedom fighters and shared their predictable defeat. Two years after the uprising he fled to the West with his wife, Maria. In February 1958 he settled in Bristol, where there was already a large Hungarian population. For five lean years Jo worked at the Parno-Yates washing-machine factory. He saved enough money to buy two lorries, set himself up as a haulage contractor, and cashed in on the 1965 Severn Bridge and Coventry Airport projects. He prospered and became known throughout the expatriate community as a generous donor to those in need. But his marriage suffered from his frequent absences and he parted from Maria. He then bought the café and became a solid British citizen.

Perhaps Jo saw in Darrell a bit of himself in his freedom-fighting days. Whatever his motives, he had become Darrell's anchorman whenever Spike sent the Welshman to the South-West's capital of crime.

The only time Darrell had ever seen a glint of anger in Jo's eyes was when he offered to pay his expenses. The Hungarian had hit the bowl of his clay pipe against the heel of his shoe and shaken his head.

'I will help you to help freedom, to hurt the dirty buggers who make trouble. I have had to leave my beloved Budapest because of them. Now you give me a chance to hit them a little. That is enough. Don't talk again of money.'

The Pit Pony was filling up with uniformed men and women. Raucous laughter and expletives; banalities in place of conversation.

'The city bus depot is just up the road,' Jo explained. 'The drivers bring their conductresses here before going home to their wives.'

Darrell spotted a tall executive type with a Dunlop travel bag. He nudged the Hungarian. 'That's him. Christ, he stands out like a spare prick at a wedding.' He went to the bar and offered David Mason a beer. They had never met before but each knew that Spike was unlikely to pick a rotten apple. The jukebox was silent now but drinkers were shoulder to shoulder and Concorde could have flown by at street level unnoticed.

Mason was thankful he had hired a Ford Escort. The Porsche would have risked more than its paintwork in the pub car park, where groups of mostly white young rowdies sat on the low brick wall looking for trouble or anything that might alleviate their boredom.

'We have two hours before Symins goes home at 8.30 p.m.,' said Jo. 'He is as regular as the clockwork. He is due back at what he calls a justice session any time now. Then home. I will take you to see what sort of bugger this man is even with his own men. Then I know you will not pussyfoot like English gentlemen later tonight.'

'Is he local?' Mason asked. 'I mean, has he always been on the Bristol crime scene?' Spike's file had been positively skeletal.

Jo shook his head and relit his pipe. 'Not local, no,' he replied, 'but in the two years he's been here, he's cut himself a strong corner of the local drugs market.'

Darrell thought Jo was wasted as the owner of a transport café. He had an amazing knack of ferreting out details, an ability that had saved Darrell time and embarrassment on a number of occasions. Symins, Jo now told him, had spent much of his youth in Australia after his family emigrated from London in the mid fifties. By the end of the sixties he was worth three hundred thousand pounds, having benefited from the burgeoning Sydney drugs scene. When the Sydney police put on the pressure, Symins, and others like him, moved to Pakistan. He thrived until, in 1975, the Pakistan police found a ton of cannabis in a boat that he owned.

Symins returned home to Britain. His first attempt to set up shop in Isleworth, West London, met with a bloody nose from the entrenched dealers' heavies. Cautiously he tested the water elsewhere, eventually deciding on Bristol, where his girlfriend, Diana, had close relatives already pushing drugs in St Paul's.

'Our Mr Symins took things slow and easy at first,' Jo explained. 'Didn't make the mistake so many of them do: rushing into someone else's kitchen. That's the quickest route to concrete boots. He settled down with his black bitch and her cousins and sussed out the ground.'

Jo explained the territories. The Bristol criminal fraternity are far more provincial than their London counterparts, seldom operating beyond the clearly defined boundaries of their often long-established fiefdoms. To find an uncontested niche took Symins quite a while. The black district of St Paul's offered a network of dark streets where white prostitutes operated by black pimps serviced a non-stop fleet of kerb crawlers. The police, in a vain attempt to control drug pushers and prostitutes, had turned many streets into culs-de-sac. Black gangs had then lured police patrol cars into these traps and beaten up the officers. *Touché*. No-go areas resulted, the territory of black capos, and no place for the likes of Symins despite the drug opportunities offered at the nightly shebeens, illegal drink parties open to anybody with fifty pence to pay for a Guinness or Red Stripe.

Westbury on Trym was a respectable, middle-class area where few drug targets existed, but neighbouring Southmead looked ripe. Built in the thirties to house folks from the inner-city slums, the place was all red brick and, to Symins, had the signs of good pickings. But he was several years too late: Southmead was in the grip of a local family, and Ronnie and his trio of hulking sons dealt summarily with would-be poachers.

'Ronnie is into the lot,' said Jo. 'Drugs, protection and toms. Nothing moves in Southmead but he and his boys know it.'

'What's toms?' Darrell asked.

'Prostitutes.'

'Not much left then for our Patrice?'

'Not in Southmead, no. But he had a go in Knowle West at the beginning of '76. After a month he was rumbled by the West Coast Chapter of the Hell's Angels, who run an HQ deep in nearby Knowle, a couple of houses knocked together by sledgehammer. They did that one day to fit in an extra-long billiard table. They hold cannabis and speed parties, immune to surprise drugs raids thanks to steel doors and a video surveillance set-up. A couple of Angels live in but thirty more arrive within minutes when summoned. They soon saw Symins off.'

'You're making me sympathetic to the poor bloke,' Mason said.

'Well he is certainly a trier ... Clifton was next, all middle-class students and rich folk. Plenty of takers, but too many police. Symins especially liked Clifton as he's a snob and Cliftonians reckon they're the cream of Bristol.'

So Symins had settled for Stoke Bishop, among the grassy heights

of Bristol's more affluent suburbs, which contain a mixture of well-heeled *nouveaux riches* and struggling middle-class families. The inhabitants mix very little, which assured Symins of privacy without suspicion.

Three years previously the government had removed the right of general practitioners to prescribe heroin or cocaine except for patients with proven terminal illnesses. Until then any junkie could obtain a controlled amount of his chosen drug legally. With this cushy arrangement ended, the street price of drugs escalated overnight, and from his eyrie in Stoke Bishop Symins masterminded a rash of break-ins to chemists all over the South-West. In Bristol itself he controlled these activities except in Keynsham, Knowle West and Montpelier, where other teams were active under mini-tyros such as Joe Lembo (subsequently caught and given five years in prison).

'What about his pushing system?' Darrell asked Jo.

'He has an expanding network of student pushers controlled by black colleagues, mostly friends of his mistress, and kept in line by half a dozen thugs who also protect his person. They are efficient, but ...' — Jo preened himself — 'there is a loophole.' With the aid of Mason's silver Parker pen and a beer-mat, Jo demonstrated how he would help the two Locals.

They left the pub and walked to the southern end of Pennywell Road. Jo led the way into a deserted yard and over a chain-link fence. This joined a high wall, the main purpose of which was to conceal an evil-smelling waterway, a dank canal that was all that remained of the once scenic River Frome. They followed the wall for a hundred yards, then scaled it using a hook and knotted line that Jo produced from an overcoat pocket. 'Natty, eh?' He looked at both men. He was in his element and needed surprisingly little help beyond a tug to the top.

From the wall they dropped into a scrapyard, or rather a garden used as a rubbish dump, and Mason knelt to unzip his Dunlop bag. He took out a ten-inch-long tubular instrument on loan from Spike, and left the bag hidden by brambles at the foot of the wall. Moving with care among the rubbish, Jo made for the rear of a low buiding with double doors. As the three watched, gaps in the doors were faintly illuminated by some low light source within.

Jo said nothing but pointed to one of the gaps. Mason nodded and screwed a telescopic monopod into his eavesdropping device. A prototype of a device later developed as the Wolf's Ear 1411 and

obtainable through the Surveillance Technology Group in Port Chester, New York, it was a 'mini-shotgun', bi-directional system capable of collecting sound from up to five hundred feet away. Powered by a built-in 1.5 volt battery, it weighed only two and a half ounces and could be used in conjunction with earplugs, binoculars and tape recorder. Mason positioned the Wolf's Ear and gave Hallett one of the earplugs. The two men listened to the action, while Hongozo watched their backs.

Four men, all smoking cigarettes, stood around as Symins stressed the heinous nature of Jason's betrayal. He ended, appearing to expect an acknowledgement from the accused. There was none because someone had liberally applied sticking plaster to Jason's mouth in readiness for the coming punishment.

'He'll be difficult to hold once we get started,' one of the heavies warned.

'That's what the tool-box is for, ya twit,' said another. 'Boss said to nail him down.'

'The floor's concrete.'

'Use your nous, Spitty. What's wrong with the back doors? Bring the lamp.'

The three men in the backyard could now see nothing and the Wolf's Ear was redundant since they were inches from Symins and his men.

Sounds of a violent struggle ended with the noise of hammering. There were no screams, merely muted laughter. One by one the points of four eight-inch nails appeared through the door frame.

Hallett's ham-like fists clenched and the veins swelled in his neck. 'Bastards,' he hissed. 'They're crucifying him.'

Mason laid a restraining hand on his back. 'Calm yourself, Darrell. There's worse to come. We don't want you bursting in there like a raging bull. They will have guns. We do not.'

They heard the unmistakable hum of a portable generator and, just distinguishable, the whine of a Bosch power drill. Although they could neither see nor hear what followed, each man felt nausea at the inhumanity of Symins and his thugs.

Mason had spent twelve months in Northern Ireland some years earlier and had, for a month, been a frequent visitor to the Vascular Unit of the Royal Victoria Hospital in Belfast. One of his friends was being treated there for a spinal bullet injury and David had often chatted to the RAMC surgeons. Over a twelve-year period the

surgeons at the hospital had become specialists in treating the hideous damage caused by kneecapping. Bullets often missed the patella altogether but still caused severe vascular trauma. Many victims were men in the prime of life whose futures were marred through osteoporosis or, where gas gangrene set in, amputation. At least, Mason thought, the poor devil in the lock-up was to be kneecapped with an electric drill, about the ultimate in low-velocity weapons. When flesh and bone is penetrated by foreign matter, the higher the velocity of the projectile the greater the damage done. Nevertheless, the long-term benefits of a masonry drill over a bullet would not at that moment mean very much to the tormented Jason. Mason felt pressure on his shoulder. Jo was tapping his watch. They left by the way they had come.

Symins addressed Jason's lolling head, uncertain whether or not he was conscious. 'We will phone the fire service in twelve hours, matey. Then us tax-payers will pay for your recovery.' He flashed his very white teeth at the others, who responded with guffaws. 'In the meanwhile you'd better talk yourself into being a good boy. When you come out of the Krankenhaus, we'll see if you're still on the payroll.'

Symins drove off in his Jaguar Mark Ten and the others followed in a stretch Ford Granada. In convoy they headed north-west for the Downs, over the open grasslands and along Lady's Mile to a prominent water tower. Here they forked left to Julian Road, home of the police forensic headquarters. An open field known as the Plateau fell away to the south, ending abruptly at the clifftop of the Avon Gorge. The heart of Stoke Bishop, Mariners Drive, is a place of secluded houses set back from the road and screened by the shrubbery of their well-tended gardens. Only the Anglican Church stands out and, not far past this landmark of piety, the Jaguar turned into Symins's drive. When the electronic gates snapped shut behind the boss, the heavies in the Granada swung away, their work done for the day.

Symins had sunk a good deal of his drug profits into this house and its comprehensive security arrangements. Apart from his driver and domestic staff there was a live-in gardener who doubled as in-house heavy.

Symins enjoyed a double brandy in front of a log fire while Diana, naked to the waist, massaged his shoulders and neck. Looking into the flames he again felt a surge of adrenaline as he remembered Jason's bulging eyeballs. The drill had slowly penetrated skin and

bone and the man's limbs, though nailed to the door, had jerked out in ginglymus rhythm. A weird smell had emanated from the drill bit which, making heavy weather of the patella itself, had heated up inside the wound. Yes, he had been right to punish Jason. Even if the man was innocent of squealing, it did no harm to show the others that Patrice Symins was not a man to cross. Word of Jason's drilling was bound to get about the city and that could only help Symins's reputation as a hard man. He felt pleasantly tired.

As he made to move, Diana slipped a caressing hand lightly over his crotch. 'Not tonight, Josephine,' he laughed. 'I'm knackered, love.' His philosophy was simple with Diana where bed was concerned: sleep with her only when horny, otherwise there was no point. Familiarity would dull the edge of his reactions to her sensuality.

Symins kept no gun to hand in his house. He trusted his security systems and staff enough to feel totally at ease. There were alarm buttons in those rooms he frequented but at home he liked to drop his antennae and relax. Tonight he lazed in the jacuzzi and then, as usual, took the day's *Financial Times* to bed with him, for he handled his own considerable investment portfolio without advisers.

Soundlessly Hallett and Mason moved out from behind the heavy brocade curtains and across the soft carpet. Not until the blade of Hallett's penknife was pressed into the side of his Adam's apple did Symins even sense his visitors' presence. His first thought was for the alarm button beside his bed. Hallett read his mind. 'The systems in your suite are both cut, so forget the heavies. The slightest move of your head and you will undergo the fastest crico-thyroidectomy since the Korean War.'

Mason pulled the duvet off the bed, placed plastic handcuffs over Symin's wrists and then lashed his feet together. Only then did Darrell withdraw his knife. On evenings such as this both Locals had often regretted Spike's dictum that they should never carry firearms when in Britain.

A pretentious chandelier of crystal baubles dangled in the middle of the ceiling. Mason applied his weight to its centrepiece. 'Solid,' he exclaimed and, locking Symins's hands behind his back, he joined the cuffs to the chandelier with a loop of parachute cord. He then pulled steadily until Symins's arms were taut and the drug baron was standing on tiptoe to counter the sharp pain in his shoulders.

'This is known in Tehran's Evin Prison as the Savaki Meat Hook,'

David explained, 'but we must ensure silence before the next step is taken.'

'How much money do you want?' Symins mouthed. 'Name your price and I'll give you cash here and now.'

'He comes straight to the point, doesn't he?' said Darrell, forcing his thumb into the side of Symins's mouth with the same action he used for training gundogs. He forced Symins's socks into his mouth, then tied the cord of his dressing gown firmly around his neck and open mouth like a horse's bit. 'Soundproof,' he muttered. Together they hauled at the parachute cord until Symins could reach the floor with his toes, but only with great difficulty.

Mason sat on the end of the bed, lit up a Montecristo Number 5 and leafed through the *Financial Times*. This was Darrell's pigeon. Jo had remained in the rhododendrons below, safe from Symins's Rhodesian ridgebacks due to the bags of aniseed powder he had sprinkled liberally between where the others had crossed the wall and the drainpipe leading to Symins's bedroom window.

'Who are we?' Darrell asked Symins and, getting no reply, jabbed him in the stomach, so that he swung back and forth gently until the tips of his toes were again able to take some weight and alleviate the excruciating pain in his arms. 'We are two of many men who have been asked to watch you. Wherever you go in this country, we will not be far away. Ten years from now we will be keeping tabs. What you do with your own people, boyo, is not our concern. If they put up with your sadism, so be it. But . . .' – Darrell gave Symins another shove on behalf of Jason – 'your drugs activities will cease completely as from tonight. To help you never to forget this evening, we will stay with you for an hour or so. If, in the future, you look back and remember this little dalliance in hell, please know that it is but a mild introduction to next time.'

He hauled hard on the cord with one hand while hoisting upwards with his other hand crooked in Symins's crotch. He did not want the chandelier fixture to break. Symins now swung free. He was not in pain – he was in agony. Most of us go through life without experiencing more than a few seconds of such anguish.

Darrell concluded his monologue. 'Make no mistake, perhaps in five years' time, in thinking there will not be a next time. If you touch the drug world again we will visit you in earnest.' He glanced at his watch then, making himself comfortable in an easy chair, he pulled out a paperback of George Borrow's 1862 travel classic, *Wild Wales.*

At home Darrell had a collection of hardback travel and adventure stories, many of them signed by the authors. Often, when he had a spare hour or two, he would phone around publishers and old bookshops to chase up titles long out of print, to fill gaps in his collection.

After thirty minutes they lowered Symins to the carpet for ten minutes. Then they raised him on tiptoe for fifteen, and finally to dangle height for a further half hour. When they departed they left him still suspended but with his feet on the ground.

Hallett silently hoped Symins would be *non compos mentis* by the time his breakfast was brought up in the morning. It would depend largely on his pain threshold.

Mason did not bother to reset the alarm circuit on their way out. Spike could hardly make a fuss over a couple of lost circuit-breaker sets. They followed Hongozo over the wall and he drove them back to their cars in the city.

'An honour to meet you, mister.' The Hungarian shook Mason's hand. They did not know each other's name. He hugged Darrell in his East European way. 'Don't make it too long until next time, my friend.'

The two Locals parted. Hallett was subdued. It would be days before he lost the vision of the eight-inch nails appearing through the lock-up doors. Mason was unaffected. The proceedings had passed off as Spike would have wanted. The result might well be as hoped. He stopped at a telephone box and called Spike's answering machine. 'Everything is fine,' he said. He gave neither the time nor his name. Spike would be in his flat listening to the machine and would recognize David's voice. If anything had gone wrong, he would have done what he could as an individual, but without Committee involvement. That was their way.

6

The Seine, the music of an unseen accordion and the Gallic bustle of the Marché Vernaison flea market drifted by the gypsy café, lulling its diners, mostly tourists, into a nostalgic haze. The waiters were gypsies clad in black berets and aprons, and there was an air of slick disdain about their trim moustaches. The head waiter, who fancied himself as a bit of a Maigret, decided that the three gentlemen at table seven were international businessmen. Their lack of raincoats suggested that they had come from the only hotel close by, the George V. He deduced they had already spent a couple of nights at the hotel since its in-house restaurant, Les Princes, served exquisite food enhanced by a famous cellar. He nudged the *sous-chef*. 'Sanch will do well at number seven. Those three are from the George. If they can afford nine hundred a night they will add twenty percent service, no problem.'

De Villiers and Davies were clearly middle-aged executives but Meier looked out of place. His heavy tweed suit was crumpled – his trousers, although a couple of sizes too large, failed to conceal a battered pair of clogs – and the lenses of his steel-rimmed spectacles needed cleaning.

'This steak tastes too sweet to be cow,' Davies muttered.

'Probably horse,' de Villiers said. 'Never mind. The fries look good.'

'Chips,' said Davies. 'You mean chips.'

De Villiers shrugged. A waiter brought him the lobster he had selected from the tank where the poor creatures waited to be boiled alive. He sat with his back to the steaming lobster vat. That way he could see the café entrance but not the tortured sea creatures. Their silent screams occurred at precisely the same time as those of Patrice Symins, by now in a state of solitary suspension. The lobsters, by contrast, had done nothing to deserve their torment.

Over coffee and cognac the three members of the Clinic discussed business, their conversation drowned between the babble at the bar and the bargaining sessions at the *brocanteurs'* stores opposite the café. Meier, unlike the others, spoke French. He reported on the

media's treatment of the murder, or rather the conspicuous absence of such treatment.

This did not please de Villiers.

'Why the silence? This is just the sort of smut they adore to headline. All the right ingredients.' He shrugged. 'Too bad; she has paid up regardless.'

Meier, who had been ferreting, had partial answers.

'The judge was involved with international rights in Mururoa Atoll five years ago. The French had burnt their fingers with their nuclear tests. They maybe have some reason for a hush-up now.'

Davies was more lively than de Villiers had seen him in years. The Paris job had suited his temperament and de Villiers, having received the client's full payment that morning, had already given both men their cheques. Fifteen percent of the total payment of four hundred and fifty thousand dollars would go to Tadnams, the agents, thirty-five percent to de Villiers and the balance was split down the middle between the other two. The ten percent differential between his slice and theirs helped to reinforce his position as leader. He maintained these percentages for any job completed by the Clinic even when only two members were involved in the action.

Meier, a naturally uncommunicative sort, came alive only when able to indulge his passion for technical innovation. He would, de Villiers knew, spend all his Paris money on advanced radio-controlled model aircraft kits and on whoring somewhere exotic.

Davies would rush back to his pretty little wife in Cardiff laden with gifts and a fat cheque made payable to her interior-decorating business. Mrs Davies, de Villiers suspected, was unfaithful to her husband during his long absences on sales tours but, realizing she might never find another man as blindly doting or as generous, she strung him along and depended on his pay cheques to fill the voracious purse of her business. She had been born devoid of taste and stayed that way despite expensive courses at London's Inchbold School of Design. Each decorating job that she obtained – and many came about through liberal application of her body to middle-aged bachelors who did not really want their penthouses redecorated – became a new glaring testament to her reputation for appalling judgement.

One day, de Villiers feared, Davies would arrive home to find his missus wrapped around some poor yuppy whose flat she wished to face-lift. The results, he reflected, would not be a pretty sight, for

when in a rage Davies did not respect the niceties of civilized life.

Although there was very little de Villiers did not know about his colleagues, his own circumstances and background were forbidden topics that both men had long since learned never to broach. They trusted de Villiers simply because he had always, to the best of their knowledge, played fair with them. He trusted them because he took the trouble to keep abreast of their problems and to know their limitations.

In a world of deceit and back-stabbing, a profession where over ninety percent of practitioners work alone, the Clinic had managed to remain an effective and cohesive working group for four years. This was, of course, largely due to de Villiers's personality which was sincere and straightforward, giving the impression of a positive individual unlikely to suffer from anxiety or indecision. This stemmed from his character, which, unlike his mien, was extremely aggressive. Deep down de Villiers boiled with a sense of fury, a rage at the injustice of Fate and a desperate yearning for roots and a mother's love.

Was he normal? Can a contract killer be normal? Normal people certainly can and do perform outrageous or sadistic acts but not repeatedly, to order. Such people almost always appear callous, shifty or aggressive in their everyday life. De Villiers's ruthlessness, by contrast, did not show through in his day-to-day behaviour. He could kill a young woman, by whatever means might suit the contract, before noon and within minutes be enjoying the banalities of lunchtime gossip and the taste of good food.

His Jekyll and Hyde character was able to support this duality without betraying a hint of outward unpleasantness. If he ever thought about it, de Villiers would claim that he killed purely to make a living. He would deny that there was an inner compulsion, a burning need to get even with Fate.

Since de Villers made a particular point of meeting would-be clients in person and carefully assessing possible contracts before accepting them, he took less leave than Meier and Davies. He averaged perhaps three or four weeks' holiday a year, which he invariably spent hunting for rare species of game alone and equipped with the best photographic gear money can buy.

De Villiers paid, adding no tip since the bill was clearly printed *Service inclus* and he was ashamed of having enjoyed the excellent lobster. The others left to find separate cabs to favourite nightspots.

De Villiers reflected on lessons learned in Paris, on contacts made that might be useful in the future. After a second cognac he returned to the hotel at 31 Avenue George V and put through a call to a number in the Cape Province. There was no answer. He put the phone down and for a moment felt a touch of loneliness. He sat in the over-plush bar for a while, indulging in his favourite activity: observing people. But the subject-matter was poor. Two gay barmen, an ageing Californian film star with her silent toy boy and an off-duty receptionist picking his nose behind a copy of *Paris Match*.

He passed through the silent foyer hung with fine Gobelin tapestries and tipped a porter who brought him an envelope on a salver. Back in his room, he exercised for twenty minutes then, with an Evian from the mini-bar, lay back and read the message from Tadnams. He was to go immediately to their office in Earls Court and be ready to fly on to the Arabian Gulf.

7

...A scum-laden lake marks the north-easterly limit of safety for joggers in Central Park, New York City. Beyond the lake you wander at your own risk unless you are poor and black. This rule of thumb held good in the autumn of 1964 but the rich kid from Oklahoma had no knowledge of the do's and don'ts of Lower Harlem. Visiting his grandmother at her spacious apartment in Park Avenue, he had agreed to take her beagle for her evening walk in the nearby park.

Some five minutes' walk into the scrub and glades that cover the region between the museum and the central reservoir, he found a grassy space, unleashed the beagle and threw her rubber ball. The dog, whose bouncy days were increasingly rare, broke into a half-hearted trot to show willing. She halted by the ball and turned back to the boy, tail wagging and grinning as only beagles can, when the six-inch bolt penetrated her neck. She fell without a sound.

The boy looked around. Three youths in bomber jackets stood in the shadows. One held a steel crossbow and, over his shoulder, an empty golfer's bag.

'You'd better give the dawg his last rights, sonny.' The speaker

had a crewcut and obviously spent a good deal of his time pumping iron.

The boy went wild and, rushing at the bowman, swung hard with the beagle's chain. By chance the linked end caught the youth across one eye and the bridge of his nose.

'Scumbag bastard,' he cried out. He was temporarily blinded but his friends pinned the boy against a tree to await his recovery. Through tears of pain, and fearing he had lost an eye, the bowman grunted his fury. 'Strip the bugger and glue him to the tree. I'll teach him who to mess with.'

Using his shirt and their own belts, they lashed the boy's arms so that he faced outwards. His handkerchief was jammed into his mouth. He wet himself with fear. Two bolts struck his right leg above the knee. A third entered his left thigh and he fainted. The jeers of the bowman's friends probably saved his life by attracting the attention of a jogger. The newcomer wore tracksuit trousers and a loose, jungle-green T-shirt. As he entered the clearing he showed little interest in the boy, the dog, or the yobs. 'Hi, friends.' He raised a hand in greeting as he slowed. 'Which way is the reservoir?'

As the bowman thought of a suitably unhelpful reply, the jogger's hand whipped up and drove a finger into his good eye. This was followed immediately by a simple karate toe-kick, the ujima, to the groin of the nearest man. The third bomber jacket's flick-knife was out but, whipping the crossbow from the ground and finding it loaded, the jogger pulled the trigger. The file-sharpened bolt passed easily through the man's guts and embedded itself in his spine. He screamed but the butt of the crossbow crashed down on the base of his neck and there was silence save for the chuckle of grey squirrels.

The jogger knelt beside the beagle and gently felt for a heartbeat. Applying counter-pressure around the entry hole, he withdrew the bolt and tied his vest round the dog's neck. 'You'll live, girl,' he crooned as he stroked the bitch's droopy ears. He laid her down and attended to the boy, suspecting heavy internal bleeding in the thigh.

He found a traffic policeman in nearby East 85th Street, gave him his name, Captain Daniel de Villiers, and the address of the fellow Marine with whom he lodged. He stayed until an ambulance came, but feigned ignorance when asked about the state of the hoodlums, the boy and the dog. He wondered to himself, would he have intervened were it not for the beagle? Cruelty to animals was a weak spot with de Villiers.

There had been a stray cat at the boys' orphange in Vancouver and, later, an ill-fed parrot kept by his adoptive mother in the Bronx, a woman whom he never understood since she beat him for the mildest infringement of her 'good manners code' yet nursed him with apparent affection whenever he came home from school with a split nose or swollen eyebrow. When she died, coughing blood, de Villiers took a daytime job as a photographer's assistant and cat-burgled by night. When the parrot died he was seventeen with savings in the bank and no ambition but to work with animals. He enlisted but his phenomenal physique and propensity for measured thought attracted the attention of a Marine Corps recruitment sergeant long before he could home in on his original target, the US Veterinary Corps.

At twenty-three, with four harrowing years in Vietnam behind him, de Villiers might well have made the military his career. Perhaps he would have done so but for a long-festering desire to seek his roots, to find his family.

For a year he held down a desk job at Bradley Air Base, spending free weekends trekking in the Catskills with Marine friends. In the winter of 1964 he resigned his commission and cashed all his savings. His only clue was his father's bible, his most treasured possession. The flyleaf was inscribed 'For Piet from his loving mother. Vrede Huis, Tokai 1891'...

8

In the days before the staff of SAS headquarters took on the responsibility for all British Special Force units, including the SBS (Special Boat Squadron), and moved to their current control centre, they were located for many years close to Sloane Square. SAS senior administrators occupied the attic level of the central block of the Duke of York's Barracks. Their offices gave on to a single central corridor reached only by a flight of concrete stairs surveyed by cameras, at the top of which were two steel doors to a vacuum-sealed 'frisk chamber'.

In the early seventies some of the SAS office windows were declared vulnerable to hi-tech snooping from the flats in Cheltenham

Terrace, across the garrison running track. Protective screening was installed but security remained generally limp. Immediately below the attic level was an empty hall which the barracks authority hired out to more or less any public group looking for a spacious rendezvous. On the morning of Wednesday 5 January 1977, Gordon Jackson and others of the cast of *Upstairs, Downstairs*, a BBC television series then showing worldwide, trooped out of the hall to make way for a meeting of a charity organization.

The two civilian security guards manning the barracks' gatehouse were affable West Africans who, noting that the Hampstead Support Group of the Royal Chelsea Hospital were due to meet that morning, happily allowed entry to any individual who mentioned the name of that charity. 'Know where to go?' was their only question.

First to arrive was Bob Mantell, formerly with 2 Commando and a retired City banker. He tidied away the crumpled script sheets and emptied the ashtrays, muttering under his breath about BBC wasters. He placed pencils and sheets of A4 paper in front of the battered chairs ranged around the rectangular table, the only furniture in the gloomy hall.

Others arrived alone or in groups. There were greetings – some hearty, some gruff. August Graves, a sixty-five-year-old black-cab driver and obsessive radio ham, made a great deal of noise before and after meetings, but unless goaded rarely opened his mouth during them. Yet his ability to find out anything about anyone in the Greater London area was nothing short of miraculous. He was also a conduit to various criminal minds, although he himself had never strayed from the straight and narrow. He arrived in the company of the Don, who had recently retired from a senior position at Warwick University.

The Twins, in their mid seventies but looking older, had first met in prison around the time the Second World War broke out. They were given probationary leave to join the Royal Engineers and after the war became plumbers. While completing a job in the late sixties, they had met up with the Founder. Like August Graves, they had street savvy and contacts that were of great value to the Committee.

Jane, whose surname nobody ever used, arrived in heated debate with Bletchley, the Chairman of the day, who was an old-fashioned and dogmatic Tory. 'Turncoat,' Jane muttered. 'He's a traitor of the worst sort. Wilson has the decency to make him Home Secretary and look what he does – makes fools of us all. And for why?'

'Because, dear lady,' Bletchley rejoined, 'he has the good sense to realize this country belongs to Europe. Heath is right. We cannot survive by ourselves now the Commonwealth is gone, and your Roy Jenkins is one of the few socialists to acknowledge the fact. Good on him, I say. Hallo, Mantell. Everything ready, I see. Good man.'

Bletchley sat down at the head of the table and busied himself with his notes. At that stage, to outward appearances at least, he was still a well man.

Jane, a prim and righteous spinster, was fastidious and worshipped the Founder. The previous two-monthly meeting had been held at the Hampstead house where Jane had selflessly nursed her mother until her death some years before. Jane, like the Don, had worked with Intelligence during the Second World War. She took ten plastic mugs from her shopping bag and doled them out around the table, placing a four-pint vacuum flask of white coffee by her own place at the opposite end of the table to the Chairman. To Jane little rituals were what life was all about.

Last to arrive were Colonel Tommy Macpherson, the Chairman of the London Branch of the CBI, together with Michael Panny and Spike Allen. 'The good news or the bad?' Panny addressed the room in his normal jovial manner. He was a man who set much store by feeling popular. Most of the others detested him but, an ex-commercial lawyer and a mine of City information, he was Bletchley's protégé and as such an unavoidable fixture. Nobody replied.

'Well, the bad news is Roy Jenkins has resigned. The good that those foul-mouthed Sex Pistols have been sacked by their own record company.'

Spike sat beside Bletchley, whom he disliked, a fact nobody would have suspected since Spike showed about as much emotion as a basking cobra. Spike preferred the alternate meetings when Macpherson was Chairman. He knew there would be trouble about the Bristol job so he had decided to report on Islington first.

Colonel Tommy Macpherson and Bletchley were, with the Founder, the initiators of the Committee. Now eight years and many successes later, Macpherson looked at Bletchley and wondered how the Founder, such a magnificent judge of men, had chosen him at all. And yet he too had originally thought the man was sound. Come to think of it, he really had been a first-class mover in the early days and a great source of inspiration. It had been he who had first coined the phrase 'the Feather Men' — 'because our touch is light'. Somewhere

along the line, however, Bletchley had undergone a subtle change.

Although he had known the Founder for over forty years and despite the fact that both men were from Highland clans, had served during the war in the Special Forces and been POWs in Germany (the Founder in Colditz), Macpherson never really knew the inner workings of the Founder's brilliant mind. His precise motives for starting the Committee were lost in the mists of time but there had been rumours of a tragedy. They concerned someone close to the Founder whose death in 1968 could have been prevented but for the inadequacy of the police. The latter's scope and budget, not their efficiency, had been to blame. There were not enough police in the right place at the right time.

The very decency of democracy hinders the prevention of numerous crimes. In Belfast, the British Army knows the identity of a dozen or more IRA killers but the law forbids the forces of the law to 'take them out'. So the killers will strike again and again. This principle also applies to drug pushers, muggers and other such predators at large throughout the United Kingdom.

The Founder knew his limitations; he was not about to take on the evils of the nation as a whole. He stuck to his own niche since charity begins at home. He was intimately involved with the family of SAS regiments, regular and territorial, and would set up a body of watchdogs to look after the well-being of the two thousand-plus ex-members of the Artists Rifles Regiment and other SAS units. This body would also respond to cries for help that were beyond the scope of the existing regimental associations.

It is a sad fact of life in democratic societies that there are no-go areas where crime thrives and innocent citizens are preyed upon yet where the police are powerless to act.

In the early 1950s 21 SAS Regiment was based close to St Pancras station and headed by the famous wartime commando, Colonel Charles Newman VC. Newman was one of a number of ex-Special Forces daredevils including Colonels Lapraik, Sutherland and Bill Macpherson, who successively commanded 21 SAS. The last-named, soon to be Chief of the Clan Macpherson, was a relation of Colonel Tommy Macpherson.

One day a veteran sergeant approached Colonel Newman and complained that his family had been threatened by local hoodlums in Notting Hill. Newman called a meeting of half a dozen stalwarts and a deputation in civilian dress visited the source of harassment.

The tactic worked and reached the ears of the Founder. Technically no law of the land had been breached, for the Notting Hill gangsters did not call the SAS men's bluff and no violence took place.

All matters for Committee business were collated by Bob Mantell from diverse sources about the country, mostly ex-SAS men in various professions, including the police. Wherever Mantell could persuade the injured party to deal with the problem through the police he would do so, but in nearly every case the police had already been approached and had been unable to help.

After the usual preamble, Bletchley began the meeting with a short list of minor cases to be handled and of actions that appeared to have been ineffective. After an hour, business moved on to two topics labelled by Bletchley as 'tender'. Both were the territory of Spike Allen.

Spike was no great wordsmith. 'Islington,' he said, looking up very briefly from his papers, 'worked well. The info from August proved reliable and the Mercedes has already been returned to our friends together with a thousand pounds in cash for the inconvenience.'

Bletchley nodded. 'The police?' he asked quietly.

Spike was ready for him. 'Our Local checked at the Upper Street Station. Mr James had reported the theft to them immediately the car disappeared. He explained how he knew that the Davenham Garage's service department were in league with the Islington mob and how it was safe to deduce the car would, over a period of at least three hours, be processed at their spray shop.'

Spike checked backwards through his report. 'The police called him back two *days* later with the usual refrain. There was no sign of the car and the police had no power to inspect Davenham's service depot without a warrant.'

'How many people did you send to Davenham's?' Bletchley asked. He always laid great emphasis on the need for minimal force.

'Three,' said Spike. 'All on the large side.'

'Are you happy, Michael?'

Bletchley addressed the former lawyer Panny, who nodded. 'August knows the Davenham brothers well. They're too small to need to make a point merely to save their egos and they can hardly complain to the police of intimidation used to force them to return stolen property to its rightful owners. No, I think Spike handled the whole thing with the right amount of pressure.'

Spike, never one to hog the limelight, thanked the Twins, who

had advised him on the level of fear likely to get the car back. In the same breath he switched to his Bristol report, hoping to bathe it in the glow of goodwill generated by the success in Islington.

'Bristol,' he announced. 'The operation which the Committee sanctioned at the September meeting last year. This was completed in November and I can now safely state there has been no comeback to or from the police, nor any media publicity. Our Local has good contacts in the city and confirms that Symins, the man directly responsible for the death of our friend's daughter, has moved from Bristol.'

Spike tapped the blue folder in front of him. 'Jane has given everyone copies of my detailed report.'

The Don looked up. 'Not exactly detailed,' he murmured. 'Two pages only and all of that deals with the target. I, for one, would like to know more of our own activities. I fully understand that they obtained the required result, but what form did they take? Since they were effected in our name, we must be sure we would approve of the methods used by your Locals, don't you think?'

There was a murmur of agreement from most of the others, as Spike had expected. 'I took the advice of Committee members as to the best means of forcing this issue.' He did not look their way but both of the Twins became heavily preoccupied with their folders at this point. 'Anything less persuasive, they assured me, would have been a waste of time with this man. There were only two Locals involved and both knew precisely how far to go. There will have been virtually no signs of physical damage to Symins.'

The Don's face was grave. 'You had this man tortured then?'

Spike explained the means used by Hallett and Mason. He did not mention their names, since Mantell, who had laid the ground rules, stressed that only Spike must know Locals' identities. Then, should any Local turn sour, he or she would be able to recognize Spike but none of the other Committee members. No Local knew Spike's real name, nor his address – only the number of his answering machine and a postbox number. Should Spike die, his trustees would send Bletchley and Macpherson sealed envelopes containing the contact details of the Locals.

'Never mind the lack of scars,' the Don persisted. 'To all intents and purposes we, the Committee, have condoned the use of torture. Yes or no?'

'Hang on, mate.' It was August, with a reddish tinge to his cheeks.

'Spike was tasked to get rid of this bastard, this child-killer, without injuring him. Well, he has and I say congratulations to Spike and his lads in the West Country. Blimey, what d'you expect, Don?' He hit the table with his folder. 'You don't crack a nut with a pair of scissors, do you?'

The Don remained calm. 'Nobody's talking of scissors. But hook-hanging is a favourite with the world's most unpleasant regimes. The Nazis used it and today it is popular throughout the Middle East. Just read through any Amnesty International report. The hook-hang can drive a person insane overnight. It is an inhumanity that I would not condone for my worst enemy.'

The fatter of the two Twins muttered, 'Your worst bloody enemy, Don, is probably your tax inspector. Your head's in the sand, man. The heavy stuff is the only thing these druggies understand. If Spikey hadn't scared him rigid, he'd not have turned a hair and he'd be latching himself back on to the Bristol kiddies as though nothing had ever happened.' He subsided, having made the longest speech any Committee member remembered ever coming from either Twin.

'We exist to deal with men of this ilk,' the Don countered, 'but not by trading violence for violence. We could, I am sure, have scared him off equally well with a heavy dose of fear. I'm not advocating cracking nuts with scissors, August, but I am recommending that we shatter glasses by emitting the right frequency. Ours should be a game of chess, of emotion and timing. First we obtain up-to-date, accurate information, then we strike by guile not force. That way we stay legal and we retain our decency.'

'Perhaps,' Bletchley suggested smoothly, 'Spike could not obtain sufficient information and had to overreact as a result?' Macpherson noticed that Bletchley's eyes were performing disconcerting saccades.

'My information was detailed and sufficient for our purposes,' Spike replied. 'Our sources in Bristol are first-class. They confirmed that our target would not respond to verbal warnings and threats alone.'

'In that case,' Bletchley snapped, 'should you not have come back to the Committee at once? We could have looked at the operation again. Chosen a different path or even aborted.'

The Chairman raised his arms in an abrupt gesture and spilled his coffee. Jane was at once on her feet to fetch paper from the nearby lavatory.

'You are raising the issue of our general policy, are you not?'

Macpherson's voice was cold. 'Can we take it you have moved on from the specific subject of Bristol?'

Spike listened with interest. He made a point of not participating in the intermittent heated exchanges between Committee members, but he never missed a nuance. Over the past three years he felt that Bletchley had become increasingly dogmatic. Only Macpherson, in Spike's opinion, had the influence to prevent Bletchley from dampening the spirits of the Committee to the point of emasculation.

Bletchley could normally count on the support of Mantell and Panny where a matter of law and order was concerned but Macpherson, as a last resort, could fall back on the casting vote of the Founder, absent but still the *éminence grise*.

Mantell had recruited and run the first few Locals in the early seventies, but then an operation on his hips had partially failed. Spike was taken on at Mantell's suggestion and became the only salaried member of the team. Macpherson alone knew the identity of the sponsor who provided Spike's pay. Spike had grown to dislike Mantell and his rigid toeing of the line laid down by Bletchley. As far as Spike was concerned, strict adherence to the law could and often did hamper their efficiency. It could also endanger his Locals. That they should never carry firearms, even if as individuals they possessed licences, was a major bugbear and one that Spike rigidly, if unwillingly, enforced. Even the least important of his operations was always recorded and, after discussion by the Committee, filed and logged at Jane's home.

Bletchley was not to be diverted by Macpherson on this occasion. Bristol should never have happened. 'The ethics of the Committee and the disgraceful goings-on in Bristol are inextricably entwined,' he growled at the meeting in general and Macpherson in particular. 'We have enough high-level contacts between us to manipulate events of this nature. A word in the ear of the Bristol constabulary would probably have been every bit as effective.' He turned to Spike. 'Was any approach made to the police?'

The Committee according unto Bletchley were so blessed with prestigious acquaintances that they could steamroller their way almost anywhere by a series of strategic string pulls. To him all criminals could be outwitted by cunning, by disinformation and checkmates. The right pressure at the right time could achieve the Committee's every aim.

Spike knew that this had been the original concept of the Founder

and of Macpherson too, but, unlike Bletchley and his disciples, they had adapted to the demands of reality when the concept had proved largely a pipedream.

'No. We did not tip off the police,' Spike replied. 'You may remember that my report last October made it clear that the police knew our target was involved in drugs long before we became involved. But they had nothing at all to hang on him, so they were powerless to move against him.'

'Chairman.' Macpherson sounded irritated. He was a man of action and could not stand time wasted in dithering. 'This matter comes down yet again to the simple question of whether we as a committee are prepared to be flexible and move with the times. Of course, I do not mean we should lower our basic moral tenets to those of the unpleasant people we attempt to frustrate. But we should look to the likes of Churchill and Kennedy, both leaders of democracy who clearly believed that some ends justify some means. The nastiness that can threaten our ex-SAS people is becoming more varied and our enemies are more sophisticated at finding loopholes in the law. If and where the police cannot provide adequate protection, we *have* to try to find an appropriate way to do so.'

There was silence but for the strains of a bagpipe lesson mingled with the muted screams of Hill House School children playing football on the grass outside.

Macpherson spoke again. 'In the last war our best Special Forces leaders were those who studied Lenin, whose sayings included "the need for 'all-sidedness' is a safeguard against rigidity". And Chairman Mao echoed this theme with "We must learn to see the reverse side of things. In given conditions a bad thing can lead to good results." This Committee will get nowhere if we remain hidebound by rules we ourselves set nearly a decade ago.'

For thirty minutes the matter of Bristol was thrashed out. Bletchley's final recommendation did not include censure of the methods used. He merely suggested a periodic check to ensure the target did not return to Bristol and that the time was ripe to notify their friend in Chippenham that his daughter's killer had been hounded from the city and would trouble no more youngsters there in the future.

The Committee passed to other matters. However, when the time came, Macpherson would trace the subsequent trouble with Bletchley back to that day.

9

With time on his hands de Villiers walked along the creek to the boat-building yard by Al Maktoum Bridge. He sat on a bale of cotton and watched the *abra* ferry crews below.

Dubai, he knew, had, long before the days of oil production, achieved an initial layer of wealth from a highly efficient pearling fleet. It was an operation that was cost-effective because of the evil treatment of the divers by their *nakhoudas* (skippers). The pearling dhows spent the diving season out on a glass-calm sea at the hottest time of the year. Daily diving rations consisted of a little water, a few dates and some rice, since underfed divers were able to stay under water for longer.

There were seldom lemons to halt scurvy – too costly – and no spare fresh water to wash off the salt, so sores erupted and deep ulcers suppurated. For some the end came from blood poisoning, while many died from the agonizing sting of red jellyfish, the whip of stingrays or a sudden shark attack.

Japanese cultured pearls ruined the market in the 1950s and deprived the divers of their thankless livelihood. The Maktoum boat-builders then turned their hands to motorized dhows, many fast enough to outrun pirate sloops and Indian Coast Guard patrol launches. These boats became the basis of Dubai's great wealth through the re-export of gold, mainly to India.

De Villiers returned to his hotel to change his shirt, for even in winter Dubai can be uncomfortably hot. He took a battered Mercedes cab to the Djera side of the creek and was quickly caught up in a honking line of jammed Toyotas. It was 12 January 1977, the day of his appointment.

He knew nothing of the client but presumed he was local and wealthy. Eight weeks earlier he had arrived in Dubai only to be told that the man was ill. The meeting was postponed and de Villiers was well compensated for his wasted time. He had worked for Arabs before, both in North Africa and the Gulf. Two years previously he had drowned an Egyptian Fundamentalist leader at Zamalek in Cairo,

and Meier had lethally rigged the stereo gear of one Saudi prince at the behest of another. De Villiers wondered if this time the target might be an Israeli. If so he would have to wage war with his principles. He respected the Israelis and might well turn down a contract to kill one. He had in the past rejected work for supporters of Pol Pot and Colombian drug kings. He had murdered many innocents for money from dubious sources but he saw no reason why he should not indulge his personal foibles from time to time.

Thanks to the carefully nurtured reputation of the Clinic, de Villiers had no shortage of jobs and could afford to be selective. Often he would split the Clinic in two and sometimes the three of them were simultaneously at work on separate contracts. Meier and Davies operated well on their own, but it was as a threesome that the Clinic was most devastatingly effective. Even the most carefully protected target was doomed once his or her details, and the up-front payment from the client, had entered the Clinic's ledger via one of de Villiers's three international booking agents, the largest of which was Tadnams of Earls Court, London.

Of the many contract killers for hire in Europe and the Americas, de Villiers had an unrivalled reputation for successful, 'no foul play suspected' results. In the increasingly competitive market of the mid seventies, this specialization began to pay off. There were too many killers chasing too few jobs, and it reached the point where in Birmingham, England, one amateur advertised, with the thinnest veneer of subtlety, in the local Yellow Pages. In 1976, in Chicago, over a quarter of the contract killings recorded by the police involved the deaths of contract killers taken out by one another. For all but a few specialists, the 'scum de la scum' to use Davies's term, it had become a buyers' market with operators accepting fees of less than half pre-1976 rates.

There was no lessening in demand. Far from it — rather a flood of amateur killers, mostly unemployed and often unemployable by reason of their emotional state, Vietnam veterans, washed up by the US withdrawal the previous year. Many were charging five hundred dollars for a straight killing which, after allowing for their expenses and the agent's percentage, often worked out at a profit of around one hundred dollars. Such low prices soon stimulated increased activity at the bottom end of the market. Frustrated citizens were now finding the local contract agency a financially viable method of ridding themselves of noisy neighbours or irritating mothers-in-law.

The cab driver, a locally employed Palestinian, turned to de Villiers. 'Abu Daoud is free,' he said, his eyes aglow with pride.

They were inching through a crowd of chanting, laughing Arabs, all Palestinians de Villiers presumed, who brandished old rifles or camel sticks and had all but paralysed the traffic. The cause of the rejoicing was the abject surrender that morning of the French government to terrorist coercion. At the weekend the Paris police had arrested Abu Daoud, the notorious founder of Black September, who stood accused of organizing the Munich Olympics terror attack of 1976, which killed eleven Israeli athletes. Now, after a hastily convened court hearing, the French deported him to Algiers – a free man and the cause of great joy among all Palestinians.

Perhaps the client would turn out to be a Palestinian. But no, there were plenty of ex-PLO killers about. More likely, de Villiers felt, a Gulf oil sheikh with a personal grudge. There was every likelihood that de Villiers would be met by a mere representative of the client. Or even the representative of a representative. That was why he never sent Meier or Davies to meet a client. You needed to be razor-sharp on these occasions. He remembered the time he had rendezvoused with a Dutch representative who had actually tried to redirect him, boomerang-like, towards his own boss, the real client. Instinct, rather than any identifiable slip on the part of the Dutchman, had alerted de Villiers, who decided to have Tadnams send him a photograph of their original client, the Dutchman's employer. Embarrassment was avoided and the outcome had been a double fee for the removal of the originally intended target *and* the disloyal representative.

De Villiers paid off his joyful cabbie in a deserted side street and walked for five minutes through the shuttered gold market. The hotel was plush and discreet. Following the written instructions received via Tadnams, de Villiers nodded politely at the reception desk, avoiding eye contact with its occupant, and crossed to the hairdresser's salon at the far end of the entrance hall. No hair was being cut, no beards trimmed. Like everyone else, around noon the barber was *hors de combat*.

The salon's inner door was labelled 'Staff Only' and hung with a planner-chart of bookings. De Villiers closed this door behind him. He was now inside a walnut-panelled elevator that responded to only two buttons, an up and a down. Ascending to an indeterminate level, he emerged into a corridor hung with Persian and Baluchi rugs where

he was met by a girl, of eleven or so, with a shy smile. He followed her down the passageway admiring the intricate sewing of her patterned jellaba. Her neck, ears and wrists jangled with beaten silver ornaments of South Arabian style, probably Yemeni.

The girl entered a long and richly furnished drawing room. The subtle scent of burnt *leban* (frankincense) was pleasing and in keeping with the general air of Arab high living that the room exuded. An elaborate brass lamp stood in each of the four corners, their bulbs hidden within giant crystal geodes, so that each cabbage-like rock gave forth an orange luminescence that glimmered back from the tapestries and the tasselled cushions.

'Come, help me rise, my little love.' The voice was gentle. As de Villiers's vision grew accustomed to his low-lit surroundings he saw the girl take the hand of an old man slumped in a leather armchair.

He exchanged greetings. The man introduced himself as Sheikh Amr bin Issa in the passable English of most Gulf Arab businessmen. His was a once strong face creased and prematurely aged by suffering and rendered ashen by illness.

'Sit close, sir, for my voice is weak.' The girl helped the sheikh without difficulty, for he was painfully thin, even emaciated. He bade her bring coffee.

'I do not know your name, only your unenviable reputation. I will waste no time with preamble, for the pain will soon come again.'

The sheikh explained that he owned an expanding chain of retail grocery outlets in the Gulf, Turkey and Iraq. Before long he would open new branches in Cyprus and Iran.

'I have sufficient profit for reinvestment to pay two million dollars annually to the Palestinian cause. My sons are at college in England, and last summer I had no thought of summoning a killer such as you.'

The sheikh coughed and took minutes to recover from the pain. If this was his client, de Villiers reflected, he would need to have a contract agreed without delay, for the mantle of death clung close.

The girl brought coffee in a silver *dhille* with an elegant beak, and tiny cups of fine china. When she was gone the sheikh continued.

'Shamsa, my granddaughter, lost her father seven years ago fighting the Sultanate troops in Dhofar, my homeland. Three of her uncles have also been killed in that sorry conflict. Four of my six sons all killed and none have been avenged.'

Sheikh Amr explained the background of his exile to Dubai. He made sure that de Villiers understood in depth the deadly seriousness

with which his people viewed his failure, as their sheikh, to follow the edicts of the *thaa'r*.

'I have visited Dubai on and off for a quarter of a century and I realize that Westerners, indeed Muslims from outside Dhofar, know very little about my country. The same is true in reverse of many of my fellow *jebalis*. They do not, for instance, share the historic hatred of the Muslim Arab for the Israeli, simply because Israel means nothing to them, does not touch upon their lives.' The sheikh paused to wipe beads of sweat from his forehead.

'I must tell you that I have not yet seen the passage of fifty years. Some seven months ago I was in good health. Then came the first pains. Within weeks the doctors told me I had a malignant growth in my belly. They gave me a year at the most and I began to think afresh about my life. Bakhait, my eldest surviving son, *is* my life. He has the gentleness of his mother and my own instinct for business. I want above all for him and his brother to enjoy the success back at home that would soon have been theirs but for our exile; an exile that I have, by my own actions, brought upon them. I have given them everything — unlimited money, the best of educations, both Western and Koranic — yet what will this avail them where it matters most, in the land of their ancestors?

He sighed and made as though to lay his hand on de Villiers's arm. But, remembering perhaps the nature of his profession, interrupted the gesture.

'You are now the key to my sons' future.' He paused. 'Their passport back to Dhofar.'

The previous August, when his sons returned for their summer holiday, the sheikh had told them of his new resolve. The *thaa'r* must go ahead. Neither son was committed to the absolutism of *jebali* traditions; both had been corrupted by their year in England and by their father's own liberalism. Nevertheless when Amr demanded that Bakhait give his pledge to avenge the murder of his brothers, a pledge of honour to be repeated on his father's grave, Bakhait did not hesitate. Devoted to his father and desperately grieved at the news of his sickness, he gave his word as Bakhait bin Amr al Jarboati that he would follow his father's wishes to fulfil the *thaa'r* and then return to Dhofar and, if God willed it, to his rightful place at the head of the Bait Jarboatis.

Dhofaris often passed through Dubai and called on family and friends living there. An increasing number flew to the United

Kingdom for training in military, engineering, social services and other skills. Amr knew from them that, in the last year, his country had undergone enormous changes. The revolution was over, the new half-Dhofari Sultan had granted Dhofaris everything that his father had withheld from them.

Business opportunities were almost unlimited and political power, at a level previously undreamed of, was now attainable. Young Dhofaris could now contemplate becoming ministers of Oman. But not Bakhait. Should he return to Dhofar — and there was no government ruling to stop him — he would for ever need to watch over his shoulder, awaiting the bullet that would surely come.

For three hours de Villiers was left alone with European magazines, chilled *loomee* juice and a plate laden with the best Sohar dates. Amr bin Issa, riven by deep stomach pains, had retired to his room. When he returned he appeared to be impatient for an answer from de Villiers.

'Listen well,' he said, 'for I am asking you to find and execute four men. The method of their killing must leave no suspicion in the minds of even their dearest friends.' If the sheikh expected surprise to show on de Villiers's face he wasted his time, for he remained expressionless as usual.

'Further,' said the sheikh, leaning forward, 'you must remind each man when you identify him, of his personal responsibility for the death of my son. You will film everything, the warnings and the executions, and for each audiovisual film that you hand to me or, after my death, to my son Bakhait, you will be paid the sum of one million American dollars by cheque from my account at the Bank of Dubai. When all four films have been satisfactorily received, we will pay you off with a final payment of a like amount.' He paused. 'Do you have any questions?'

De Villiers remained impassive. He thought he had heard every motive under the sun as to why one man should wish to kill another. This was merely a variation on the fairly common theme of revenge. But with what a difference! He could see why the sheikh wished for 'no foul play' methods since suspicion of a chain of connected murders might lead to the involvement of Interpol and thence Royal Oman Police interference. If Amr became suspect his family might be exiled officially by the Sultanate and that would defeat the whole purpose of the killings.

De Villiers also understood why the sheikh needed evidence on

film. He must show those who had exiled him solid proof of the 'trial' and termination of the guilty parties. But, from de Villiers's point of view, the act of warning intended targets that they were about to be killed added a whole new dimension to the act. He could picture the reaction of Meier and Davies when they learnt of this particular contractual requirement. On the other hand the fee was exceptional.

'I have two questions,' de Villiers said. 'Who are these men and by when must they be killed?'

Sheikh Amr explained.

Part 2

10

... All night the fires raged along the upper ramparts of Table Mountain. Dogs howled in the valleys and de Villiers sat naked on his window sill to catch the breeze and savour the night scent from the bougainvillaea terrace below. He could not remember a time when he had been so happy as these past few months at the estate of La Pergole.

In the Cape spring of 1969 he obtained a temporary job as groundsman at the Kenilworth racetrack and, using his one-room flat there as a base, combed the Tokai district in search of Vrede Huis and the de Villiers family.

He found a good many folk sharing his name but none who remembered Vrede Huis. For months he persisted and had all but exhausted his options by the time he came to La Pergole. The estate owner, Jan Fontaine, was a dyed-in-the-wool Boer despite his name but he was proud of his war medals from General Smuts and the British king. He had served in the desert with the First Army and made good friends with the Yanks. He liked the look of the tall young foreigner who was searching for his Boer origins and agreed to take him to Vrede Huis.

'You mean the house exists?' De Villiers was sceptical as ever, yet his face flushed with eagerness.

'Hold it, man. Don't get excited.' Fontaine raised a restraining hand. 'I can take you to the old place, yes, but it is only rubble these days. I have been here forty years and, even in the thirties the roofs were gone, and the doors. Our Kaffirs have long used the materials for their homes. I know nobody who remembers the original occupants.'

A scarred Xhosa from Transkei, a good six feet six inches tall and houseboy to Fontaine, had wheeled his master out to the battered Chevrolet and helped him transfer to the passenger seat, his legs trailing doll-like since he was paralysed from the waist down. The Zulu drove.

'Where to, Baas?' he grinned.

'The old place by the quarry, Samuel.'

They drove down the avenue from the house, past spacious stables and along narrow dusty lanes to the main Fontaine vineyards, stretching as far as de Villiers could see to the west and east. Ahead the land climbed gradually to the forests of Tokai and the foothills of Table Mountain.

The scenery took away de Villiers's breath. This was his homeland but even were it otherwise, he decided, he would want to live here for ever. It was surely the most beautiful land in the world.

Vrede Huis, when they bounced their way into its clearing, was an anticlimax, for there were not even ruins, merely low heaps of rubble overgrown with bracken and thick clumps of bamboo clustered with the hanging nests of weaver birds. Lizards sunned themselves on the rocks, and carpets of flowering nerine colonized what had probably been a central courtyard. De Villiers wandered into a glade behind the bamboos, a place of wild strawberries, moss and seeded mulberry trees. In the face of a carved granite stone he traced the single word VREDE.

He realized then that he did not mind the disappearance of the de Villiers clan. If his cousins had died out, so be it. He would in time buy this site from Fontaine, build another Vrede Huis and raise a family to continue his blood-line. The fact that his savings were hardly enough to purchase a second-hand car did not detract from the scope of his plan.

Since his lonely orphan days in Vancouver, de Villiers had recited to himself, as a Jew might the lineage of Moses, his known parental history as lovingly passed on by his parents during his Alaskan childhood. When Jan Fontaine asked him the fate of the original de Villiers owners of Vrede Huis he was able to reply almost by rote. Of Matje and Anna, his great-grandparents, he knew little save that they lived in South Africa and came from *voortrekker* stock. But his grandfather had been his boyhood hero.

In 1897, a year of declining relations with the British, Matje's youngest son Piet responded to a romantic call from the far side of the world, his chance to make a fortune in the Gold Rush. Working his passage to Seattle in the autumn he joined the main body of the Klondikers, as the '97 prospectors came to be known, from the Indian *Thron-diuck* or 'Hammer-water'. On a crowded stern-wheeler, the *Skagit Chief*, Piet followed the Inside Passage route north. Young

Danny had heard the tales a hundred times from Piet's son. Swirling mist and deep green water, calving glaciers, killer whales and sudden clearings with Indian villages and grotesque totems. Past Wrangel and Sitka and Juneau until they reached Dyea: a narrow sand bay subject to a twenty-foot tidal bore that had trapped many a Klondiker trying to haul his year's supply of goods from ship to shore up the mile-long reach of that lethal inlet.

Piet made it to the beachhead and began the nightmare haul, one human ant in a struggling file of forty thousand, sliding and cursing in the mud and snow. Faltering souls would repeat the refrain: 'Seventeen dollars an ounce. Seventeen dollars an ounce.' The trail was marked by the frozen corpses of emaciated packhorses.

By the spring of 1898, Piet and all his stores had reached the foot of the Chilkoot Pass. A 3,250-foot-high climb in four demanding miles. Piet made this exhausting portage thirty-eight times. On 3 April, carrying his twenty-sixth load, he was struck by an avalanche of wet snow that buried an area of ten acres of the Pass to a depth of thirty feet. Several hundred Klondikers were swept off the precarious ice-steps known as the Scales. Piet clawed his way to the surface but many, unconscious or upside down, stayed where they were. Sixty-three bodies were recovered and the Rush went on.

At Lake Bennett Piet and four colleagues fashioned themselves a boat from two twenty-foot logs and, when the ice broke up on 29 May, they joined seven thousand other such boats, all overloaded, all heading north for gold. There were whirlpools, sharpened snags, ice-blocks, windstorms that whipped up five-foot waves and, all day long, mosquitoes. Old hands told stories of Yukon mosquitoes so large that they carried off eagles as food for their young.

In the White Horse Rapids, Piet's boat, thankfully laden with none of his stores at the time, sank and three of his friends were drowned. He spent the winter in the mud, bars and bordellos of Dawson City. That year Piet found no gold though he tried his luck at Bonanza and Eldorado, at French Hill and Cheechako.

In the summer of '99 he decided on a change of scenery and responded to a new Rush — to Nome. A paddle-steamer took him and hundreds of others as close to the shoreline as the skipper dared and, after a two-week wait off the shallow beach, Piet gained a place on a landing barge. He waded his gear in for the last hundred yards.

The beach was black with men and women sieving the sand for gold. At Nome there was no law except force of personality. No

legal claims existed in the tide flats but a man could work the sand within a shovel's length of where he stood. For miles there was no forest, so Nome consisted entirely of tents. There was no sewage system. The public lavatories cost ten cents per visit and their effluent drained into the drinking-water supply. Typhoid and malaria were rampant and the local bar was owned by Wyatt Earp.

Piet's luck was consistently bad and when on 7 September 1900 his tent, all his gear and most of Nome were washed out to sea by a great storm, he finally called it quits and settled at the mouth of the Yukon in a village where the fishing was good. He married a nurse at the mission and Daniel de Villiers's father was born before the year was out.

The giant Xhosa's shadow fell across de Villiers as he wheeled Fontaine into the clearing.

'You like it here, de Villiers?' Fontaine did not wait for a reply. 'Since the *skollies* did me in, I have needed a strong hand to be my foreman on La Pergole. What about it?'

De Villiers did not hesitate. There was nothing to lose; everything to gain. If he did not like it, he could leave.

Fontaine did himself a favour, for de Villiers had only to be told once. He was a quick learner and a willing worker. The estate's mixed bag of Cape Coloureds and blacks found their new foreman unbiased, so they worked well for him, and recognizing the cold alertness in his manner they did not try to fool him. After some months he learnt that it was not *skollies*, roughnecks, who had crippled Fontaine but his own predecessor as foreman, an Afrikaaner who, cursed by Fontaine in front of the men for some inefficiency, had attacked him one dark evening and left him for dead on the floor of the stables.

Fontaine had survived but he would never walk again: a knobkerrie blow had done permanent damage to his spine.

De Villiers was given comfortable rooms on the attic level and ate his meals with the Fontaines. He enjoyed their company, for Jan was a well-educated man and, though opinionated and scornful of most other Afrikaaners, he seemed to respect de Villiers for his North American outlook. Anne, his wife, was heavy going, for she had little to say and when she did begin to comment, Fontaine made a habit of speaking over her. De Villiers learned from the farm boys that Madam had come to La Pergole from abroad when she was little and was taken in by Fontaine's late parents. She wore her long, blonde hair in a bun and spent a great deal of time on horseback about the

estate. De Villiers found her presence increasingly awkward, for she was the most beautiful woman he had ever seen.

Fontaine, at sixty, was some thirty years older than his wife and openly jealous. De Villiers knew better than to show the slightest interest in Anne, since his existence in this paradise depended upon Fontaine's continued support and approval. Nevertheless he found his nightly fantasies increasingly centred on Fontaine's wife.

There were no children and de Villiers had glimpsed a look of utter loneliness on Anne's lovely face. This turned his stomach with pity, a sentiment that did not normally impinge on his life.

The dreamy months passed by, amid the vines, the blue mountains and the wonderful, balmy climate of the Cape. The screaming images of Nam ceased to trouble de Villiers's sleep and he learned to ignore the black rages into which pain and frustration increasingly drove Fontaine.

One summer evening when Fontaine was sedated in bed, de Villiers tried to draw Anne out. He asked her about horses, for he knew they were at the centre of her life, but she remained reticent, even uneasy. At the end of the meal when the houseboy brought them coffee on the stoep and the bullfrogs chimed from the *vlei* (swamp), she spoke to him in a low voice.

'The servants receive a tip when they tell my husband things. They do not miss a glance between us. Please be careful for both our sakes.'

'Of course,' he said. 'I understand.' As he spoke their eyes locked for the first time in all these months and de Villiers knew that he had gradually come to love her.

There were days out in the fields when he felt his blood surge at the mere echo of distant cantering hooves. He began to hate his ailing benefactor Fontaine. When the doctor in Weinberg first muttered about hospitalization, de Villiers had consciously to hide his delight.

On New Year's Eve, when the Cape was merry with bonfire parties and, after nightfall, the clatter of rifle fusillades, no flicker of revelry disturbed La Pergole. Farmers traditionally brought in the New Year by shooting the bounds and the Fontaines' neighbours were no exception.

The guns excited the dogs of Tokai and the surrounding homesteads. Their feral cousins, gone wild in the foothills, returned a primordial chorus in praise of the moon and sleep came hard to de

Villiers. He pulled on his work shorts and wandered down to the stoep. There he sat on the steps that faced north towards the mountains. Midnight came and with it a surge in the sounds of distant celebrations. This tailed away and soon the crackle of donnerball combs in the pinewoods close by was all that prickled the night.

She came without a sound, her bare feet smooth on the cold, red tiles. They kissed without a word, without preamble. He knew only that she must feel as he did and sensed the urgency of her need.

Hand in hand they walked through the garden and past the oleander terrace to the fringe of the woods. She led him to a place that she knew, her nightdress wet from the grass-tip dew.

'Do you love me?' she asked him, her face uptilted and her wonderful hair reaching down to the small of her back.

She has *never* been loved, de Villiers marvelled to himself. He spoke in a whisper the better to retain the magic of it all.

They knelt together in the forest and the words of love tumbled out. Neither had known such depths of feeling before, for both had lived lives devoid of human warmth. The words that they exchanged were a necessary foreplay to their mounting passion. Their shared knowledge of what was to come was in itself sublimely sensual.

Then de Villiers smelled the sweat of the Zulu. He flung himself sideways but the giant's cudgel glanced off his shoulder and a sharp pain shot down his arm. The Zulu padded back to the shadows and wheeled Fontaine into the glade.

'Samuel should have used his assegai,' he snarled, his lips rigid with fury. He wore a dressing gown of blue silk and a double-barrelled twelve-bore shotgun lay across his wasted legs. Quite why he let de Villiers go, neither of them would ever know.

De Villiers was driven to Weinberg by a silent Samuel, his only possessions packed in the rucksack he had carried the first time he came to La Pergole nearly a year before.

Fontaine made it known throughout the tight-knit Cape community that de Villiers had somehow abused his hospitality. He would not easily find further employment within many miles of La Pergole, or, as important to him, Vrede Huis.

De Villiers knew the strict religious code of the Afrikaaners. Anne would never leave Fontaine. The dream had been shattered even as it materialized and, with nothing to hold him in South Africa, he returned to New York.

A Marine Corps friend introduced him to an association that found

work for Vietnam veterans. By 1971 he had entered the fringes of the contract-killing business and within nine years he was working internationally for a US-based agency. After a complex job in Greece, he teamed up with Meier and Davies and the Clinic was born. . . .

11

In London de Villiers met up with his colleagues and explained the new job. Meier's immediate reaction was, 'How did this old sheikh get on to the agency?'

'Simple,' de Villiers replied. 'He has a son at school in England who watched the movie *The Day of the Jackal*. The boy tells his dad that Europeans kill each other for cash. The sheikh then moseys along to his PLO friends, thick as flies in Dubai, whose office, as you know, has done business with the agency before. Bingo.'

'How do you rate our chances of finding the sheikh's targets?' Meier asked.

De Villiers favoured neither optimism nor pessimism since he found both equally unreliable.

'If it had been straightforward, I am sure Sheikh Amr would not have come to us. His sons were killed over a six-year period by government forces.' Meier and Davies listened intently, for they knew de Villiers disliked repeating himself. 'The sheikh gave me an outline of each death and all four occurred in areas held by Omani units or British Army Training Teams known as BATTS. These are small, specialized groups of SAS men.'

'So our targets are either Brits or Omanis?' Meier pressed.

'Not quite true,' de Villiers spoke slowly. 'BATTS include a smattering of Fijians and the Sultan's Armed Forces [SAF] officers are Omani, Brit, Dhofari, Aussie, Paki, South African, Indian and Baluchi. Since our targets may by now be dead or retired from their military work, our search area could be quite wide.'

Davies whistled through his teeth. 'It would be easier to locate four fleas on a rhino,' he murmured.

Meier grunted. 'No one will pay you five million dollars for that.'

'Remember,' de Villiers broke in, 'we have no time limit other than

the premature death of our targets before we can trace them. So we can continue with normal work as we wish and concentrate on the Dhofar targets when other business is slack.'

'It may be easier to trace men who are still in the forces,' Davies mused, 'but, when retired, they'll be a lot easier to hit.'

'We must computerize this problem,' Meier said. 'We cannot just search at random.'

De Villiers looked at the Belgian. 'I don't intend to.' His voice was toneless. 'We have four months free before we need start on the Miami contract. To make the most of our team we will split up. Davies will cover the case of Sheikh Amr's second son, who died in 1972. His killer was almost certainly the SAS commander at the Dhofar garrison of Mirbat. The SAS are based in Hereford. Davies, being Welsh and ex-British Army, should have little trouble in making some discreet enquiries there.'

Davies nodded his head but his habitual half-smile was not in evidence.

'You and I,' de Villiers addressed Meier, 'will trace the man who killed Amr's first son in 1969. This incident was an ambush in a remote part of the Dhofar *jebel* covered by a single company of the sultan's army. The sheikh has no idea where the Omanis keep records of their military actions, what we call war diaries, but that should not be difficult to find out. We will fly to Muscat as soon as Tadnams can arrange visas, or No Objection Certificates as the Omanis call them.'

Meier seemed to find no holes in this programme or, if he did, he kept them to himself. 'And the other two targets?' he asked.

'Not so easy,' said de Villiers, frowning. 'Amr's third and fourth sons were killed in 1975 during the last year of the war. They died in bitter and confused fighting close to the South Yemen border.'

Sultan Qaboos, seven years after sending his reactionary father to exile in London's Dorchester Hotel, had dragged Oman out of the Middle Ages and, thanks to determination and mounting oil revenues, installed the full panoply of twentieth-century benefits — schools, roads, hospitals — where there had so recently been only stagnation and suffering. Qaboos, the fourteenth ruler of the Abu Saidi dynasty since its inception in 1744, retained absolute power. The law of the land was Koranic and handled by *qadhis* in regional courts. The sultan allowed virtually no tourists into Oman, so his police were able to

enforce rigid control over foreigners likely to cause trouble.

In his mid thirties the Sultan was equally handsome in his Savile Row suits at London functions or when clad in full sultanic regalia at ceremonies in Muscat. He spent most of January 1977 at his new palace close to the town of Seeb and conducted daily interviews with ministers and advisers. One of the latter was the retired Deputy Commander of the Sultan's Armed Forces, Brigadier Colin Maxwell. After twenty-five years with the forces, which he himself had formed in 1952, Maxwell had retired to become a defence adviser to the Sultan.

For an hour the two men discussed the Omanization of the Sultan's Armed Forces, a process whereby the number of British officers was to be reduced as quickly as their Omani replacements could be trained.

Maxwell left the palace, with its lofty, modern lines and acres of fountain-fed pools. He never ceased to thank the Lord that, as Allah, He had given Qaboos to the people of Oman. Maxwell loved the Omanis and rejoiced that their centuries of strife and backwardness had, through this one man Qaboos, come to an end.

Maxwell's Omani driver dropped him off at his home in Ruwi, part of the first modern block built in the area. Said Fahher, uncle to Sultan Qaboos and Deputy Minister of Defence, also lived there.

From the front of the apartments the old town of Ruwi sprawled seawards and, just across the nearest *wadi*, as though Beau Geste was a neighbour, the crenellated ramparts of Bait al Falaj fortress slumbered beneath the red flags of the Sultanate.

Maxwell lived alone but for his staff. For thirty years, since post-Second World War service in Somalia, he had suffered from chronic arthritis but this had never diminished his natural warmth of character. The expatriate administrative officers of the Sultan's Armed Forces were known for their internecine feuds and backbiting, but Maxwell was universally liked, for he possessed not an ounce of malice nor cynicism towards his fellow men. On that particular day in January 1977, this was perhaps rather unfortunate.

Towards 7 p.m., as Maxwell relaxed on his balcony, his houseboy announced the arrival of two American military historians who had telephoned earlier in the day. This was nothing new. He had received many such callers ever since his appointment as official historian to the Sultan's Armed Forces.

Maxwell was delighted that interest in his favourite topic should

be spreading as far afield as the USA and he spent the next half hour waxing eloquent on the origins of the forces he had created. The two Americans apparently specialized in the worldwide communist expansion of the fifties and sixties. They were especially curious about late 1969, when Marxism had come within a whisker of engulfing Dhofar. The critical factor that had delayed a guerrilla onslaught in that post-monsoon period, when all but a nine-mile coastal strip of Dhofar was under Marxist control, involved a sudden thrust by a small Sultanate force deep into their eastern territory. This incursion, known as Operation Snatch, sparked off what was to become a flood of ex-guerrillas who changed sides and joined the government forces, at that time numbering under three hundred fighting men.

The Operation Snatch force killed a senior political commissar and the leader of an Idaaraat torture squad named Salim, the eldest son of Amr bin Issa, the sheikh of that region.

Maxwell searched through one of his files and at length gave a cry of success.

'Yes,' he said, lighting a stubby French cigarette, 'that was a brilliant operation handled by our intelligence officer Tom Greening and commanded by Peter Thwaites. Quite threw the *adoo* off guard for months.'

'The field commander was Thwaites, you say?' asked de Villiers, taking notes.

'No, no.' Maxwell breathed out a cloud of smoke as pungent as burning camel dung. 'Peter commanded *all* the forces in Dhofar. I am uncertain who the actual man on the ground was but you could find that out from the relevant regiment. They will still have all their old contact reports.' He extracted a military deployment chart from his folder. 'Ah,' he beamed with pleasure, 'a company from the Northern Frontier Regiment was the only unit stationed anywhere near the area of Operation Snatch. They were my old regiment, you know. In 1955 I formed them from the Batinah Force and led them in their first action, an attack on the Imam at Rostaq.' A small, nostalgic smile creased the brigadier's sun-ravaged cheeks.

'But come now. You are after the sixties, not the fifties. You must go and see the current CO of NFR. He'll tell you all you need to know.' He paused. 'But wait. NFR are at Simba now.' He shook his head and frowned, but then brightened up. 'There is no problem, my friends. I will telephone Ted Ashley at JR – that is, the Jebel Regiment.

Ted is their colonel and you will find him at Nizwa, just up the road to the Interior. He will help you as much as he can. So will his officers, many of whom are old Dhofar hands. NFR would, of course, be better but they are down in Dhofar now, beyond your reach as it were.'

They parted company with much shaking of hands and mutual affability.

Tadnams had arranged three No Objection Certificates for de Villiers, Meier and an Indian driver. They had learned from Charles Kendall's of South Kensington, UK agents for the sultanate, that a major new fisheries project was about to be launched and workers were being taken on by the American Temple Black Corporation. The boss's wife, Shirley Temple, had once been the golden girl of Hollywood and, as idle rumour had it, a teenage idol of the current Minister of Fisheries.

'What are we now,' Meier grunted as they left Brigadier Maxwell's apartment, 'fisheries inspectors or military historians?'

'We are well on our way to the first target,' de Villiers replied. 'These Brits are a pushover. Get them reminiscing and they'll tell you anything.'

Their driver, Karim Bux, waited at their hotel, the Al Falaj, together with his rented Nissan pick-up. They drove south-west along the newly metalled road leading to the oilfields of Fahud. After an hour they crossed the great German-made bridge that spans the Wadi Sumail, a valley subject to spectacular perennial floods.

De Villiers leant across Meier and pointed north up the dark-green line of the wadi.

'Be sure to remember that deserted village, Karim Bux, and the date-palm grove below it. If we need an RV [rendezvous point], that's it.'

The road was now flanked to the north by ten-thousand-foot-high cliffs that soared sheer to the plateau of the Jebel Akhdar. At Izki they bore west and entered ancient Nizwa, the eighth-century citadel of Oman.

Thanks to Maxwell's telephone call the Nissan was expected at the Jebel Regiment garrison and a soldier escorted them to the officers' mess. The adjutant, Captain Mohanna Suleiman, was waiting for them.

'I will give you whatever help is possible.'

They sat in comfortable chairs in the mess, a place of brass ashtrays,

countless stale newspapers and white-robed messboys.

The captain explained that Colonel Ashley was away. Soon, he said with pride, Major Ibrahim would be taking command, the very first Omani regimental colonel.

After some talk of little consequence, de Villiers broached the key question. 'Captain, Sah'b,' he said. 'Brigadier Maxwell tells us that, in October 1969, there was a company from the Northern Frontier Regiment stationed in Dhofar. We are writing an account of those times for an American publisher. Do you know anybody who may remember those days?'

The Omani captain smiled. 'You are in God's favour. There is a police officer from Seeb who sometimes visits because he used to command one of our companies and, like our second-in-command Major Mackie, this man was once a British Royal Marine. His name is Milling – John Milling.

'This John Milling was with which regiment?' de Villiers asked.

'He was with NFR at the time you are asking about. He was transferred to this regiment in 1971 in order to put together our first company. He will be happy to meet you, I am sure. You will find him at the Police Air Wing with their helicopter detachment. *Insh' Allah*, all will be well for you.'

As they were leaving the Chief Clerk passed by. The adjutant stopped him. 'Chief,' he said, 'these gentlemen are enquiring about Dhofar for a history book. Maybe you can help them.'

The Chief Clerk told de Villiers all he could and that was enough. Captain Milling had indeed been in the northern *jebel* in October 1969 and had at that time led a dangerous mission involving the very first *adoo* informer to help the army.

'Was this action known as Operation Snatch?' Meier asked.

'That I cannot say, but I can assure you there were no other operations in the area at that time and John Milling was definitely the officer in charge.' He chuckled. 'Nobody could mistake John, then or now; he is a giant of a man. Why don't you go and see him for yourselves. I will phone him if you like.'

De Villiers hastily thanked the Chief Clerk. A phone call would not be necessary. They took their leave and headed back towards Ruwi. The sun dipped below the western *jebel* and the valleys receded into dim and cheerless voids.

12

The Marches is the ancient name for the country on either side of the Welsh–English border. Here the wild ridges of the Black Mountains give way to hop fields, orchards and high-flowering hedges. The deep gorge of the Wye cuts through the Forest of Dean and the cathedral city of Hereford, Queen of the Marches, remains serenely prosperous through the deepest of recessions elsewhere in Britain.

Hereford, a somnolent little city, is the home and the heart of the SAS Regiment. Certain pubs in and around the town are patronized by SAS and ex-SAS men, but an outsider would not easily identify them, for the majority are quiet, affable individuals who take great pride in anonymity and, unlike special forces the world over, hardly ever become involved in public brawls.

In 1988 the Bunch of Grapes public house, on the north side of town, was closed because of structural damage and ceased to be a haven for SAS men in civvies. But on 11 February 1977 both bars throbbed with life and music. In a corner of the main downstairs public bar Bob Bennett, on leave from his regiment in Germany, held his mug of John Smith's beer aloft and, with his friend Ken Borthwick, toasted the Queen.

'May she thrive for another twenty-five,' said Ken. 'God bless her.' He was a member of the Territorial Army Volunteer Reserve and a policeman from neighbouring Worcestershire, but both men had met up at the Grapes to join friends for a Royal Silver Jubilee Party, one of thousands held across Britain that year.

'Cheers, boys.' The landlord, Tony Burberry, joined the toast. 'Long time no see, Ken. How's the Force?' Tony was a bluff, professional publican with no army ties of his own. His personal chemistry and an aptitude for discretion had first attracted the SAS fraternity to the Imperial, a pub where he was tenant in the mid sixties. Then, when he moved to the Grapes, the SAS followed him. No man could wish for a better clientele, for they spent good money, drank sensibly, behaved well and their reputation scared off the town's less savoury elements.

There was the down side, an ever-present fear of IRA bombs, but the boys kept their own security roster, and were more alert and capable than the most expensive security money could buy.

Tony knew three generations of SAS: the Malaya boys, the Borneo crowd and more recently the Oman BATT-men. Memories of the wars in which they had served bound them together as tight as ticks. Of course, they had all operated in other theatres of combat, fought skirmishes in those territories that had taken the fancy of the Foreign and Commonwealth Office for a while, but always in small groups of two, four or six. These groups did not exchange their war stories with one another, nor with anyone else for that matter, which left precious little mutual ground for reminiscence other than the three major campaigns of the post-war years where whole squadrons had acted together.

Bob Bennett, whose home was in Hereford, knew many of the local characters and discussed them with Ken Borthwick. Some of their party began to drift away to other pubs as the evening wore on. A Welshman with a local crumpet clutching his waist found some sitting space at their table. The girl was very drunk but the Welshman still made sense. He crooned her a love song from the Valleys and was cheered by the crowd for his pains.

One of the drinkers, a bear of a man with a hand that completely eclipsed his pint beer mug, was a Fijian whom Bob recognized as an SAS sergeant. He and his friends began to swap memories of long-lost friends from Borneo days, and the Welshman was visibly enthralled. The conversation shunted around to talk of a Fijian named Labalaba whom everyone seemed to know, and then somebody mentioned Salalah.

'I was in Salalah,' the Welshman interjected, 'posted to the Muscat Regiment from the Fusiliers. Small-arms instructor to help introduce the boys to the new FN rifle.' He beamed. 'It's really nice to meet people who were there too. Doesn't happen very often.' He bought them a round. Bob Bennett was included but Ken took his leave.

The Grapes emptied well after closing time and Bob followed the Welshman's red Escort at a discreet distance. After dropping his girl off in the centre of town the Welshman headed west on the A438 towards the village of Brobury. The Escort turned into the drive of Brobury House, at which point Bob parked by the roadside and disappeared into the shadows of the well-kept gardens. He knew the place well. It had recently been bought by an American couple.

The Escort passed by the main house and parked in front of two small cottages down a tarmac lane. Bob had seen enough. He returned home to Hereford and his wife Lyn.

Spike Allen spent forty minutes six mornings a week jogging in Hyde Park. He seldom enjoyed the exercise but, in his mid-forties, he had to compensate for his love of good food or join the pear-shaped majority. At 8.30 a.m., when he returned to his flat, his wife had already left for the British Museum, where she worked as a curator's assistant.

As always, Spike checked his answering machine. He was to call a number in Worcester. The number was not that of a Local but it did figure on his Informant Sheet. This was a list of non-Committee individuals, mostly from the Midlands, Wales and the South of England, who volunteered pertinent information to which the Committee might wish to react.

The number responded.

'Hallo, Ken. Spike calling back.'

Ken Borthwick, an ex-SAS sergeant-major and currently a Detective Constable, did not waste time on pleasantries. 'Spike, you may think this is a long shot but here goes anyway. Last night I had a drink at the Grapes with Bob Bennett, an ex-B Squadron lad on leave from Germany. I left the pub early but Bob called me early this morning with a potential problem. He does not know about you or our connection. He called me merely because I'm with the Force and because I saw the Welshman before I left.'

'The Welshman?' Spike queried.

'Yes. He had a light Borders accent and made out he'd been with the Welch Fusiliers. He mingled with some of the lads and said he'd been seconded to the SAF in the early seventies. Bob thought nothing of it at first but, for a Sultan's Armed Forces man, this fellow was pretty damned ignorant. He kept referring to the lads down in Dhofar as 'SAS' not 'BATT' and he told a story about an SAS officer whose name he had forgotten but whose batman was a cousin of his. Since no SAS officer has ever had a batman, this grated on Bob.'

'Hardly enough to brand the Welshman as undesirable,' Spike commented.

'True, but as the evening progressed the fellow kept muttering about Mirbat and in particular about the 1972 shindig there. Bob thought he was fishing and, since Bob was himself involved that day

at Mirbat, he decided to follow the Welshman. He left him at a bed and breakfast on the Hay road.'

There was a pause. 'So?' said Spike.

'So we may have another case like Tim Shand. Remember, the lad from G Squadron who the IRA traced to his home in Ross last year. We put a watch on him for a week but nothing happened, so we cleared out and, a month later, he found a key-set two-pound car bomb clamped to his Peugeot.'

'But, ' Spike said, feeling he was missing the point, 'I thought you said this Welshman was fishing for Dhofar, not Belfast, connections?'

'Poor Spike,' Ken's voice oozed sympathy, 'menopausal run-down and haemorrhoids of the brain. If *you* were trying to identify which of the Grapes clientele were with the Regiment and not merely ex-Army, would *you* sew your web of Belfast silk? Course not. Give the Provos a break, mate.'

Spike did not rise to this. 'So you go along with Bob's suspicions, do you, Ken?'

'In principle,' was the firm reply. 'I saw the Welshman, only briefly, but I sensed unease and the guy had a hard, mean cut to his features. Listen, Spike, us boys in blue would not react to this sort of random suspicion without more evidence of intent. There's no point in my even trying to alert my bosses. I'd merely get a lecture on the current lack of manpower and the sorting out of priorities.'

'OK, Ken,' Spike sighed. 'Give me the details of the bed and breakfast and I'll do what I can.'

Spike ate a bowl of Alpen cereal laced with maple syrup and washed down with percolated Douwe Egbert coffee. Mastication always helped him think. He decided on John Smythe, a freelance photographer, who had left the SAS Territorials a year before because of a heavy demand for roof insulation. John was on the lump and dabbled in any highly paid work, normally scaffold erection, that could be done without the tax man's knowledge. He had phoned Spike a couple of months before to complain that life was slow and what was the point of being a Local if Spike never called him.

Although Hertford, John Smythe's home town, was close to Hitchin and a recruitment basin for C Squadron, 21 SAS, Spike had received no calls in that area for many months. He would leave Hallett, the usual West Country Local, alone, but respond to Borthwick's call by putting Smythe on to the Welshman.

*

At 5 p.m. Muscat time de Villiers took a booked call to England from one of the booths at the Cable & Wireless office in the town centre, the only available way of placing an international call from Oman.

Davies, at Brobury House, was waiting and explained in cryptic terms that the SAS were a closed-mouthed, hyper-suspicious crowd of bastards and he had nothing to report.

'Never mind,' said de Villiers, '*we* have positive identification and need you over here like yesterday. The office will give you details but you must speed up your visa by going to the embassy soonest.'

Two hours after Smythe was installed with binoculars, vacuum flask and his car radio tuned to Radio 4, the red Escort turned right out of the drive of Brobury House and sped east.

Smythe had learnt a good deal about surveillance merely through past failures. He now carried a box of accessories to improve his results. When Davies parked the Escort in Trebovir Road, close to Earls Court underground station, Smythe stayed with the car. Once the Welshman was gone, he took a slightly crushed Coca Cola can from his box of tricks and placed it in front of one of the Escort's rear tyres. Back in his own car, he settled down to sleep as soon as he had switched on the receiver unit of his Coca Cola gizmo. A green light pulsed at him. It would continue to pulse until a set of contacts in the can were mated by pressure. The light would then go out, to be replaced by a series of beeps loud enough to waken Smythe from the deepest of slumbers.

On 27 February 1977 eight of the Committee met at Bob Mantell's home in Richmond, a quiet semi-detached house close to the East Sheen Gate to Richmond Park.

The meeting had been called by Spike at short notice and absentees included Bletchley, who had been hospitalized for a check-up, according to his housekeeper.

Colonel Macpherson, who detested meetings on Sundays, was in a testy mood and keen to speed up procedures. This suited Spike. He explained the Hereford background to Smythe's surveillance activities.

'The day after the Welshman arrived in London, he visited 64 Ennismore Gardens, the Omani Embassy, and our Local followed him into the Visa Section. After a long wait, during which both men filled in No Objection Certificate application forms, the Welshman was summoned into the inner office. Mr Alfred Jones was the name called

out by the Omani official. We have no further details other than the number of his rented Avis car and a rather poorly focused photograph taken by our Local.'

'When does this Welshman Jones fly to Oman?' Macpherson asked.

'That is the reason I asked for this snap meeting,' Spike replied. 'Calling myself Alfred Jones, I telephoned Gulf Air Reservations and asked for confirmation of when my secretary had booked my flight to Muscat. I said she was sick and had taken my diary out of the office.' Spike paused to check his notes. 'Jones is scheduled to fly to Muscat via Doha and Dubai on Gulf Air Flight 006 next Saturday.'

'Do we have contacts in Oman?' Michael Panny asked.

'No one,' Spike said, having checked with Mantell. 'But I have a friend at Kendall's who handles contract officers' liaison with the Omanis. He can fix visas for me without too many questions being asked.'

'Why should we need a visa?' Macpherson's bushy white eyebrows were raised.

'We have only one suspect,' said Spike, 'the Welshman, whose current whereabouts are unknown because our man lost him shortly after he left the embassy. Either we have someone follow the Welshman when he catches his flight for Muscat or we drop the matter.'

'Never mind dropping it,' the Don commented acidly. 'I can't see why you picked it up in the first place.'

'Then you have no business with your intellectual airs, Don.' August Graves was, as ever, Spike's dependable ally. 'Even I can see this Welsh geezer is up to no good.'

Macpherson, seeing a slanging match shaping up, cut in. 'Spike has taken the effort to get this far. Now we must decide if we should follow up. We have a chance surveillance of a possible IRA threat to one or more of our Hereford fraternity developing into something very different. So now we have a conundrum. Why should anyone go to the trouble of fishing around SAS-frequented watering-holes with the apparent intention of identifying SAS soldiers through their involvement with some long-past incident in Dhofar? And why should this same character then rush down to the Omani Embassy with the likely intention of going to Muscat as soon as he can get a visa?' Macpherson looked around the room. 'Any ideas?'

There was no immediate response and Macpherson did not wait for the inevitable speculation.

'Since there are no clues at all,' he continued, 'other than the

probable involvement of the SAS in some unknown context, I suggest we send a suitable Local, if there is one, with a brief to watch the suspect's actions in Muscat and learn what he can.'

'I have an excellent man who once served in the Sultan's Armed Forces.' Spike was on cue. 'He speaks passable Arabic and is unmarried. If he is prepared to go, I will need to pay his basic expenses.'

The Committee were obviously intrigued by a matter unlike any previous project to have come their way. There was enough of an existing, if questionable, threat to the SAS community to warrant their interest. No police force would be remotely likely to follow up so indeterminate a lead and the only obvious obstacle was that of funds.

'We have more than enough in the slush fund to cover a return flight and two or three weeks' basic accommodation,' Jane offered without being asked.

So it was agreed with less bother than Spike had anticipated. Now he had only to locate the best man for the job.

13

At 9 p.m. on the last day of February, Mason drove the Porsche with studied legality through the streets of East Berlin. He was in uniform. He had dined with a cavalry friend at an *echt Berliner* restaurant with an unpronounceable name. The occasional shabby Trabant loomed up in the gloom and the white faces of the drivers stared at the Porsche with palpable hostility.

Mason passed through Checkpoint Charlie on his ID card, joining Heerstrasse just beyond the Brandenburg Gate. The wide and ramrod-straight Heerstrasse is governed by synchronized traffic lights. If you cruise at a constant thirty miles an hour you can travel its entire length without having to stop. Mason had quickly cottoned on to the principle that sixty miles an hour was a simple mathematical progression. When that speed had succeeded without an hitch, he wagered and won fifty pounds from brother officers by covering the same distance at a hundred and twenty.

Two minutes' drive to the north of Heerstrasse, Mason arrived at

Wavell Barracks, home to a major portion of the British Berlin Garrison which, in March 1977, included a parachute battalion, a battalion of the Welsh Guards and a cavalry squadron. The armoured might of the British in Berlin totalled twelve tanks. Their allies, the French and the Americans, were similarly equipped while, ranged against them, were the twelve thousand battle tanks of the Warsaw Pact. The fatalistic attitude of Mason's CO, Lieutenant-Colonel Charles Guthrie, and most other allied officers in Berlin was understandable.

Mason was scornful of the neighbouring Allied forces, the French to the north with their canteen full of cheap and nasty wine that ate through its plastic bottles after three weeks in storage and a majority of thoroughly useless conscript soldiers. He made an exception of their regular officers and NCOs, many of whom had been crack Foreign Legionnaires in their day.

The Americans to the south he briskly summarized as 'lots of kit, lots of money, and enormously fat wives with a non-stop diet of fries and junk food.'

The Porsche growled by the battalion sties where the battalion pig-corporal was feeding his charges on battalion swill. Mason parked outside the officers' mess and shivered in the raw Berlin chill.

He glanced at his pigeon-hole in the Foyer of the officers' mess. Nothing there: nobody loved him. He went upstairs to the ante-room. Even the snooker table was deserted. Guardsman Coleman appeared from nowhere, smart as a laundered penguin, and gave him a gin and tonic without being asked.

'Message for you, Captain Mason, sir. About an hour ago. Please contact your uncle in London.'

Mason's only 'uncle' never went to London. He sighed but experienced the familiar prickle of anticipation that went with a call from Spike Allen. He picked up a copy of The Times, determined to enjoy his drink for five minutes.

His moment of peace was interrupted by two tiresome second lieutenants who flung themselves into neighbouring chairs.

'Nearly made it with Angela last night,' one said in an undertone, preening himself in an especially nauseous way that Mason detested.

'Bad luck actually,' the subaltern continued. 'Just as the adorable Angie was stretching out those quite wonderfully long, brown legs, one of those bloody wild boars from the Grünewald executed a raid on the Everleys' dustbins directly below her room.'

The Everleys were a married couple from one of the resident units whose nanny from Kent was then the rage of most unmarried officers in Wavell Barracks. Quite how the hugely unimpressive subaltern had attracted the girl was a mystery to Mason. The last time the garrison had been called out at night for a 'Rocking Horse' (the NATO code-name for a rehearsal response to a Soviet attack), Angela's current lover had failed to appear and was accordingly confined to barracks for three months.

Mason's *bête noire* continued his lament. 'The Everley children woke up and screamed at the crashing bins. Angela froze on me. She quite dried up. Those damned pigs ought to be shot.'

Mason grunted, mentally congratulating the dustbin-loving pigs, and left the room to book a call from the phone booth beside the ante-room. Because of the late hour, he was put through almost at once. Spike explained the background to the Muscat mission. Mason was obviously suited for the job. Spike had provisionally reserved him a seat on the 10 a.m. flight from Heathrow on 5 March. Could he make it?

'Your timing is as lousy as ever.' Mason cursed his luck. He was due to start his annual leave on 4 March. He and another officer would be skiing in Italy for a fortnight. There was no way, he knew, that he could hand over his Berlin duties until midnight on 4 March. On the other hand he tried never to let Spike down. He made up his mind.

'I will check out the timings, Spike, and phone you back in an hour or two.'

Mason made a number of calls and his mood began to improve. His second conversation with Spike was a reverse-charge call placed from a booth outside the barracks. The ante-room phone was anything but confidential.

'By absconding on my leave some seven hours earlier than permitted,' Mason spoke with some relish, 'by bribing a Royal Military Police NCO and by driving extremely fast during the night of 4 March, I will just about be able to make the flight. My skiing friend, if asked at some later stage, will insist that I was indeed in Italy with him drinking *Glühwein* and scorching the black runs. He assumes, I imagine, I'm going to have two dirty weeks with some married woman.' Mason inserted a hardness into his tone. 'So I'm all set providing that you, Spike, will bend some of your normal rules.'

Spike responded with a sigh. 'If you are thinking of taking any items with you, as per Cyprus, forget it.'

'No item, no Muscat, I'm afraid Spike. I have great respect for your maxim in the UK but I have risked life and limb for two long years in Oman and the reason I am alive today is *my* maxim of self-preservation.'

Spike never wasted time in pointless repartee. 'I have told you to travel legally. If you have other intentions, I know nothing about them.'

'Good,' said Mason. 'The other matter is my expenses. Travel, accommodation, two thousand Deutschmarks for a gift to my RMP friend, and all incidental expenses.'

'No problem,' said Spike. 'I will use your second passport to process your No Objection Certificate through Kendall's and have it ready for you at Heathrow along with a photograph of the Welshman.'

Mason placed a further reverse-charge call to a close friend, Patrick Tanner, at his London flat. He apologized for the late hour but he urgently needed Patrick's help along much the same lines as the previous year and involving more or less the same equipment. After some good-natured banter, Tanner copied down a complex shopping list. Most of the gear was to be had from Mason's own safe-room on his parents' Oxfordshire estate. Mason's father was a touch old-fashioned and did not take kindly to strange civilian friends of his son turning up to stay overnight unless, of course, David was with them at the time. On the other hand he was immensely proud of his son's service record and any brother Guards officer was always welcome. For this reason, the previous year David had ensured a friendly welcome for Patrick Tanner by having him stand in for an actual Guards officer named Douglas Erskine-Crum, whom his father had heard of but never met. Tanner agreed that he would again present himself as Erskine-Crum and Mason called his parents to warn them of his arrival the following evening. He would be needing a bed but no breakfast, as he must leave in the small hours for Scotland.

Patrick Tanner's alarm sounded at 4 a.m. He left a thank-you note to the Masons on his bedside table and descended to the study for the safe-room key. David had told him exactly where to find it. Quietly, lest David's father should be a poor sleeper, he unlocked the heavy safe-room door, disabled the inner alarms and, with admiration and a touch of envy, surveyed the guns that lined the walls.

photograph by kind permission of Bridgie Milling-Smith)

Superintendent John Milling flying with the air wing of the Royal Oman Police in 1977.
Superintendent Milling died on 20 March 1977 'in an air accident' off the coast of Oman.

(*photograph by kind permission of Mrs Nancy Kealy*)

Major Mike Kealy climbing in Wales *circa 1976*.
Major Kealy died on 1 February 1979 'of exposure' on the Brecon Beacons in Wales.

(photograph by kind permission of Rose May Cassel-Kokczynska)

Major Michael Marman in Midway, Dhofar, in 1975.
Major Marman died on 11 November 1986 'in a road accident' on the A303 in Wiltshire.

(photograph by kind permission of Pauline)
Corporal 'Mac' in Dhofar in 1975.
Corporal 'Mac' died on 12 December 1987 at his Hereford home 'of asphyxia during an epileptic attack'.

He was thankful for the checklist David had given him the previous year. On that occasion he had retrieved the Colt Python .357 Magnum revolver.

There were a number of shotguns — .410s, 20-bore and 16-bore — but the prize items were a pair of 12-bore Purdeys with thirty-inch barrels and made in the 1920s, the best period for English game guns.

Patrick smiled as he read through the checklist. David was a connoisseur. The list was almost a homily:

'S&W .45 ACP auto, 9 shot. Good auto, quick firing etc, but like all autos is more prone to jamming than a revolver.

Walther PP .32 calibre. Excellent small auto, but needs very accurate shot (or 2–3 rounds) to stop quarry. Any pistol with a smaller calibre than this is frankly no use for anything other than firing into one's mouth if one needs a new tooth filling.

Walther .22LR semi-auto rifle with sound moderator (silencer) for vermin (ideal for rabbits).

Colt Python .357 Magnum revolver. Heavy and deadly accurate. I get 4-inch groups at 100 yards. The best revolver made. Fires heavy 160-grain slug.

Stephen Grant .22 Hornet for slightly larger vermin. *Deadly* accurate up to 120–150 yards, then trajectory falls off quickly. Converted by J. Rigby & Co., from the original .250 'rook rifle' calibre.

Parker–Hale .243 rifle. Cheap but accurate. Good flat trajectory for vermin out of range of .22 Hornet.

Rigby .275 Mauser action rifles. I have three of these, one with an extra long barrel and two with standard barrels. Superb rifles, ideal for deer-stalking. One has a Zeiss 4 × 40 mm scope, one a Pecar 4 × 30 mm and the long-barrelled one has open sights only.

Daniel Frazer .303 double rifle. Collector's item. Very accurate.

Rigby .350 Magnum Mauser action rifle. Oldish (1920s). Very reliable. Open sights. For big game.

Rigby .375 H&H Magnum rifle. Converted from .350 special (an obsolete calibre). Marvellous rifle — will stop just about anything. Kick like a mule. 1.5–6 × 40 Zeiss scope.

Pair of Purdey .450 double rifles. Collector's items (turn of the century).

Rigby .470 Nitro Express double rifle. Fantastic weapon. Beautifully made (*c.*1930). Mint condition — very valuable. Will stop *anything*. Makes a noise like a nuclear explosion when fired (500-grain bullet @ 2,150 fps).

You will notice from the above that the majority of my rifles are made by John Rigby & Co. For a century now they have in my opinion been

the best rifle-makers of all (they still are) although in terms purely of accuracy rather than quality of workmanship there are quite a few other good names.

Those are the rifles and handguns I have at the moment. As far as military weapons are concerned, my favourite is the Russian AKM assault rifle (brilliantly simple, no-nonsense design, never jams, small and manœuvrable, lightweight ammo, etc.), and my least favourite is anything that has been issued to the British Army since they replaced the .303 Lee Enfield rifle and Bren LMG, with the honourable exception of the L42 sniper's rifle and to some extent the GPMG, although both would be better if they used .303 ammunition modified to rimless, instead of .308 Winchester (7.62 mm NATO). The SLR, the Sterling SMG and the Browning 9 mm 'Hi-Power' auto pistol are all badly designed, fault prone, bloody awful weapons, although the silenced version of the Sterling has its uses ...'

Patrick folded away Mason's note, unclipped the .22 Hornet from its rack and removed sufficient materials and tools to make up ten rounds of .22 ammunition from a box in the drawer immediately below. He selected a hardened-plastic rifle case from the relevant rack and spent the better part of an hour centralizing the smaller items on David's ancillaries list. Finally he removed a battered brown suitcase containing clothing. Not all the gear Mason had requested was in evidence but Patrick had put together a shopping list to attend to later in the day. He replaced the keys, let himself out of the house and drove his VW camper as quietly as the gravel allowed down the driveway of Eynsham Park.

At 5 p.m. on 4 March, having handed over his duties as early as was feasible, David Mason left Wavell Barracks in a hurry. He was technically seven hours AWOL since his two weeks' leave did not officially begin until midnight. Fifteen minutes later he arrived at Checkpoint Bravo, entry point to the Berlin Corridor, and frowned with irritation at the line of cars awaiting document checks. He jumped the queue and flashed his ID card at a queuing Burgermeister type who showed signs of indignation. The RMP Duty Warrant Officer was immediately on hand and Mason passed him the two-thousand-Deutschmark Eurocheque to which he had previously agreed in return for keeping a space for 4.30 p.m. for Mason's green Porsche 911, British Forces Germany registration number EZ 242 B. The warrant officer took details of Mason's BFG licence, his ID and

Green Card insurance cover. The Berlin Corridor system was rigidly controlled to ensure no car driver had time to spare, after leaving the checkpoint at either end of the Corridor, in which to leave the road for nefarious purposes, such as smuggling locals to the West.

The regulations also ensured that no speeding could take place by stipulating a *minimum* time limit of two hours for the one-hundred-mile drive. Mason left the checkpoint at 5.30 p.m., not at 4.30 as stamped on his pass by the warrant officer. He was therefore able to average a hundred miles an hour along the potholed Corridor and still arrive at the 'correct time' of 6.30 p.m. at the Helmstedt Volkspolizei checkpoint out of East Germany.

The East German border guards were perfunctory in their check and the British NCOs at Checkpoint Alpha passed Mason through without a second glance. He then settled down to some serious autobahn driving via Hanover, Dortmund and the Belgian border at Aachen, passing through that unmanned border post at 135 mph.

He reached Zeebrugge at 10.15 p.m. and caught the 11 p.m. ferry. On board he purchased twelve rolls of Kodak 'Tri-X' film and four rolls of Ilford FP4 film, both 35 mm, at the duty-free shop and slept for two hours.

After clearing Dover Customs at 4.30 a.m., he set off along the A2 and M2 to London then, via the M4, to Heathrow where, at 7 a.m., he drew up behind Patrick's VW camper on the access road to the long-term car park.

Inside the curtained and locked rear of the van the two men drank black coffee from Patrick's vacuum flask and Mason lit up a cigar, and placed the .22 rifle, with all the other items that Patrick produced, on the camper's kitchen table. He carefully explained to Patrick exactly what must be done over the next two hours.

Patrick switched on the car's ignition to activate the extractor fan in the hope that it would deal with the cigar smoke before he died of asphyxiation and to ensure that their conversation was inaudible outside the van. A BBC newscaster wished them good morning with the news that thousands had died in an earthquake in Rumania.

The rifle, Mason explained, had been manufactured by Stephen Grant & Son of 67a St James's Street, London, in the early 1930s. It had been made as a .25 rook rifle and was later rechambered for .22 Hornet bullets. The outside of its barrel was octagonal, giving it an antique appearance that belied its efficiency. The action worked from

a side lever and opened like a modern shotgun, being single-shot, not magazine-loaded.

To dismantle the weapon Mason removed the wooden fore-end piece in front of the trigger guard and, breaking the gun by pushing down the side lever, he hinged the barrel down and away.

The camper's built-in cooker had two gas-rings over which Mason held a twenty-four-inch length of eighth of an inch diameter 8 SWG steel rod and, in his other hand, the barrel of the rifle. Patrick heated a black candle so that its melted wax dripped down into an egg-poacher.

Mason smeared a chewed wad of gum with engine oil and pushed it into the barrel's muzzle end. He then held the heated barrel upright with its muzzle on the floor and inserted the twenty-four inch rod into the twenty-six-inch barrel until it disappeared. He shook the barrel a touch and the rod rattled audibly. Patrick then poured the melted wax into the barrel through a funnel so that it filled the entire area between the rod and the inside wall of the rifled barrel. Once the rifle and the rod cooled down the wax solidified and the rod was rigidly sealed into position.

Removing the wad of gum, Mason applied varnish with an artist's brush to both ends of the captive rod, dabbed on gun-black as a final camouflage coat and tapped both ends of the rod with a screwdriver. The effect was that of a police-plugged barrel. To all intents and purposes the weapon was now merely a decommissioned antique. As such, it could travel legally and document-free as air cargo. Mason reassembled the rifle, having first removed the firing pin and mainspring. Then he locked it into the plastic rifle case and stubbed out his cigar.

'The next stage,' he told Patrick, 'will take longer.' He removed four cassettes of Ilford FP4 film with their plastic containers and began to force their tops off gently with a standard bottle-opener. 'I wasted hours when I first tried this with Kodak cassettes. They come off OK but they're buggers to reassemble. Also the hollow area inside the spools of these Ilford cassettes is more spacious.'

Mason used a modelling knife to cut away the main central portion of the take-up spool. He retained only the now truncated ends, each of which looked rather like a miniature black top hat. He set Patrick to work on a second Ilford cassette and turned his attention to the components of the ten .22 Hornet bullets. First the empty cases, new and unprimed. These he prepared one by one with Eley primers by

placing a primer on to a Lyman ram tool and pushing it firmly down into an empty case held in the slot of a Lachmiller priming clamp. When five of the cases were primed he bound them into a tight bundle using surgical tape. He then positioned an Ilford spool 'top-hat' on either end of the bundle and forced it into the original Ilford cassette casing. The caps, which he had earlier removed by bottle-opener leverage, he now replaced by simple pressure until they once again mated over and around the 'top hats'. Since the Hornet cases were exactly thirty-five millimetres in length they fitted with precision into the space vacated by the film.

The finished cassette looked as good as new although it now weighed thirty-three grammes instead of twenty. When Mason had primed the remaining five empty cases he fed them into the guts of the cassette that Patrick had successfully doctored. Cutting five inches of film leader from one of the discarded films, he inverted it to protrude in the normal manner. Loading the cassette into one of his Olympus OM-1 cameras, he made sure that the leader covered the camera's take-up spool without actually entering the winder slot. After closing the camera he pulled back the film-advance lever a dozen times. Although the film itself did not move, the exposure-counter window now registered twelve. He fed the second camera with the other five disguised bullet cases. On the security X-ray, the intricate components of the cameras would disguise the presence of the cartridge cases.

Only the bullets themselves and the gunpowder remained to be dealt with. Mason used small balance scales to weigh out eleven grains of IMR 4227 gunpowder, which he poured into a small, square plastic bag labelled silica-gel desiccant. He sealed the bag with instant glue and repeated the process twelve times, allowing two extra bags for damage or wastage at a customs inspection. The bags went into a side pocket of Mason's camera case. If inspected for drugs, the gunpowder was tasteless and, like silica gel, hygroscopic. The case also contained a foldaway developing tank, trays, chemicals, paper and the parts of an enlarger.

The ten Hornady forty-five grain (2.9 gramme) .22 Hornet hollow-point bullets fitted perfectly into the central space of two packets of Polo mints that Mason put into his trouser pocket.

Thirty more minutes were spent checking and packing all the equipment, and at 8.50 a.m. Patrick left Mason at the Terminal Three Departure Lounge. The Gulf Air check-in counter took his large

suitcase and the rifle case as cargo baggage and he passed through to Emigration.

At the X-ray machine, Mason placed his hand luggage on the conveyor belt and entered the walk-through metal detector, which bleeped loudly at him. A security officer had him empty his pockets on to the side table and try again. Next time the machine was silent but he was 'patted down' and the contents of his pockets were checked over item by item. These consisted of keys, wristwatch, steel Parker pen, coins, sunglasses, penknife, handkerchief and Polo mints. All were passed as innocent.

Mason's hand baggage was opened by an efficient lady in a well-filled grey sweater. She switched on his razor, dictaphone and radio and inspected his cameras and lenses with care. She ignored the silica-gel bags and various other small, harmless-looking items.

Immediately Mason finished with Security he headed for the toilets in the Departure Lounge, where he taped a polythene bag to the inside of one of the cisterns. The bag contained all his 'guilty' items, including bugging gear, firing pin, Polos and doctored cassettes. He reloaded his cameras with genuine Ilford film.

No sooner was he seated behind a newspaper in the Departure Lounge than his name was called out on the Tannoy. He must return to Security. Once there he was taken to a side-room and confronted with his rifle case. This he unloaded, explaining that the gun was a decommissioned antique for which he had an exchange-buyer in Muscat. He intended to bring back a six-foot-long matchlock if the sale went well.

The officers seemed satisfied but rechecked all Mason's gear. This went ahead without a hitch and he returned to the toilets to retrieve his equipment. He recalled that the previous year he had felt guilty during the recheck *en route* to Cyprus. This time he had been troubled by no such twinges.

Davies had still not boarded by the time of the last call for their flight, but Mason spotted and identified him with considerable relief soon after it was made. The Welshman travelled First Class, Mason in Economy.

The TriStar was half-full until Doha but then filled up, mostly with Asians, for the final legs to Dubai and Muscat. It touched down at Seeb International Airport shortly before midnight. The night air was cool and Davies was met by a cab driver holding a name-board. While Davies returned to await his baggage amid a milling bustle of

Asians, Mason asked the Welshman's driver if he was free.

'Sorry sah'b, I take another man to Gulf Hotel. But no worry. Many more taxi outside for you.'

Mason relaxed. Spike already had him booked into the Muscat Gulf, the best of the only three available hotels in all Oman. There was now no need to worry if Davies's bags appeared before his own.

14

Bill Bailey, Chief Superintendent of the Air Wing of the Royal Oman Police, watched the helicopter disappear towards the mountains on an emergency medical evacuation requested by the Army. He had sent John Milling because no one knew the Jebel Akhdar better.

Most of Bill Bailey's helicopters were Augusta Bell 205s, modelled by the Italians on the American Huey and extremely reliable even when flown well beyond their specified limits. They were designed to carry, under normal conditions, a maximum of twelve fully equipped men but Bill had once counted twenty-four Dhofaris, all with bundles of personal gear, spill out of one.

Bill knew John Milling of old, for both men had served with the Royal Marines in Europe. John had not been his normal cheerful self the last couple of days and Bill put this down to the recent news of the death, in a helicopter crash, of Queen Noor of Jordan. During a Royal visit to Oman the previous December, John had flown Queen Noor to all the main places of interest and grown to like her. Most of his pilots, Bill knew, would simply have said, 'How sad.' But, John took such things very much to heart. If he liked you, he was the most loyal of friends. A bit of a romantic too, Bill had always thought. It was probably due to his genes: he came of a devoutly Protestant family from Ballymoney, in Northern Ireland, where his father was the North Coast Warden for the National Trust. Tall and very good-looking, John had conquered more than one heart on his travels over the years.

The reason for his current introspective mood had in reality nothing to do with the late Queen of Jordan and everything to do with his wife. Bridget, or Bridgie as she was generally known, was

seven and a half months pregnant with their second child and showing worrying signs of a premature delivery. With the leaden heat of the Oman summer less than a month away, John was anxious for Bridgie to have the child in Europe and, until then, he must ensure she was treated like porcelain.

A natural sportsman, John had rowed at Henley for his school and then joined the Commandos. After service in the Far East he was seconded in 1969 to the Sultan's forces and decorated for bravery under fire. For a while he flew helicopters in the West Indies until, leaving the Royal Marines in 1975, he joined the Air Wing of the Royal Oman Police. After eighteen months his restless soul was already becoming bored. He sought new and distant horizons.

The Bell flew through the Sumail Gap. To the south lay many hundreds of miles of sand and igneous rock, the Wahiba and Sharqiya regions; to the north the great escarpment of the Jebel Akhdar and Nakhl. On landing at Izki camp, John collected a generator spare part, then, departing slightly from his official flight plan, flew north for the lush gardens of Birkat al Mawz, Pool of the Plantains. To the delight of his Omani crewman Ali, they headed for a valley that cleft the sheer face of the Jebel Akhdar, ten thousand feet high.

John's face visibly relaxed, the tensions of his personal worries dropping away as the need for his flying skills became paramount. This was split-second flying deep in the heart of the most spectacular scenery in the world. The canyons of Colorado were mere runnels compared with the spiralling chines of the Akhdar.

The atmospheric change within the ravine and its effect on the Bell was immediate as the hot air of the plains confronted katabatic gusts from the escarpment. John juggled his controls with the skill and delight of a teenager at an arcade video game. But this was very much for real, a test for any pilot.

The floor of the valley, the Wadi Miyadin, zigzagged below, mostly in shadow, a crooked corridor of waterfalls, deep pools and enormous boulders tossed there by bore waves in years gone by.

This was life at its best, an exhilaration John had experienced only from flying and from the heat of battle in Dhofar, now over six years ago; a lifetime away. John was disdainful of many of his expatriate colleagues in the Omani services. They seemed to care only about their pay and perks, showing little or no interest in this wonderful land and its friendly people. For his own part he regretted the disappearance of the old Oman. While he could appreciate the

enormous benefits of the progress brought about by the accession of Qaboos, he missed the charm, the unique atmosphere that had drawn him back to this country. Omanis still wore their traditional white robes, the head-dress known as a *shemagh* and curved waist daggers, but Polaroid sunglasses had sadly become part of the national dress. Cola bottles, telephone lines and motor scooters were infesting every corner of the land. All were doubtless blessings to the local people but a bit of a let-down to the romantic observer.

John spoke and wrote classical Arabic. He could perhaps teach English in the mountains of Royalist North Yemen, where the only sign of twentieth-century progress to have shown itself had been deadly clouds of Tabun nerve gas from Egyptian fighters ten years before. Bridgie might find such a life a touch lonely to begin with but she would soon grow to love it, for she was plucky and adaptable. John had the knack of wishful thinking down to a fine art.

The Bell climbed free of the shadows of the deeper ravines and John touched the controls to bank west over the pool of Salut, half-hidden by groves of tamarisk and oleander, where camels and goats watered. Within minutes, the view widened to an airy panorama of the *jebel* ramparts. Massive crags and cliff-hanging villages, cascades of plunging water and a slash of green where terraced orchards defied gravity.

On a ledge below, John spotted the remains of an RAF Venom bomber, a casualty of the 1959 mountain rebellion. The Sultan now kept a permanent army detachment at Sayq on the *jebel* but in '58 a rebellious imam, with Saudi help, had taken and held the mountain fastness with a heavily armed force of seven hundred guerrilla fighters. For nine hundred years no invaders had ever taken the mountain by force, though many had tried. In 550 BC the Persians had first arrived and fought their way by sheer weight of numbers to the upper plateau. Even the easiest of the existing twenty-three access routes was no wider than a single-file pathway.

In January 1959 two troops of SAS men, fresh from the Malayan jungles, surprised the imam's fighters by a night ascent of a climbers' route from Kamah village. The attack was led by Captain Peter de la Billière, who, in 1991, was to command the British forces in the Gulf War.

John landed at Sayq Battle Camp. A messenger from the commandant ushered forward an Arab teenager with frightened eyes, a dirty *dishdash* (a checked skirt-like wraparound garment) and bare

feet. This, said the messenger, was the husband of the evacuation case. John shook the boy's hand and addressed him in his own tongue. He was of the Beni Riyam tribe and lived in Shiraija. His wife had been bitten by a cobra and was very sick. He had run up to the army camp but all three of the medics were on exercise elsewhere on the *jebel*.

'Did you kill the snake?' John asked the young Arab and was relieved when he nodded. Knowing the geography of Shiraija, John could see the wisdom of helicopter evacuation to a hospital with a range of serums capable of countering the venom of most Omani vipers. Whenever evacuating snake-bite cases, he tried to give the hospital authorities the snake's body along with the patient. This ensured the use of the correct serum without delay.

John handed the generator spare to the commandant's messenger, strapped the boy into the rear of the Bell, with a set of headphones, and left for Shiraija. The village was no more than a mile from Sayq camp but tucked into the upper reaches of a near-vertical ravine. The mountainside below fell away in giddy tiers of irrigated steps. Every layer was tended by artificial channels that overflowed from level to level to the very last of the tiny fertile orchards three thousand feet below.

Plants and trees with exotic foliage hung heavy with fruit: figs, peaches, almonds, walnuts, berries, bananas and pomegranates to name but a few. Sugar-cane groves thrived on the lower tiers and lawns of lucerne waved in the cool, scented breeze at every level.

Crewman Ali conferred with the young Arab, who, face pressed to the Plexiglass, kept making downward motions. The girl must have been working in the very lowest of the orchards. John circled slowly, banking so that the boy could see the terraces below. At length the young Arab shouted into the headsets so that both airmen winced. He had spotted his wife.

Six hundred feet above the victim's location, John found a lucerne bed just wide enough for the helicopter to land without the rotors smashing into the wall of the next terrace. The three of them scrambled down through the orchards to where the girl lay in long grass. Her face was tinted with the yellow dye of the saffron flower. He saw at once that she was dead. The poor lass, John thought: she had died alone and in great pain. Her body was rigid and arched, her eyes wide open and her tongue extended. She looked so young to be married — no more than twelve, he estimated. Her throat glands

were horribly puffed out, so John felt her wrist for a pulse. There was none. He touched one of her eyes but there was no reaction. The snake's body, broken and battered, lay in the dirt. John saw that it was an eckis, not a cobra, and almost certainly, with its broad flat head, a highly poisonous Schneider.

The boy knelt beside the dead girl. His hands came together at his mouth and tears ran down his face. John clenched the boy's shoulders and as the deep, dry sobbing began, held him close.

They carried the little body with care to the helicopter. John spoke with the Sayq duty signaller and, when they returned to the camp, a Land Rover with a stretcher and body-bag awaited them.

John's lasting memory of that day was the face of the boy, as lost and alone as a wounded gazelle. He and Ali were silent as they flew back to Seeb. John said nothing to Bridgie that evening, but he felt especially tender towards her and their three-year-old son Oliver.

15

Mason paid the cab driver at a point where the morning traffic, a honking mish-mash of camels and motors, passed through a gap torn in the town wall. Matrah, an ants' nest of commerce, had changed greatly in the year since Mason's Omani service. A modern harbour, Port Qaboos, was under construction and bulldozers were sweeping away much of the old town to make space for modern office units.

Davies was not in a hurry and behaved like any expatriate worker newly arrived in so fascinating a city. He wandered at will through the babble of Asian building workers, gazed a while at the old and the new in the harbour area and ambled to the inner walled market of the Khojas, the Sur al-Lawatiyah. Generations of Khoja merchants, originally from Sind, had retained their language and customs while masterminding Matrah commerce from the tangled and labyrinthine corridors of the Lawatiyah.

Mason was forced to close in or risk losing the Welshman. The narrow, scented passageways seethed with humanity and Mason began to sense a certain urgency and purpose to the hitherto random course of his quarry. A head and shoulders above most of the crowd

he managed to keep in touch, but only with difficulty and many a hostile glance from the white-robed denizens of the *sooq*.

At a divergence of three corridors Mason was unable to wedge a passage between two women in black-beaked Ibadhi masks. '*Min fadlak*,' he shouted, '*indee mushkila*,' but the women, both as heavy and round as Soviet shot-putters, ignored him. Their fishwife gossip merely gathered strength, each talking, neither listening. Davies disappeared.

A half-hour search of every stall in the Lawatiyah and its adjacent streets proved fruitless, so Mason took a cab back to the Gulf Hotel. Davies would return there in due course and Mason had things to prepare that were better done without delay, now that Davies was showing signs of activity.

In his bathroom he reassembled the ten rounds of ammunition with his Lyman crimping tool and heated the rifle barrel over a flat iron obtained from the chambermaid. The black wax melted and he knocked the steel rod loose. Later he would pull the barrel through with petrol-soaked swabs. After packing a travel bag with the detached stock and the barrel, he added some clothing and equipment, then ordered a taxi.

'*Muaskar al Murtafa'a*,' he instructed the driver, referring to the Northern Headquarters complex of the Sultan's Armed Forces. At the security gate his taxi was waved past; Mason looked like the officer he had once been. Over four hundred British officers and NCOs worked for their Omani superiors within the sprawling barracks and the turn-over rate was such that no one knew everyone else.

In the lavatory of the officers' mess, Mason changed into the uniform of the Desert Regiment, which differed from that of other SAF regiments only in the colour of beret and belt. He was pleased that during his time back in Europe he had not put on weight. He walked through the camp, returning salutes as appropriate, to the lines of the Motor Transport Section. Hundreds of Bedford lorries, Land Rovers and Land-Cruisers were parked beside a like number of civilian Datsuns and a smattering of Mercedes for use by more senior officers.

A fairly strict vehicle sign-out procedure existed, but Mason had ignored all red tape in days when resources and manpower were smaller and control much tighter, so he found a Datsun with keys in the ignition and drove back to the Gulf Hotel without troubling the 'official channels'. He left the car in the hotel parking lot, far enough

away from the main entrance for the SAF number plate not to be noticeable, and in any case it appeared to be one of many white Datsuns. He entered the foyer. Davies's key was still missing from its pigeon-hole, so Mason settled down with a Scotch and slightly stale *Newsweek* in a far corner of the lobby. Without his brown Desert Regiment beret, he was merely an army staff officer taking it easy.

The Khoja merchant was as fat as a Sumo wrestler and his bald scalp glinted under the fluorescent bulbs as a result of daily application of scented unguent. He was solicitous in the extreme and twice interrupted the meeting with offers of more coffee before de Villiers bade him leave them in peace.

He emerged from the *majlis*, the inner room used for entertaining and business, glad that he had overcharged the supercilious sons of bitches. He joined their 'local representative', Karim Bux, in the small room immediately behind his stall.

'This tall man was English?' Karim Bux asked the Khoja. 'You are certain?' The merchant shrugged. 'It is as I told you. My sisters saw only this tall foreigner behind your friend, so, as instructed, they blocked his way. He spoke to them in good Arabic but like an *Ingleezi*.'

Karim Bux sipped at his *loomee*. Despite the fans, the cushioned room was rank with the smell of lovemaking and he wished de Villiers would hurry up. He decided to make no mention of the man who had followed Davies. There was always a smattering of Europeans about the Lawatiyah. The Khoja and his sisters were probably merely fishing for an extra tip.

Karim Bux was Tadnams' only agent in the subcontinent and had plenty of overdue work in Delhi. He objected to his current role in Oman, for he was not accustomed to playing second fiddle to Europeans. But he kept his feelings to himself for Tadnams paid him well and he knew his three charges were veterans, possibly with influence in Earls Court.

Davies leafed through the photographs of John Milling, his wife and two other men: they showed the men in uniform, or simply relaxing by the seaside. 'Big fellow, this Milling, looks like some Greek god,' Davies commented.

De Villiers shrugged. 'Tomorrow we will test his immortality.'

Davies was content with the plans. He preferred methods that the Clinic had successfully used in the past, and de Villiers had, in Milling's case, settled for a simple domestic accident.

For two weeks the Millings had been subjected to an intensive and annotated study. It was the custom of the Clinic to spot repetitive patterns of activity in their prospective targets' lives or, if none were apparent, to gain access to some pointer to their future plans such as an office wall-chart, a diary or a personal secretary who could be encouraged to gossip.

Once a pattern or a specific intended activity was identified, the Clinic would select a time and place where the target would be alone and vulnerable to an accident.

On arrival in Oman, de Villiers had settled in at the Intercontinental Hotel and Meier at the Falaj Hotel. De Villiers looked after Milling's home life and Meier his Police Air Wing activities.

A sign at the Air Wing perimeter gate announced maintenance works by J. & P. Contractors, so Meier went to their recruiting office in Azaiba. His excellent references, including seven years with Mercedes, probably helped, but electrical and mechanical engineers were anyway much sought after. As luck would have it, that morning J & P had sent a European engineer home on compassionate leave. The company's considerable connections in high places enabled it, under the current circumstances, to circumvent the normal immigration rule that would have required Meier to leave the country while his work-permit application was being processed. He was able to start work within a few hours of the initial phone call to J & P's sponsor's office. He was assigned to the maintenance team handling the contract for the Royal Flight and Police complex, including the current alterations to the Police Air Wing workshops.

Subsequent comparative studies indicated that, while Meier was keen and confident that he could sabotage Milling's helicopter in such a way as to produce 'accidental death', a more certain method would be a visit to the target's home at a time of day when he was normally alone.

Davies was to provide back-up and removal facilities while the other two would complete the killing in a manner they had carefully prepared and rehearsed.

The Clinic agreed all the details and Karim Bux dropped them off, each within walking distance of their separate hotels.

At 3.45 p.m. John Milling, a green and white *wizaar* wrapped about his waist, watched his wife set off for her usual Thursday shopping spree at the Matrah Cold Store supermarket.

He felt a pang of quite unnecessary jealousy as his friend Geoff

Leggatt, six foot four inches tall, helped Bridgie into the front passenger seat. Even seven and a half months pregnant she was stunningly attractive. The long slim legs, the golden blond hair, the large green eyes and the sparky Irish temperament had earned her the tag of the loveliest, sexiest girl in Oman.

Cha Cha, their albino Kashmiri houseboy, sat in the back with three-year-old Oliver, whose features already showed the Milling stamp. Geoff slammed the door and waved to John. They had been friends since schooldays in Enniskillen. Four years ago John had fallen headlong in love with Bridgie, who was then Geoff's girlfriend. A passionate affair followed, punctuated by Bridgie's worldwide travels, for she was then a BOAC hostess. Geoff accepted the situation and they all remained the best of friends. He had called in at their home in Seeb a week earlier on his way to teach English in Japan.

John Milling closed the front door of the bungalow and settled into an armchair with his feet on the drawing-room table. In an hour or so he would go jogging along the coast road. This was not his normal practice on Thursday afternoons but the pilot, James A. Sims Junior, with whom he usually jogged or went scuba diving twice a week, was on leave. Jim was a tall, dark native of Tennessee and unmarried. John was quite looking forward to this outing since he found it hard going to keep pace with the athletic American and today he would accompany the forty-five-year-old George Halbert, a retired RAF navigator and one of the Air Wing's fixed-wing pilots. George liked to drink and to keep fit so he indulged in binges of each activity on alternate months. He lived just down the street from the Millings.

The *Economist* magazine fell to the floor as John nodded off to the gentle rattle of the air-conditioning. Some minutes later he woke with a start at the chime of the doorbell. Perhaps George had arrived early, the silly bugger, in the full heat of the afternoon.

Milling recognized neither of his visitors. Both wore slacks and clean white shirts and the balding, shorter man with spectacles carried a briefcase. Both were profuse in their apologies. They had not realized Superintendent Milling would be resting. They would come back later. They were American military historians writing a definitive account of guerrilla wars in the mid to late twentieth century. Colin Maxwell and Ted Ashley had suggested they seek Milling's advice. John's curiosity was pricked.

'Come in,' he waved them into the cool, curtained living room. 'I can offer you a beer, *loomee* or iced tea.'

He indicated the armchairs and padded to the refrigerator in the kitchen. The bungalow was mostly open-plan. The refrigerator was tucked against a side wall in the kitchen and just out of sight of the living room. As Milling returned, grasping two beer cans and tankards, he noticed the snub-nosed revolver in the hands of the taller man.

'Put the beers down, Superintendent, and lie face on the floor.'

Milling did so.

'Now clasp your hands together, fingers interlaced, behind your back.'

One of the men bound his fingers and then his wrists together with an elasticated material that felt like electrical tape. Although there was no discomfort, the bindings were rock solid and did not respond to his subsequent attempts to dislodge them.

He was helped into one of the chairs and the armed man stayed behind him. The other set up an 8-mm cine camera on a tripod, then moved around the bungalow bolting windows and doors. He moved a single sunblind aside to allow more light on to Milling's face.

Meier took his briefcase into the bathroom and quickly made his preparations. Two days earlier, while the Milling family were at the beach, with Cha Cha handling their barbecue, de Villiers had taken a plaster-cast impression of the corner of the shower plinth, six inches above floor level in the bathroom. Karim Bux had then prepared, with molten lead, a truncheon head shaped in the plaster-cast mould.

The death scenario was simple. Milling had decided to take a pre-jog shower, slipped on some spilled shampoo, tore the shower curtain loose in falling and struck the plinth corner with his occiput, the point where skull joins neck. The resultant depressed fracture of the skull would cause brain damage and death. Since only one blow could be struck, Meier had an ample supply of polythene in readiness to induce asphyxiation if necessary.

Satisfied that all was ready in the bathroom, Meier returned to the cine camera and gave the go-ahead to de Villiers, who moved the revolver and his head into frame, close behind Milling's. He spoke slowly and clearly. 'On 18 October 1969 you murdered Salim bin Amr Bait Na'ath in an ambush at the Dhofari village Qum. Do you admit this?'

Milling was silent for a moment, digesting this totally unexpected

and preposterous accusation. When he replied his voice was controlled.

'In 1969 I was an army officer fighting communist terrorists. I remember leading part of my company for the Qum operations and I remember that two *adoo* were killed but *not* by me.'

Only the whirr of the camera and the faint clatter of the air-conditioning disturbed the silence. De Villiers tried again.

'As the officer in charge of the Qum ambush you were in overall charge of all your men. If, under your orders, one of them fired the bullets that killed Salim bin Amr, you are as responsible for his death as if you had personally murdered him.'

The events, nearly eight years ago, came back to John Milling in a rush. He knew exactly what had happened, but if he gave a name he would endanger someone else. He took the middle course.

'Whoever you are, you are crazy. Nobody is *murdered* in battle. Soldiers eliminate their enemy in military, not moral, circumstances.'

De Villiers did not hesitate. 'You could have accepted the surrender of Salim bin Amr. There was no need to shoot him down. You will now be executed as decreed by the father of the man you murdered.'

A part of Milling's mind toyed with the idea that these men were mad, obsessed with some vendetta, or even involved in some weird Esther Rantzen-inspired joke. But Meier's eyes, the hard, flat tones of de Villiers's voice and the quiet economy of movement of both men, militated against such theories.

'There *was* an officer who ambushed a Marxist commissar at Qum. I remember the event but not the name of the officer.' John remembered the name very well but was damned if he would reveal it. 'If you do not believe me, check it out for yourselves. The officer wrote a book about that ambush and the events leading up to it. He clearly described the whole affair.'

'Do you have this book?'

Again John found he could not save his own skin at the expense of another man. The book was some two paces behind his chair with many other titles on Arabia.

'No,' he replied, 'but it is easily obtainable through the Family Bookshop in Muscat.'

De Villiers had seen it all before. Faced with imminent death, most people find rational thought elusive, but there are many who remain cool and capable of creating a web of deceit in their bid to stay alive. Knowing that Milling was indisputably the only British officer in the

area and that Salim bin Amr died at the hands of a white Caucasian, de Villiers was unmoved by Milling's evasions. He looked at Meier, who nodded. The film was in the can.

De Villiers took no chances, since Milling was unquestionably fit and powerful. The revolver remained out of sight and out of reach.

'Stay on your knees and go to the shower room.'

Milling hobbled in a kneeling position into the bathroom and was tied face down over the lavatory seat. The barrel of the revolver nudged past his lips and against his teeth. A wad of lavatory paper was then forced into his mouth. Behind him he heard one of the men opening the briefcase and then, a wonderful sound, the loud chime of his doorbell.

Meier and de Villiers acted without hesitation. With the briefcase closed again, they shut Milling into the bathroom and quietly left the bungalow via the kitchen door. After crossing the rear courtyard, they vanished through a gate in the wall and made their way over wasteland to the nearby Seeb road junction where Karim Bux and Davies were waiting.

George Halbert, on receiving no response to the doorbell nor to his repeated shouts, went to the rear of the house and entered through the kitchen door, to find his friend in the bathroom. With a bread knife he quickly cut through the tape.

'What on earth have you been doing?' Halbert was amazed.

'Good question,' John replied. 'Very good question.'

He filled the basin and plunged his face into the cold water. He needed time to think. If he told George, everyone would know in no time, including Bridgie, and that must be avoided at all costs. The doctor had warned them that she must avoid shocks of any sort or she might lose the baby. She must not become distressed and he well knew how she would react to the news of an attempt on his life. He dried his face and changed into jogging gear.

'I suspect those buggers from MAM HQ,' he told Halbert, 'we messed them about a bit at the Blackpool Beach [the nickname for a local beach] party last week and they probably thought it would be clever to tie me to my own loo for a while.'

'I'm surprised you let them.' Halbert sounded unconvinced.

'They must have come in through the kitchen and caught me dozing. There were five of them.'

John made an effort to appear normal to Halbert, chiding him for the state of his girth, but his thoughts kept dwelling on the nightmare

visit by the 'historians'. He tried to telephone Colin Maxwell and Ted Ashley but both men were out. He decided to warn the officer who in reality had killed the *adoo*, as soon as he returned to the UK.

That evening John was especially attentive to Bridgie. They went to a St Patrick's Day hooley at the house of some Irish friends where many rebel songs were sung, and John began to relax. Though nominally a Protestant, he was no political animal, and happily joined in the singing.

Bridgie left for a breath of fresh air. She was of the O'Neill Wallis family and a believer in the usual Celtic superstitions. She stopped short in the hall with a small gasp of horror. A vase of flowers gave colour to an alcove in the side wall. But what a colour, and in an Irish house. They should have known better.

Bridgie clasped her hands about her stomach as a shiver ran down from the nape of her neck. St Patrick's Day, and the flowers were red and white. A sign for sure of an impending death.

16

Mason was not in the best of moods on Friday 18 March. For twelve days the Welshman had lounged about the hotel as though on holiday with all expenses paid. He had chatted up the Gulf Air hostesses who invariably overnighted at the Gulf Hotel, and scored with at least two. Mason, from a sixth-floor window, had photographed him by the poolside, using an Olympus OM-1 with a 300-mm telephoto lens. Since his own bathroom was impossible to black out, he had developed the Tri-X film in the nearest broom cupboard with reasonable results. In every other respect his Omani outing had been a failure, a waste of time, for he had nothing at all to report to Spike.

On the only day the Welshman had ventured beyond the hotel confines, Mason had promptly lost him in the Lawatiyah. He had returned to his room at 6 p.m., by which time Mason, no locksmith, had borrowed the Welshman's key at the time of midday prayer and returned it before the receptionist was back at work. In the one and a half minutes Mason was inside the Welshman's room, he taped one

of his voice-activated transmitters, smaller than a matchbox, to the underside of the bedside table. The nine-volt battery gave twenty-four hours of continuous transmission or three hundred on stand-by. More than enough for Mason since he would have to return to his regiment in Berlin by the following Tuesday at the latest.

Mason's mood was not improved by the fact that Davies netted a third Gulf Air hostess that night and evidence of the Welshman's considerable virility and remarkable imagination were delivered via the earplugs of his receiver unit, on and off through the small hours.

At 7 a.m. both men swore when Davies's phone buzzed. It was a summons to a rendezvous with de Villiers. Mason heard enough to understand that the Welshman was shortly to be collected from the hotel by a third party.

He dressed in his SAF uniform and, carrying his two pre-packed travel bags, made his way to the far end of the car park. Wearing Polaroid sunglasses and his green SAF *shemagh*, he sat back in the Datsun and waited.

Davies emerged at 8 a.m. and walked down the road until out of sight of the hotel. A few minutes later Mason watched as a light-brown Nissan pick-up collected the Welshman. He followed at a discreet distance, thankful that the rutted dirt roads of his day had given way to tarmac, eliminating the dust cloud that acted as a smoke signal to any moving vehicle.

Some miles south of Seeb the Nissan veered west on to the Nizwa road, which it followed as far as the Sumail Bridge. Here the Welshman's driver took a series of side tracks running behind the village of Fanjah and skirting a dense wall of aged date palms.

Mason required all his concentration to shadow the Nissan without being seen. At length, in rocky scrubland, it eased to a halt in a gravel wadi bed between thickets of acacia and thorn. Mason swerved from the track at once and switched off, the Datsun well concealed by low *ghaf*.

The larger of Mason's travel bags served as a knapsack since its handles were designed to fit over the shoulders. There was no waistbelt but his hands were free to carry the .22 Hornet rifle and a lightweight Zeiss monocular. He removed his Polaroid glasses. He had wandered this terrain with his cameras when based at nearby Bidbid and knew the area as well as any local, most of whom seldom ventured beyond the cool and verdant Sumail.

Since there was no habitation nor point of any interest to the likes

of the Welshman in these rocky steppes, Mason assumed that he and his companions were there to meet someone. He saw three men climb out of the Nissan but did not notice Karim Bux squatting in the shade of the acacias, chewing tobacco. Mason wore an ancient pair of Clark's suede desert boots, 'brothel creepers' as they are fondly known, by far the most cool and efficient footwear commercially available for patrol work in sand or on rocky ground. He approached the Nissan soundlessly and found its cab locked. On the front seat, he noticed a battered bolt-action .303 of the type carried by many Omanis both as a symbol of their independence and for rough shooting in the hills.

Mason followed the Welshman's group to a flat plateau where he watched them kneel by a mound of earth similar to a large anthill with its crown excavated into a crater. Other similar spoil-heaps dotted the plateau at intervals and Mason knew them to be the openings of short vertical shafts giving access to a *falaj* or underground water canal.

Mason took a dozen photographs of the Welshman's two accomplices. One wore spectacles and a white, floppy hat; the other was a tall, athletic character who hauled at a rope, lifting a suitcase from the shaft.

The three men returned by their outward route carrying the suitcase and, having passed the rocks where Mason hid, stopped in the shadows of the first camel-thorn bush that they reached.

As they settled down, Mason, crouching below the silhouette of the rock outcrop, circled a hundred and eighty degrees until, approaching their position with the sun behind him, he monkey-crawled in the dirt of the scrub to within twenty paces of the bush.

Camel thorn is sharper and tougher than any rose thorn and Mason could get no closer even when he eased his travel bag along the ground behind him. He unzipped it and removed a pocket-sized bug-gun. He could hear conversation but no words were clearly audible, so he loaded a transmitter dart and cocked the powerful crossbow mechanism. He could see his target at ground level only and he aimed at the roots of a thorn tree close to the floppy hat, which lay in the dirt near its perspiring owner. The dart struck the ground quite close to the hat and, donning the earphones of his receiver, Mason was soon able to tune into the conversation.

The transmitting bug's position was by no means ideal and Mason could distinguish the words of only one man. A German accent, he

guessed, but could not be sure. The meeting lasted some forty-five minutes. Mason learnt little, although a few bits of information were of immediate interest. The speaker was a worker at a police helicopter hangar, his boss was called Chief Superintendent Bailey and he was to fix his machine to crash on the morning flight.

Mason felt elated. He would locate the relevant police chief and warn him of his danger. Meanwhile, if he glued himself to Floppy Hat instead of the Welshman, he might yet identify the leader and the motivation behind their activities.

He kept well behind until he heard the Nissan drive off. Then he broke cover and jogged, as fast as the rifle and travel bag would allow, to the Datsun. Placing the rifle beside him, he leant sideways to throw the travel bag on to the rear seat. This action may well have saved his life, for a bullet shattered the windscreen. Mason reacted with speed. Grabbing travel bag and rifle, he dropped from the passenger door to the ground and slithered into the scrub.

Almost immediately a second bullet smashed into the bodywork of the Datsun. Mason spotted the only possible position of cover from which his car was visible, a jumble of rock no more than a hundred and fifty yards to his front and across the low wadi. The sun favoured neither party but Mason was a marksman and the .22 Hornet was his favourite weapon.

With such a small-calibre bullet he needed a head shot. He took careful aim at the most likely rock. In a few seconds he saw a dark face and white-shirted shoulder appear just left of his aiming point. He realigned in an instant and squeezed the trigger.

The rifle was zeroed for 100 metres, so the 45-grain hollow-point bullet, muzzle velocity 2,400 ft/sec, required two and a half inches' elevation aim-off. There was no further sound. No movement. Mason left his bag in the scrub and loped across the wadi, having reloaded his rifle.

The body was that of an Asian. He must have been in the Nissan with the others. Mason shrugged. He noticed that the bullet had entered an inch or so higher than his aiming point. Intended to hit the thinnest part of the skull, the left eye socket, the bullet had in fact penetrated the eyebrow and the thicker bone and sinus cavity beneath, and gone into the brain.

There was no pulse at the carotid artery under the jaw. A drop of blood had issued from the wound, and a thin trickle from one ear, but there was no exit wound: the bullet, probably fragmented, was

somewhere inside the skull. A quick body search revealed only a Parker pen and a tin of tobacco. Mason had begun to consider whether to dispose of the dead man or to attempt to catch up with the Nissan when that vehicle reappeared at speed around the nearest bend in the wadi.

Uncertain of whether or not the men were armed, Mason took no chances. Wedging the Asian's .303 behind a rock, he struck west and directly away from the negotiable floor of the wadi. He headed, by a circuitous route, for the plateau of the *falaj* mounds, the only solid cover within miles.

No bullets chased him but he did not look back until, reaching the mound with the hidden suitcase, he found a climber's rope affixed to a steel peg and disappearing down the *falaj* shaft. Before lowering himself, he spotted the three men not far behind.

The *falaj* system was developed in Persia in 400 BC and introduced to Oman two thousand years ago. The diggers were known as *muqanat*, 'men of the killers', for many died of rockfalls or escaping gases. They were often young boys, blinded at birth, who developed an uncanny accuracy when digging through solid rock with simple tools so that the narrow channels ran straight and dipped only imperceptibly to maintain gravity. Some *falaj* were up to one hundred and fifty feet deep and fifty miles long, taking water under the hottest of deserts with little loss from evaporation.

Since the last of the Persian invaders were expelled, centuries had passed in which many *falaj*, especially minor offshoots to long abandoned villages, became neglected and partially blocked. Mason had no way of knowing how far he would be able to travel within this *falaj* but he was certainly safer below than above ground in his present circumstances.

He reached the canal floor, or rather a heap of spoil and a goat carcass, some eighteen feet down. The diameter of the shaft had been sufficiently narrow to enable a tall man to chimney his way upwards without help from a rope, and Mason assumed other shafts would be no wider. He headed south in the knowledge that the canal would gradually rise as it led away from the mountains.

There were numerous rockfalls but none entirely blocked the way. Mason was aware that various types of viper and water snake infested the Omani *falaj* system but kept his mind on other things. A loud shout or a rifle shot might trigger a major rockfall.

Perhaps nobody would follow him. Well past the second vertical

shaft he waited and listened, cursing silently when he clearly heard a clatter of rocks down the tunnel behind him. He increased his speed and blundered into a waist-deep pool where the channel floor was faulted. Beyond this and close to the third vertical shaft, Mason's head, bent forward and low, made painful contact with an earthen wall.

Swearing aloud, he rubbed his scalp. At the same time he felt apprehension surge through his stomach, a fairly rare experience since he was blessed with an unusually high threshold of fear. The cause of his dread was the sound of hornets, many hundreds of them, stirring in anger.

Two years earlier, on a patrol in central Oman, Mason had witnessed the agonizing death of two young Omani girls attacked by *jebel* hornets in a deserted hovel. The nest had hung from the ceiling like some giant inverted cone of mud. Now the memory made him fall to the tunnel floor and scrabble forward. To his relief the way was clear, with sufficient space beneath the nest to make his way forward. Knowing the smell of his fear would leave a scented trail, he forced himself to lie calm and still along the damp surface of the channel. He was not stung and the nest quietened down. Gingerly he continued, and minutes later heard the terrified screams of his pursuers roaring down the echo chamber of the tunnel. The sound of splashing water followed, and then silence but for an occasional low moan.

Two shafts to the south Mason came to a pile of spoil that helped him gain a chimneying position at the base of the man-made tube. He waited patiently for two hours, then, with his back and his arms inching up one side, his braced feet up the other and his rifle hanging below him from its strap, he reached the surface panting and filthy.

The plateau was lifeless in all directions, a midday heat shimmer raising inverted mirages to the south. He returned cautiously to the Datsun, collected his bag from the bushes, knocked away the remnants of the windscreen and drove back to the main road. There was no sign of the Nissan. Mason took his second travel bag down to the wadi a mile upstream of Fanjah and, washing with care, changed into the standard expatriate uniform of cotton slacks and shirtsleeves.

From the pocket of his dirty army trousers he took the empty case of the only bullet he had fired and buried it in the wadi bed. Lighting a Montecristo cigar, he cleaned the Rigby thoroughly and sat back

to enjoy life in general and especially the magnificent view of the great mountains to the north.

At 3 p.m., back in his hotel room, Mason telephoned Enquiries. There were two numbers for Chief Superintendent Bailey of the Royal Oman Police Air Wing. He took both and tried the home number first.

The Baileys' Kashmiri houseboy, Said, who spoke good English, answered and apologized that the Sah'b was out and would be quite unobtainable for the rest of the day.

'But this is *very* urgent.'

'Sorry, sir.'

'Could you give him a message?'

'Very happy, sir. Yes, a message.'

'Please tell him he must on no account go flying tomorrow morning. In fact no flying at all until he has spoken to me on this number.'

He gave the Kashmiri the hotel number and his room extension, but not his name.

Mason had been pre-booked into the Gulf Hotel as 'MOD VIP ex-Kendall' and, on arrival, had told the receptionist his passport was at the British Embassy for renewal. Three subsequent and generous tips to receptionists for minor services had helped avoid any reminders about the passport. He had called himself Mr D. Messon and given the management to understand he would be staying for a further three weeks.

The Kashmiri repeated Mason's message back to him and then added, 'Chief Superintendent Bailey will not be flying tomorrow, sir. You must not worry about that. He is not to fly for at least two more days.'

'Are you certain of that?' Mason was bewildered.

'Certain sure, sir. Oh yes indeed, he will not fly. I know his programme. I look after him.'

Mason thanked the Kashmiri. The man sounded honest and reliable. There was nothing more he could do to warn Bailey until the next day. At no stage in the Sumail had his face been visible to the Welshman or his cronies. Of that he was certain. Nothing would connect him with the dead Asian and he felt fairly sure that the opposition would dispose of the body themselves. That evening, when traffic in and out of Northern Headquarters was at its busiest, he returned the Datsun to the Motor Transport Section and borrowed

a Land Rover in its place. If anyone noticed the soiled state of his uniform they might feel disdain but not suspicion.

After an excellent dinner, Mason settled back in his room to an evening of Tolkien and listening out for the return of the Welshman.

Bridgie wore a cleverly cut white dress that accentuated her narrow shoulders and superlative cleavage while playing down the current size of her midriff. She was a touch troubled by John's mood. He was as gentle and attentive as ever where she was concerned, but definitely out of sorts for some reason. He had been a touch upset by his recent Jebel Akhdar mission but this was altogether different. If she did not know him better she might have thought him nervous. This and the memory of the St Patrick's Day omen made her especially anxious when John failed to turn up at the embassy dinner. The Ambassador, Sir Peter Treadwell, was leaving and his wife had laid on a splendid affair, a distant echo of the Raj.

John had flown down to Salalah that morning with Geoff Leggatt to inspect a sailing boat and to bid farewell to RAF friends. After forty-nine years, RAF Salalah, one of Britain's remoter outposts, was packing up and hauling down the flag. Its very existence had saved the sultanate from a Marxist takeover in the late sixties.

The guests took their seats and Bridgie was beside herself with worry. She had every confidence in John's flying abilities but she could not shake off the sense of foreboding that increasingly weighed on her mind.

The third course had been served when the animated hubbub puttered to near silence. Every woman in the room found her eyes following the splendid figure of John Milling in his white tuxedo as he strode to the ambassador to apologize for his unavoidably late arrival. He laid his hands affectionately on Bridgie's bare shoulders then sat down between two ladies, both of whom addressed him at once. Many members of the Muscat expatriate community were secretly jealous of one or other of the Millings while finding both the best of fun.

The post-dinner cigars and superlative port from the embassy cellar soon gave way to boisterous games, and a number of guests, including John, ended up fully dressed in the pool.

Back at home John and Bridgie were asleep by midnight. Their worries put aside, they were both looking forward to spending a free Sunday with young Oliver on their secret beach. Twenty minutes

by helicopter to the south-east of Muscat, John had discovered a deserted cove of white sand and surf. There they had spent many a perfect day wandering naked along the limitless shore, collecting seashells and lazing with a picnic in the dunes.

17

Mason awoke early on the Saturday and telephoned the Bailey house at 7 a.m. This time the Kashmiri houseboy fetched the Chief Superintendent from his breakfast.

Mason went straight to the point.

'I am very glad to make contact. I need to speak to you at once, for I have good reason to believe your life is in danger.'

'I must thank you for your concern,' Bailey's voice sounded cool, 'but, forgive me for asking, who are you?'

David was keen to avoid knowledge of his presence in Muscat leaking out. There were still a few British, mostly ex-army officers on contract, who would remember him, and people talk. It would not be long before someone in the Welsh Guards heard the gossip.

'Please understand that it is difficult to talk on the telephone. I can come to see you immediately anywhere that suits you.'

Bailey began to sound standoffish.

'You told my houseboy I was not to go flying.'

'Correct.' Mason was emphatic. 'Your machine has been damaged, sabotaged by one of your own workers. I can show you a photograph of the man.'

'Have you told the police?'

Mason hesitated, 'I have no proof ... but I know you are in danger. We must meet so I can explain the situation.'

Bailey was impatient now. 'Look, I have a very busy day today and it does not include any flying. Quite honestly, I think this is a police matter and you should contact them at once. The earliest I can see you is tomorrow morning and then I'm afraid it must be brief. This is a very busy time of the year for us.'

Mason agreed to meet the police chief at 8.30 a.m. on the Sunday. He spent Saturday morning developing the film shot in the Sumail.

Davies was back and using room service for all his meals. Mason was forced to curb his curiosity as to whether the hornets had altered the man's appearance.

Davies had in fact been lucky: saved only by plunging into a subterranean pool and staying there until the hornets had gone. The Clinic members had split up as soon as Mason went underground. Davies had followed him down the *falaj* but the others had remained above in case their quarry re-emerged. Davies had eventually crawled from the pool, but could not see through his swollen eyelids. Hearing his cries, the others had descended and hauled him up on the rope.

They had left Karim Bux's body in the gravel wastes of the Wadi Umayri, off the Fahud road, for the wolves and vultures. Then they had driven to the Gulf Hotel and helped Davies to his room where the in-house medic had removed two dozen hornet stings from his face and hands. He would be of no further use to the operation.

Meier had passed a good deal of time in idle conversation with the European ROP aircraft engineers. Milling, he learnt, was highly regarded and nearly always nominated as pilot-instructor to the police cadets on their first helicopter flights. Meier had decided therefore to go ahead with the operation that night since three cadet flights were planned for the following morning.

Meier and two Joannou and Pariskavides contract workers spent the morning installing ducting for a new intercom system within the ROP hangar. All normal duty personnel left by 1.30 p.m. Only three people would remain, the Operations Officer who left at 6 p.m., and two engineers, one fixed-wing and the other a helicopter specialist, who covered the afternoon shift. They would spend their time continuing tasks left over from the morning shift and preparing the aircraft for the following day's flying programme including, that day, twenty minutes checking the Bell to be flown by Milling. Just a standard inspection of oil levels and control integrity.

Meier and his two J & P colleagues worked on during the afternoon, concentrating on the intercom installation and leaving the two engineers to do their work. There was no flying that afternoon, and by 4 p.m. the engineers had completed the daily inspections and reroling of the aircraft for the next day's programme and left. Meier was relieved to see them go. He had delegated the relatively simple task of fixing the ducting to his two Indian co-workers while he worked separately, sorting out some wiring in another room. Soon after the

Airwing engineers had left he suggested to the two J & P workers that they might wrap it up, but he would stay on for another half-hour or so to finish what he was doing. Meier told them to take the J & P pickup and said that he would get a lift with the Ops Officer to the airport roundabout and hitch from there.

By 4.30 p.m. he had let the Operations Officer know that the J & P workers were leaving. After making sure that they were off the premises, he went down to the general workshop underneath the Operations Room, laid a mat on the floor, closed the door and fell asleep. His wristwatch alarm was set for 7 p.m.

At 5.30 p.m. Meier was woken by a metallic clanking. At the far side of the well-lit workshop a tall man was checking through an engineer's tool-box. Meier recognized Brendan O'Brien, one of the aerobatic aces of the Rothmans flying team, on a visit from England. Their four Pitt Special bi-planes were parked inside the hangar and O'Brien was probably carrying out some repair to his machine.

Meier remained motionless, uncertain of whether or not he had been seen. He was worried on two counts. Chief Superintendent Bailey was holding a buffet supper party that evening, to which the Rothmans people had been invited. If O'Brien had seen him, he might well mention the fact to Chief Bailey. If, on the other hand, O'Brien intended to work overnight on his bi-plane, Meier's own plans would be scuppered.

After an hour or so Meier heard O'Brien laughing with the Duty Operations Officer and then the sounds of their leaving the hangar. He double checked that he was alone in the building, then climbed the stairs to the executive corridor and the operations room, where he checked the daily roster board. For the following day, 20 March, the main duty was marked up as 'Police Cadet Helicopter Familiarization Flights', with Milling's name entered as pilot-instructor. The first take-off of three separate flights by that machine was scheduled for 8.00 a.m., but he knew the flight engineers would arrive at least an hour earlier to check and prepare the machine. Meier had twelve hours to himself. A single armed guard patrolled the compound by night but he would only enter the hangar if given reason for suspicion.

Meier stripped off his clothes and donned an ROP set of engineer's blue overalls with tactile gloves and flip-flops. He then placed his tools and instruments on a trolley and wheeled it to the machine with the correct tail number. His plan was simple enough. He would

create a mechanical defect, and Milling would crash, but the event would be blamed on pilot error, not sabotage.

Meier eased himself upwards from the hangar floor and into the innards of the machine by way of the heavy rubberized ring that protects the helicopter from the pendulum motions of the swinging cargo hook. The hook itself was not fitted. If it had been, Meier would have had to work on top of the helicopter's roof by removing the gearbox cowling in full view of any surprise visitor to the hangar.

Once inside the area known to most helicopter aficionados as the 'hell-hole', Meier used the rubberized bumper as a conveniently placed seat. He carefully positioned himself in the rear left-hand side of the hell-hole with his back against the apex of that corner. Reaching upwards, he hooked a fluorescent inspection lamp over a hydraulic ingress pipe and strapped his ready tool-bag around his waist.

Oman is relatively cool in mid March, and the hangar, despite the lack of air-conditioning, would remain around sixty-four degrees Fahrenheit most of the night. Inside the hell-hole Meier worked in a cramped position and was soon smeared with grease impregnated with grit and dirt.

The hydraulic system of the Augusta Bell 205 A-1, a civilian version of the Vietnam-famed Huey, has two oil reservoirs feeding three hydraulic actuators or 'jacks'. Each of these cylinders is attached to the gearbox and to the non-rotating star that is situated on the mast and beneath the rotor head.

The jack that Meier intended to doctor was the one that assisted the pilot's collective control level, the function of which was to lift the aircraft in its vertical plane.

The Bell maintenance manual made it clear that the relevant cylinder was situated to the rear and left-hand side of the static gearbox body. Meier located the hydraulic input pipe where it entered the collective jack and, using two open-jaw 5/8 AF spanners, disconnected the mating union and blocked off both pipe ends with blanking caps. There was a slight seepage of MIL-H-5606 hydraulic fluid from the jack, which Meier mopped up with a rag.

After resting his arms for a while and adjusting his spectacles Meier began the search for a lee-plug. In the casing of each cylinder there were four or five steel bungs, or lee-plugs, originally drilled so that the manufacturers could carry out interior fitments. Each hole was only 3 mm in diameter and since the head of each bolt had been chamfered flush with the cylinder wall and then sprayed with a light-

green paint, Meier realized that he might not find a lee-plug by touch alone. If unsuccessful he would sound-tap but that was a time-consuming process.

After a number of false alarms he struck lucky, locating a bung almost opposite his position and fairly low down the face of the cylinder. Between the lee-plug and the inner side of the hell-hole's bulkhead there was a gap of some nine inches in which Meier had to work; a challenge of the sort he loved best. Manipulating a right-angled drill head with a 3-mm-diameter tungsten-steel bit, he removed the plug with total precision. This task alone took him two hours, for he had to ensure no metal detritus entered the jack.

With painstaking care he tapped a thread into the wall of the hole he had exposed, greased it and screwed in his own home-made lee-plug. This steel bolt was a mere quarter millimetre longer than a standard 4-mm-long lee-plug and, to the eye, no different in size or shape.

Meier's substitute lee-plug had at this stage two important ancillary features: an alloy male thread welded around its entire length, like a coil around a magnetic bar, and a 2-mm-square steel nut with a hole drilled through its centre. The threaded lee-plug screwed into the hole in the nut for a distance of 0.25 mm, the limit of the nut's female threading. The nut was 1.5 mm in depth and two small holes had been drilled into two of its opposing outer sides.

The skin of the hydraulic cylinder was itself 4 mm thick. Meier tightened his two-part lee-plug into place using a torque spanner to avoid wrenching the alloy thread loose from its steel core. Then, producing his second home-made device he placed it over the square nut so that male plungers in its base slotted home into the small holes drilled in the nut's outer sides. The end of an open steel tube protruding from the base of the device entered the hole in the top of the nut with precision.

The apparatus was a miniature explosive hammer with just enough power to focus a 3,000 psi blow directly on to the cuckoo lee-plug, sheering its alloy thread and forcing it down into the oil-filled cylinder. The device measured 4 inches square and 3 inches deep. Its explosive unit contained a hollow ring primed with a fraction of an ounce of treated PE4 and a Kaynor .008 detonator no bigger than a grease-nipple. Slightly proud of the unit's upper surface was a Seiko micro timer-switch. Meier had pre-set its twenty-four-hour alarm trigger, using the end of his ballpoint pen, for 10.05 hours, at which

119

time the helicopter was scheduled to be in flight with its load of police cadets.

With the device locked on to the bolt-head, Meier positioned his third and last contrivance, a 6-inch square, 2-inch deep, pad of bullet-proof Kevlar that clipped over the rest of his appliance. This would minimize damage to the inner wall of the bulkhead and help ensure that, once blown, all traces of the apparatus and the steel nut would fall down the hell-hole and hit the ground well away from the subsequent crash site. The only item left behind by Meier would be the lee-plug, and that would be *inside* the punctured cylinder.

Meier knew by listening to the ROP engineers that Milling was a well-respected pilot and one who believed student-training flights should be realistic, low-flying 'events to remember'. He estimated that, some four or five seconds after the induced hydraulic leak, the helicopter would become accident-prone. The very next time the pilot attempted to pull out of a hedgehopping routine he would find the collective control no longer gave the required instant response to gentle pressure. Suddenly there would be severe handling problems, not insuperable under normal high-flying conditions, but lethal in the wrong circumstances.

Meier spent another two hours recoupling the input pipe and cleaning up every sign of his presence. Very little hydraulic fluid had been lost, perhaps a quarter of a pint, and this would not be noticed. No topping up would be required. There would, Meier knew, be air in the pipelines but the system would self-bleed as soon as the steering column was moved during pre-flight checks.

There was no shortage of rags and kerosene in the workshop and, by 4 a.m., Meier was scrubbed clean and dozing in the lavatory with a dozen greasy copies of *Flight International* magazine for company.

18

Cha Cha brought tea and gently woke John Milling.

'Six o'clock, sah'b.'

'Thank you, Cha Cha.' John smiled at the thought of the day ahead. 'We go to beach today. OK? You make us picnic. We take Oliver. You have free afternoon. OK?'

The Kashmiri spoke little Arabic and even less English. 'OK, fine, sah'b. Excellent picnic but not today.'

'Not today?' John's eyebrows rose.

'Not today,' the albino's thin eyebrows mimicked John's. 'Today you fly helicopter. Telephone call from headquarters ... so I bring you early cha.'

Milling's heart sank. The bloody office had changed the duty roster again.

In deference to the Kashmiri he flung his *wizaar* about his middle and stomped to the telephone. A few angry words with the Duty Operations Officer confirmed his worst fears. Richard Shuttleworth or one of the others had been taken off cadet training and now his Sunday was ruined. Bridgie was surprisingly mild in her reaction. After they were all dressed and breakfasted he drove her and Oliver the short distance to the Royal Flight swimming pool and told her he hoped to be back for lunch. They were both disappointed by the dashing of their plans. John suspected a last-minute request by the Cadet Training Major that Milling, and only Milling, be in charge of the familiarization flights purely because he spoke fluent Arabic, whereas his brother pilots spoke little or none.

He drove to Air Wing HQ deep in thought. While still adamant that no word should reach Bridgie of the attempt on his life, if that is what it was, he was distinctly worried lest the two nutters show up again when she and Oliver were at home during the four or five days that remained before their leave in Europe. He made up his mind to see a discreet friend of his, a major in the local Criminal Investigation Department. Maybe some unobtrusive surveillance of

his house could be arranged just for these four days. Yes, he would fix it first thing tomorrow.

At 7.20 a.m. Meier called Davies. Local-anaesthetic cream had eased his discomfort but he was relieved to hear de Villiers's instructions, since he was bored stiff with the confines of the Gulf Hotel. He was to arrange three separate bookings for the earliest available flights. De Villiers to Amsterdam and the two of them to Paris.

'And the action?' Davies asked.

'This morning,' Meier replied and rang off.

Mason, who was in the act of ordering a taxi for later that morning, just missed the short conversation.

At 7.30 John Milling poked his head round the door of Chief Superintendent Bailey's office. 'Morning, boss,' he said with a meaningful grin.

'Sorry about the flight change, John,' Bailey said, 'but that's the way it is. All well with Bridgie and Oliver?'

'Yes, fine, but I can't say we're not looking forward to our leave.'

John changed into flight gear and met up with his crewman Ali. Together they went to the Ops Room to complete pre-flight preparations, then out to the flight lines where their Augusta Bell 205 A-1 had been thoroughly checked by the engineers.

Two minutes' pre-start checks.
Two minutes' wind-up.
Wave away the external start-up facility.
Open throttle to Flight Idle.
Call Air Traffic for take-off to depart east to Qurum.
Immediate clearance received.
Lift-off from dispersal and down taxiway, climbing to 500 feet.
Over Qurum Police Training School in seven minutes.
Land on H circle on parade ground and shut down engine.

John would relay the above sequence of instructions in Arabic, without notes, to an assembly of police cadets, men who had progressed through the ranks and been selected for commissions. Air familiarization was one of the more exciting sections of their training. John would be able to take only thirteen cadets at a time so three flights were scheduled in tight succession.

This was to be an introduction to helicopter usage. Safety rules.

Magazines off and weapons cleared before mounting. Only approach from where the pilot can see you. Never approach from the rear, not even the baggage bay, without the crewman in attendance. Watch out for uneven ground where clearance is minimal and decapitation occurs in an instant.

John's manner was easy, confident and humorous. The cadets soon warmed to the subject and the more apprehensive among them began to relax.

Mason arrived at the Air Wing thirty minutes early but the police chief was occupied until 8.30 a.m. They shook hands and Bill Bailey did not press Mason for his identity. He could sense at once that this was no impostor and decided he was probably a spook from either Whitehall or ORD (Oman Research Department), the local equivalent of the UK's Special Branch.

Mason kept it simple and unambiguous. A group of dubious characters were under surveillance. Two days previously one had been heard to say he had fixed the machine of Chief Superintendent Bailey. Not in so many words but that is how it had clearly come across. The man was employed by J & P and working in this very building. Why Bailey should have been chosen as a target was not known. Mason handed Bailey a sheaf of photographs, saying, 'I am afraid your worker is the man wearing the hat. His features are partially shaded in all the shots but hopefully you might click as to his identity.'

'We have a number of transient workers here but none who would be able to sabotage one of my helicopters. The machines are always checked thoroughly by my engineers before each flight.' Bailey was pensive for a minute. 'On the other hand the hangar workshop is being altered at present and the J & P people have a pretty free hand ... Come down to the hangar with me. You never know, you may recognize the man right away.'

There were two J & P electricians at work but neither had been to the hangar before and they could not identify Meier from the photographs. Bailey took Mason around the hangar. A number of pilots, engineers and staff were about but no one familiar to Mason. Back in Bailey's office Mason thanked him for his time and agreed there must have been some mistake. Nevertheless Bailey said he would hold on to the photographs for a while and watch out for any man fitting the description of Floppy Hat. He would also have his flight engineers keep an especially keen eye open for any irregularities.

'How do I contact you if this man should turn up?' Bailey asked.

'Call this number in the UK, leave a message and we will call you back.' Mason gave the police chief Patrick Tanner's home number. If any of Mason's stray pigeons ever did come home to roost, Patrick was a past master at denial. Mason needed to know if Floppy Hat should reappear after he was himself back in Berlin.

The two men shook hands and Mason returned to his hotel. He was booked on the next flight back to Europe. He could do no more. He would risk a great deal for Spike and all that he stood for, but not to the extent of a court martial for absence without leave. Once back in Europe he would write out a full and meticulously detailed report to give, with all the photographs, to Spike.

The cadets were excited. John had explained how low they would be flying. The first thirteen moved out to the parade ground in their smart khaki uniforms and blue berets. They practised embarking in the correct fashion and Ali strapped them to their seats. Nine faced each other in the forward hull section and four faced outwards in the compartment either side of the hell-hole.

The helicopter left the ROP Training Centre at Qurum, heading north for the nearest point of the coastline. It was on schedule: 10.00 hours by John's battered Rolex. At Ra's al Hamra, Cape Donkey, he banked sharply east and the real flying began, as reflected in the faces of the wide-eyed cadets in the main cabin. John Milling was at his happiest, his most confident, when flying low and fast with total concentration. The helicopter hugged the beach, skirted cliff-faces, and skimmed the glassy sea with as much precision as a sports car on the contorted course of Germany's Nurburgring. The rotors often scythed within yards of rock walls and the students thrilled to their pilot's expertise.

Mina al Fahal Bay flashed by, where the dark outlines of the stingrays and sharks were briefly visible. John scanned the instruments. All felt and looked well. They continued at one hundred knots, fifteen feet above the white sands. Darsait Headland loomed ahead. For mid March the temperature, eighty-five degrees Fahrenheit, was well above average and, in such high-density altitude conditions, the Bell was close to its maximum 'all-up' weight. The rocky bluff of Darsait now filled the entire width of the forward windscreen. Immediately south of the helicopter and on the rim of Fahal Beach, secretaries and executives glanced out from the windows of the Shell

Market offices. At the last minute John raised the Bell's nose by pulling back on the cyclic control and sacrificing air speed to gain height. At this point his intention was probably a sharp torque turn to seaward. But one hundred knots at the bottom of the climb reduced to a mere forty knots at the cliff top, so he immediately reduced the collective lever, allowing the torque reaction to turn the helicopter's nose left and seaward while he pushed the cyclic control forward to regain his speed by a shallow, thirty-degree dive. Having gained one hundred knots of air speed, he would pull out just above sea level.

Things did not go as planned. At the back of his mind John registered an abnormal sound. Not alarming, but not standard either. A muffled and unattributable thud. He turned briefly to check if a cadet had done something silly but all seemed in control.

The pressure that is normally trapped within the actuator to resist the feedback loads from the rotor is between 500 and 700 psi. With the lee-plug blown, hydraulic fluid was excreted in a thin, solid jet. Within seconds all hydraulic assistance to the collective control ceased to exist.

Some thirty feet above the surface of the sea John began to raise the Bell's nose and to pull in the collective pitch with his left hand. To his surprise the collective felt extremely stiff. He knew the still air and heavy load were rendering the control responses a touch sluggish, but this was something else altogether. Frowning, he glanced at the air-speed indicator. The needle registered ninety knots. With a mere fifty feet to go, ample leeway had the lift response been normal, he hauled with all his considerable strength to exert the necessary pull on the collective, in excess of thirty-five pounds, despite the constraints of his seated position.

Aware of sounds of uneasiness in the main cabin, John found time to shout over his shoulder, 'Maa shekhof. Maa shekhof. Kull shay ba stawi zehn, insh'Allah' ('Don't worry. All will be well, God willing).

But all was far from well for, at this critical moment, a combination of unrelated factors came together: John's relative inexperience of high gross weights at higher than normal density altitudes combined with the sudden hydraulic failure.

John fought hard and nearly won the aerodynamic battle. He turned the dive into a bouncing blow with skids and belly. His mind raced to stay ahead of the developing emergency. He would not accept that the situation was irretrievable. His greatest fear was that the helicopter's nose would contact the water and, to avoid this, he

needed a delicate response from his controls; this he did not have.

John's concentration centred on the stubborn collective lever and this had the subsidiary effect of coarsening his handling of the cyclic lever. He pulled the Bell's nose up a little too far and became immediately concerned lest the tail rotor strike the water.

To level out he pushed the cyclic forward. Once again his touch was a little too heavy. At two or three feet above the water, a little too far was *too* far and the nose touched the sea.

John's veins stood out on his forehead as he wrenched up on the stubborn collective with his left hand while simultaneously attempting a delicate correction to the nose with his right.

A lesser pilot would have lost control at that point. John kept his head to the last. Somehow he managed to claw the Bell out of the water but was still caught in a lethal dilemma. Above all he needed delicate controls to lift the nose without ditching the tail. Once again a minute and unavoidable over-correction made the nose touch the leaden surface of the sea.

Although the Bell's hull had levelled out at the moment of impact, the deceleration effect of the initial immersion was catastrophic. The gearbox was torn from its mountings and smashed its way forward to sheer through the roof of both cabin and cockpit. The massive control feedback caused a momentary surge of pressure to some 5,000 psi and dislodged a number of lee-plugs within the other two undoctored cylinders.

John and Ali, haltered by lap but not shoulder straps, catapulted forward and were knocked senseless by the instrument panel.

The stricken Bell floated for some seconds. Then, in less than a minute, she sank to the seabed some forty feet below. The cockpit filled with water. John and Ali drowned without regaining consciousness.

A rescue operation was swiftly mounted. Within minutes men with scuba gear, including George Halbert, were inside the hull, hoping for survivors trapped in an air bubble. Five cadets failed to escape; the rest surfaced and were quickly rescued. Had the machine nosedived on the first impact, all on board would certainly have died.

The meticulous investigation and the resulting accident report concluded that the crash was caused by many factors. The blown lee-plugs were noted but no suspicion was aroused.

Three days later in Berlin, after reading of the accident in *The*

Times obituary column, Mason phoned the Air Wing in Seeb. Bill Bailey was away but another officer told him, 'There is no question of sabotage. It was either pilot error or some mechanical defect.'

Bill Bailey was sure that the accident could not have been connected with sabotage. He was uncertain of Mason's identity or whereabouts since there was no response from his answering machine and Mason himself never reappeared. He realized that there could be no connection between Mason's visit and the unfortunate accident but even so he passed the photograph of Meier to one of the Omani police officers peripherally involved in the accident investigation. No follow-up action was possible, for there was no starting point nor indeed any reason for any enquiries.

The Times obituary on 22 March 1977 for John Milling was straightforward: 'On 20th March, as a result of an air accident in Oman, John, late of the Royal Marines serving with the Royal Oman Police Air Wing, beloved husband of Bridget (née Wallis) and dear father of Oliver, much beloved son of Desmond and Diana, Co. Antrim.'

An article in the *Globe and Laurel*, the Royal Marines' magazine, stated, 'It is a fitting tribute to John and a measure of the respect and fondness in which he was held that the news of his death brought messages of sympathy from His Majesty Sultan Qaboos and Omanis and Britons throughout both countries.'

John was buried in the Christian burial ground that overlooks Mina al Fahal and the Gulf of Oman. A great many friends, Christian and Muslim, were present. Eminent Omanis and simple soldiers were saddened by the loss of a true friend of their country.

Part 3

19

... In the Second World War diamonds were needed for tools in new armaments factories, so the value of suitable stones shot up. Then, during the Korean War, people throughout the West bought diamonds, often mortgaging their homes in order to do so, for they thought the Third World War was about to start. When there was no war the price of diamonds slumped, and many suicides followed. Until 1979 there was no further spectacular rise in the diamond price but then the world situation caused the great 1980 boom. The price for a one-carat 'D' flawless diamond rose as high as sixty-five thousand dollars. Only a year later the value of such a stone had fallen as low as seven thousand dollars.

Because diamonds, like drugs, are so much easier to conceal and transport than gold, they are the root of much crime.

In April 1976 a successful Rhodesian restaurateur, Derryck Quinn, joined the rising number of whites wanting to get themselves, their wealth and their families — often in that order — to a safer country. At the time South Africa appeared to be a safe haven compared with Rhodesia, but June of that year saw the first great Soweto riots and then there was little to choose between the two countries. Both offered decidedly insecure futures for whites.

The international embargo against Ian Smith's UDI (Unilateral Declaration of Independence) was officially supported by South Africa but a sufficiency of critical materials, including oil, continued to reach Rhodesia by truck and train over the Limpopo river.

Quinn had for years benefited from being in a cash business. He stashed his money on his estate in the Bulawayo suburbs, a practice totally alien to the inflation-wary people of most Western countries but a common enough safety device of many a Rhodesian and South African ever since the mid fifties. Their greatest fear, undermining any ability to live an unworried and secure existence, was a black take-over, possibly with time to escape but more likely sudden and

bloody, with wives and daughters raped against a backdrop of villa and possessions in flames.

An old school-friend from South Africa, a hotelier with resorts in Mauritius and Namibia, gave Quinn an address that galvanized years of vague intention into excited action.

Quinn was without children but proud of his pretty Eurasian wife, Davisee. He took her into his confidence at once, and made her an integral part of his plan.

Twice over a period of four months he flew to Johannesburg, each time to the plush offices of diamond dealer Krannie MacEllen. These were situated within the Diamond Exchange Building at the corner of Quartz and de Villiers Street on the northern edge of the city. Mentioning the name of his hotelier friend, Quinn discovered, made him checkable and therefore more acceptable to MacEllen, a naturally suspicious person.

Had Quinn wished to settle in South Africa, he could have done so without too much trouble but he believed in the domino theory. Once Rhodesia fell, South Africa and Namibia would not be long in following suit. He wanted his money in the safest of places, and this he believed was Geneva. Davisee, who would be classified as Coloured in South Africa, persuaded Quinn that they should settle in London.

On his third visit to Johannesburg Quinn handed MacEllen a suitcase containing two million US dollars' worth of Rhodesian dollars. MacEllen, an optimist who rated Ian Smith's chances of winning through as high, had agreed to exchange Quinn's Rhodesian money, then at an all-time low, directly for diamonds. Because Quinn was buying with cash he avoided the standard government duty of twenty-five percent and so had good reason to keep clear of Internal Affairs and their Customs agents.

The meeting was held in MacEllen's office. The room was electronically monitored. Even if Quinn had been a police plant, any recording device, whether a passive recorder or an active bug, would have been identified, warning MacEllen to conduct no unofficial business. Equally, if Quinn were to have announced that he was a Customs agent only at the very moment MacEllen handed him diamonds in exchange for his money, then MacEllen could easily maintain that the relevant stones *were* officially registered. After all, a quantity of stones of all varieties passed legitimately through his hands most weeks of the year.

Like many diamond dealers the world over, MacEllen's business

was mainly official, his polishing work above board and his stock of unofficial stones, well hidden by supporting documents, were stored alongside his official supply. Because he held a government warehouse, or VSJ, number he could buy and sell without tax payments but only in business with other VSJ number holders. As he also held a standard rough-diamond dealer's licence he could always state, should the Quinn deal fall foul of the law, that he was *intending* to 'prepare a full and legal invoice shortly'. He was as knowledgeable as any IDB (Illegal Diamond Buying) policeman from John Vorster Square as to the exact statutory powers that he possessed.

MacEllen counted out Quinn's money and handed him a parcel containing almost a thousand carats of polished diamonds, all large, brilliant, flawless stones with the highest-grade colours and quality. He then gave Quinn the address of an elderly Jewish jeweller in downtown Kerk Street. The Quinns went there at once by taxi and received the jeweller's receipt for the diamonds. He sketched them various designs for possible settings and Davisee selected her favourite. The jeweller promised to have everything ready in five to six weeks, exactly as specified by the Quinns.

Two months later they flew to London, the most popular destination for South African émigrés since, despite the generally foul weather, it has always remained a daily destination for South African Airways and has a population generally sympathetic to the lot of white South Africans. On top of which few South Africans ever learn to speak anything but Afrikaans or English, so that their choice of a new country is limited. By the end of 1976 London was the third biggest 'South African' city after Johannesburg and Soweto.

The Quinns stayed at the Savoy Hotel within easy walking distance of the Hatton Garden diamond market. They experienced no trouble at all with Customs at Heathrow, simply wheeling their trolleys through the Green section. Over half their diamonds adorned the curvaceous body of Davisee, fashioned by the Johannesburg jeweller into a body set. She felt wonderful, like a film star, but she had fasted throughout the thirteen-hour flight, including the Nairobi stopover. Despite this precaution the act of walking was decidedly awkward due to the presence of a condom containing cotton wool wrapped around the three best stones. These had been kept back from the jeweller at a last-minute whim of Davisee.

In the backroom of a Hatton Garden diamond dealer recommended by his Mauritius hotelier friend, Quinn deposited the jewellery and

the three unset stones. He watched as the in-house setter deftly extracted the stones from the low-carat gold clasps and setting, turning the jewellery back into a mere scattering of polished diamonds.

The dealer then spent half an hour checking every stone, his face registering neither pleasure nor disappointment. The Quinns were on hot coals but refrained from showing their impatience.

At last the dealer gave a peremptory sigh. 'The three stones that you kept separate are fine and I am prepared to give you two hundred thousand dollars.' He looked up at Mr Quinn.

There was a pregnant silence, broken at length by an exasperated Quinn. 'And the rest? What will you give me for the rest?'

The Jew's heavily jowled face was expressionless, his grape-black eyes marbled by thick lenses.

'Nothing, Mr Quinn. I can give you not a cent for the rest of these items. You will not find a dealer anywhere in Europe who will buy these from you. They are all fakes. The chemical name is cubic zirconium. Since you are obviously no fraud yourself, I assume you have been duped by the person who sold you these stones.'

The Quinns were devastated. Their world had collapsed and their dreams of a happy, secure future built on a lifetime of hard work turned quickly to bitter resentment, to blind hatred and finally to an all-consuming desire for revenge.

Quinn obtained an introduction to the London criminal fraternity through a lawyer friend of the dealer and, after parting with five hundred pounds in cash to a middle man, received a visit from a representative of Tadnams Light Removals.

A lack of current employment and an ever-gnawing curiosity about Anne Fontaine attracted de Villiers when his agent mentioned a South African job. He met up with the unfortunate Mr Quinn and, having been briefed as quickly as possible, took a British Airways flight to Johannesburg.

Within a fortnight de Villiers had homed in on the fairly common malpractices that had so impoverished his new client. He anticipated an easy job with no need to summon Meier or Davies.

Krannie MacEllen, he discovered, had given Quinn real diamonds, but at a heavily overpriced value. He had to all intents and purposes *stolen* several hundred thousand dollars of Quinn's money.

The Johannesburg jeweller, a crafty craftsman, had substituted CZ (cubic zirconium) for the real diamonds, knowing that, once they

were set, the fakes would be very difficult to detect, even by an expert, until removed from their settings. The refractive index of CZ, and therefore its fire and brilliance, matches that of real diamonds.

De Villiers telephoned Quinn with his findings. Did he wish both men terminated? Quinn burst out that he wanted his diamonds or his money back. If that was not possible, then he wanted revenge. De Villiers pointed out that he dealt in removals, not retrieval work, but that, for twice the initially agreed sum of $100,000 plus expenses, he would do his best. Either Quinn's goods would be recovered or the guilty parties targeted.

The fraudulent jeweller, being of a nervous disposition, gave de Villiers all of Quinn's original stones that he still possessed and a cash payment in place of those he had sold. His personal policy was to yield and live to thrive another day.

Krannie MacEllen appeared to be timidity personified on de Villiers's first visit, promising he would collect a suitable amount of cash by the following day. De Villiers sensed trouble. Five hours before the agreed time for the cash hand-over, he arrived in a hired car and parked outside the Cinerama building, directly opposite the Star Cinema Complex and the Diamond Exchange that housed MacEllen's office. De Villiers watched the plainclothes members of the Hillbrow Flying Squad slip a tight and unobtrusive net around the building. He gave them six out of ten for the subtlety and camouflage of their agents. MacEllen had blown his survival option.

MacEllen and his family kept a powerboat by their riverside house – he called it their dacha – on the banks of the Vaal river outside the city. With or without friends, they went there most weekends to relax, float on air-beds or cruise with a *braiifleis*, or barbecue, hamper.

De Villiers bought himself diving gear and struck on a Sunday morning when the dealer and his rowdy colleagues were water-skiing.

When MacEllen's podgy corpse was laid on the river bank there were clearly no marks of violence nor any other reason to suspect a cause of death less mundane than a heart attack or severe cramp.

De Villiers made arrangements for Quinn to retrieve his diamonds and cash. He kept both the original killing fee and the subsequently agreed retrieval bonus. With time on his hands he took a South African Airways flight to Cape Town, intending to photograph the wildlife and some of the two and a half thousand species of mostly

flowering plants that grew in the Cape mountains. For a week he camped out, exploring the Hottentots–Holland range. He came away happy, with what he knew to be superlative shots of baboons, dassies – the rock hyrax of the Bible – long-tailed sugarbirds and multicoloured sunbirds, all against a riot of blurred background colour.

The urge that was de Villiers's real reason for coming to the Cape grew steadily more undeniable during the days and nights in that lofty paradise and, on the eighth day, he drove his rented Moke to Tokai. He would revisit the Vrede Huis ruins, with a packed lunch, take some pictures and return to Cape Town.

The ruins were unchanged and de Villiers again felt that intense feeling of belonging, but now a stronger, keener need interfered with his sense of well-being. All day he dallied at Vrede Huis and, for the first time in ten years, allowed himself to think back to his days at La Pergole.

In the late evening as rolling mists, the mythical pipe smoke of pirate Van Hunks, closed over Devil's Peak and the ramparts of Lion's Head, de Villiers found his feet and his heart were set for the distant spinney of silver trees, the landmark he had used many times to return to La Pergole through the vineyards.

The Anglo-Arab stallion was Anne Fontaine's favourite horse. Four evenings a week she rode around the estate and, in fine weather, further afield through the Tokai pinewoods and the gum groves of Platteklip. These outings were her only pleasure. She rode bareback in a thin cotton dress, the better to savour the power of the horse.

Sometimes, and despite her surroundings, Anne wished that she had never been born. She craved children yet could have none; the doctors did not know why. She yearned for love and there was only jealousy. She craved sexual satisfaction but her natural sensuality was denied outside marriage because of the stern moral code of her formative years. Only once had she known a man with whom her loins could have run wild and Luther be damned.

Within the cold walls of her marriage there had been a great deal of sex, all quick and mechanical. The remaining mystery was how disgust had not driven her permanently frigid.

A crescent moon edged into view above the distant silver grove and Anne murmured to the Anglo-Arab, pressing her thighs inward

and gently shortening the rein. She would cool the stallion by walking the last mile of vineyard.

Jan Fontaine was more often than not in hospital these days and, because of his evil temper, changed from one clinic to another with an alacrity that depended on the flashpoint of the relevant staff. Anne dreaded each visit, the bedside interrogations, the increasing and irrational bitterness. Divorce was inconceivable to her, amounting almost to mortal sin, but many a time she found herself fighting off the wish that her husband would die.

Anne had been a virgin bride, as was then to be expected. Her first sex with Fontaine had been a brutal shock. The man was sensitive only to his immediate lusts and these were quickly quenched, for Anne was satin-tight. The early years were hellish enough but, after his injury, he could no longer perform an active role and things became even worse. Now he expected her to satisfy his urges as though she were a paid whore or some tikki-a-time hotel girl.

The rhythmic motion of the horse faltered and Anne slipped easily to the ground to check his front hooves. She found a chip of granite in the frog and prised it loose with a nail file she carried for that purpose. The stallion snorted, nosing the air, and Anne clearly saw the figure of a man on the sandy track to the house.

She passed him by, attempting to avoid eye contact, for this was no time nor place to chat to a stranger. She would, on reaching home, alert Samuel to the presence of a trespasser on the estate.

The man had stopped, statue-like, when he heard her approach, but only when she had thankfully passed him did she hear him call her name. She had heard that voice so many times in her dreams. Was it possible or was this the ghostly robber, Antje Somers, come down from his legendary lair in the foothills?

Few words were spoken. Time ceased to exist. They were back in the forest clearing of ten years earlier. The stallion grazed beside the track and the world was far away.

Their bodies moved as one in the moonshadows of a bamboo island. As wild as animals, as gentle as hedonists, as abandoned as their instincts dictated. Each had long nurtured fantasies of this act — the one through many killings, the other through a thousand hot nights of hopelessness.

For three wonderful weeks they met in the evenings: out of sight of prying eyes, for there is no gossip machine, no jungle-drums telegraph system, half so efficient as the Cape grapevine.

When de Villiers was forced to leave for overdue work in Europe, he told her the date he would return.

'I will live for that day,' she said, her eyes abrim with tears of pure love.

De Villiers was a sensitive, loving human being when he left South Africa...

20

The *khareef* flies, as small as European midges or Canadian 'no see-ums' but more aggressive, crawled over his forearms and sucked blood from his neck. His shirt was soaked with the monsoon drizzle and his spectacles were misted up. On June 1, 1972 Mike Kealy, SAS troop officer at the *jebel* outpost of Tawi Ateer, the Well of the Birds, was squatting in the orange mud in a glade above the camp. His SLR (self-loading) rifle lay within easy reach but his concentration was focused entirely on the iridescent plumage of the hummingbird that hovered less than two paces from his knees. Wingtip to wingtip, Mike estimated the body size as two and a half inches — a tiny masterpiece of nature — and he sorely regretted that for once he had failed to bring his camera.

Khaki rivulets veined the clay soil around islets of fern and *bidah* gladioli. From the overhanging cliffs above, to the edge of the clearing, lianas fell in dank profusion. Tamarind trees and wild citrus shed their burdens of rain in a non-stop and rhythmic tattoo while all manner of crawling, hopping insects animated the undergrowth.

Mike's lifelong fascination with Nature ensured that he was never bored during the long, grey days of the 1972 monsoon. At home on the Sussex Downs, around his home at Ditchling, Mike's father had lovingly taught him all he knew about the then abundant fauna of the area. Mike's only sister had died young and the Kealys' world revolved around their son. After Eastbourne College he had passed into Sandhurst, keen for a career in his father's old regiment, the Queen's Surreys.

In 1965 he was commissioned and, after six years as an infantry officer, joined that small but élite group selected, from the many who

try, to be SAS officers. With four months of intense specialist training under his belt, he was sent to B Squadron, then commanded by the jovial little dynamo Major Richard Pirie.

Mike did well but he found life far more tense and competitive than during his years of infantry soldiering. Then he had commanded mostly amenable teenagers on humdrum exercises. With the SAS he found himself appointed to 8 (Mobility) Troop, generally considered the regiment's best. A dozen or more veterans of several wars and secret operations around the world constituted the twenty-seven-year-old officer's new charges. These were men who accepted nothing at face value, who questioned orders with a cool appraisal based almost always on experience, whereas Mike's thinking was often the result of classroom military dogma.

His first few months with the Troop were a far tougher test than even the SAS selection course. He was on sufferance from day to day and he knew it. Not a few aspiring young officers, elated by success at selection and proudly sporting their newly awarded winged-dagger badge, have found themselves unacceptable to their designated troopers. In such cases the officers always moved on, not the troopers.

Unlike in infantry regiments, where each officer has a personal batman-orderly to attend to his needs, the SAS officer will often find himself cooking for his radio operator while the latter is busy with codes and ciphers on arrival at a 'basha' (improvised tent) site for the night. One way of speeding the process of acceptance into a troop is, of course, for the officer to prove himself in battle. This was Mike's first four-month 'tour' in Oman and so far the *adoo* had opened fire on his men only once.

On 8 June, 8 Troop were helicoptered down from the *jebel* to the coastal town of Mirbat. This village of fishermen's shacks huddled in isolation on a stormy promontory under the shadow of a three-thousand-foot escarpment. Two small mud fortresses protected the *jebel* side of Mirbat and the broiling monsoon breakers prevented any attack from the south. A tangle of barbed wire ringed the forts and the town from west to east, starting and ending in the sea.

Mike and his eight men took over a lone mud hut known as the Bat-house between and slightly to the south of the two forts. The village itself squatted in poverty and squalor between the Bat-house and the sea.

The sultan's *wali*, or village headman, lived in the fort to the north-

west of the Bat-house with a garrison of thirty ancient *askars* (militia). The second fort, seven hundred yards to the north-east of the Bat-House and mere yards from the perimeter wire, housed two dozen Dhofar Gendarmerie troops. These fifty-five men, armed with outdated bolt-action rifles, formed the *wali*'s entire defence force. The small SAS presence was intended to provide only civil aid and military training. Their own defence consisted of two roof-mounted machine-guns and a mortar pit close by the Bat-house.

A few mortars and rockets were occasionally fired at Mirbat by night but, by the time 8 Troop were due to hand over to a new SAS team, Mike had still undergone no baptism of fire. A roster of guard duties was rigidly followed but the months of inactivity tended to reduce a man's alertness.

The Eagle's Nest, the summit of Jebel Samhan, towered six thousand feet above Mirbat. At dusk on 18 July, seventy men picked their precarious way down its mist-swathed face, all heavily laden with weapons and ammunition.

Ali, second son of Sheikh Amr bin Issa, led the sixth and last sub-unit of the Wahidaat a Wasata wa Sharqeeya. The previous week his men had completed the nerve-racking task of locating and removing the many PMN plastic anti-personnel mines the PFLO had previously sown on the vertiginous trails.

Every man was proud to be a part of this historic attack. Omani and 'Ingleezi' blood was to gush and the shock troops of the PFLO would be heroes for years to come.

Ali was himself from Arzat country to the west and knew little of this arid region north of Mirbat. For three days he and his men had worked out of the cavernous hollows of the upper Samhan. The *jebel* here is limestone on a bed of chalky dolomite. Erosion had worn away the softer strata into innumerable crags and winding tunnels.

Ali's heart was proud as he led his men down the precipitous and slippery route. In places there were fixed ropes; further evidence of the intricate preparations involved with the operation.

The previous morning Ali had heard the news on Radio Aden of a major reverse. The perfidious President Sadat had ordered the Soviet supporters of Islam out of Egyptian territory. So be it: tomorrow the PFLO would show the world what Arabs could do without a single Soviet adviser.

Ali did not stop to consider the arsenal that his men and other converging PFLO units were carrying that night. The grenade and

rocket launchers, the heavy mortars, the motley array of machine-guns of various calibres, the recoilless anti-tank weapons and their personal AKM and AK47 rifles – all were of Soviet origin.

The PFLO leaders had laid their plans with care. The attack coincided with maximum mist cover from the *khareef*, making it all but impossible for government aeroplanes to support the Mirbat garrison.

A diversion the previous day had drawn out the Mirbat *firqat*, the fifty or so ex-PFLO turncoats normally based in the village. These men were now several hours' march away to the north, an important factor since, unlike the *askars* and Dhofar Gendarmes in the two Mirbat forts, they were all armed with fully automatic rifles.

The 'Ingleezi' element would be a pushover since they were less numerous than the fingers of a single man.

Long before midnight Ali's men crossed the ravine of the wadi Ghazira. Ali remembered a visit to this wadi when he was a child. His foster-father had brought him and his brother Tama'an down from Qum to see the great flood. They had quivered with fear, long before they reached the wadi, at the distant reverberating roar of the storm water descending from the escarpment. He would never forget that noise, the very sound of God. No man alive who had heard and seen those floods could ever swallow the Marxist claptrap about Allah being merely an invention of British imperialists. They had clung to their father's waist, their mouths agape at the boiling maelstrom that filled the forty-foot-high gorge, changing its shape forever, destroying everything in its path and driving its plunder of dark detritus far out into the Indian Ocean. Looking back at the mountainside, they had gasped at the glistening sheets of falling water, Niagaras spumed by the wind and plunging down from the *jebel* to the drainage wadis as though it was once again the beginning of time.

Ali was called back. One of his men, crossing the wadi, had been bitten by a snake, a large cobra. He bade the man, a black freed slave from Darbat, to remain still. They would return for him after the attack was over. Meanwhile he apportioned the man's spare ammunition among the others. Each man carried well over a hundred pounds of lethal hardware. Ali trod with extra care now. In these days of mines, one was inclined to forget the snakes. Yet a venomous cocktail of vipers infested the scrub of these coastal wadis, including the rare *Thomasi*, with its sharply etched black rings, the Boulenger

or Spotted Rhodorhachis, which climbs near-vertical rock as fast as a windblown leaf, the minute, almost invisible, threadsnake and sixty or so other equally unfriendly species.

After crossing the wadi they took up positions in an outcrop of boulders and Ali counted over two hundred men pass him by in the semi-darkness. Some carried long tubes or other awkward loads, parts of the heavy long-range weapons.

Two hours before dawn the attack lines were ready. Two hundred and fifty of the PFLO's finest fighters, trained in Moscow and Odessa, took up position overlooking the silent village and its puny forts. A killer squad left the main body and silently climbed towards the only government watch-post north of the perimeter wire.

The Dhofar Gendarmes who manned the posts were caught by surprise. Four were held fast while their throats were slit but others escaped into the night and one, before he flung down his rifle the better to flee, loosed off a magazine to warn the *wali's* men.

With speed the *adoo* forces spread out across the whole length of the perimeter wire and eight hundred yards to its north. Ali found himself immediately opposite the Dhofar Gendarmerie fort, the first main target of the attack along with the twenty-five-pound field gun dug into an adjacent sandbagged pit.

Ali checked and exhorted each of his men, then delved into his pack for the Chinese field cap of which he was so proud. He pulled it tightly down to his ears and gently checked the cocking lever of his AK47.

With a burst of sudden *son et lumière* the PFLO heavy mortars began the offensive as the first stirrings of dawn came to Mirbat.

Mike lay half awake, pleasantly aware that life was about to take on a rosy tint. Tomorrow 8 Troop would be relieved. In only a few days he would be home in his beloved Sussex. Idly he ran over the things to be done in preparation for the handover to G Squadron.

He heard the crump of incoming mortar bombs; another symbolic action by the *adoo*. Nothing serious was expected. There had been no warnings from the 'green slime' (SAS argot for Intelligence).

When several heavy mortar rounds landed close by, Mike rose and fumbled in the dark for his spectacles. Donning shorts and rubber flip-flops he grabbed his FN rifle and clambered up a rickety ladder to the Bat-house roof.

The pre-dawn sky crackled with high-velocity bullets. To his

immediate front Mike watched a patch of perimeter wire disintegrate in a mortar explosion, while 12.7-mm Spaagen rounds dug great chunks of masonry from the Dhofar Gendarmerie fortress and shrapnel screamed over the Bat-house. This was no low-key attack.

Mike was mentally well prepared. He had spent time over the previous month plotting imaginary reactions to hypothetical attacks on Mirbat. He knew exactly what to do and so did the men of 8 Troop. A lot of 'muck' was already being flung at the fort, a sure sign that the building was a priority target for the *adoo*. The poorly armed Dhofar Gendarmes were unlikely to survive a frontal assault without immediate aid. If they fell, the twenty-five-pounder would go too.

Mike knew that his Fijian sergeant, a giant of a man named Labalaba, had already departed into the gloaming to help the single Omani gunner in the pit beside the fort. Laba, as he was known, was a humorous soul, given to boasting that an ancestor of his had once feasted on the missionary John Wesley. He was one of a number of Fijians who had been recruited by the British Army when good jungle soldiers for Borneo service were at a premium.

Mike approached Corporal Bob Bennett, the quiet West Countryman in charge of the Bat-house mortars. Mike had established a close rapport with Bob over the previous three months.

'High Explosive and White Phosphorus, Bob,' Mike ordered. The WP mortar shells would provide an instant screen of white smoke among the *adoo*, upsetting their aim and giving Labalaba time to prepare the twenty-five-pounder for action.

'Right, boss,' Bob replied and radioed his mortar-fire directions to Fuzz Pussey, an Oldham man, down in the mortar pit.

Mike could see major trouble was imminent. He turned to the powerfully built trooper lying behind the sights of the .50 Browning machine-gun.

'Pete, see if you can establish comms with HQ.'

Pete Winner was a Northerner with a fiery nature. In May 1981 he was to lead the Alpha Assault Group raid on the Iranian Embassy in Kensington, London.

Pete left the Bat-house roof and tapped out a morse message to SAS Headquarters near Salalah: 'Contact. Under heavy fire. Wait. Out.' Sand and mud showered his face as a brace of 120-mm Katyusha rockets exploded nearby.

A dull monsoon dawn had broken over the shore and the village.

The SAS men wore shorts, shirts and desert boots. All were bare-headed.

For half an hour the attackers poured bullets, mortars and rockets at the forts and the Bat-house. Bob and Fuzz returned mortar fire as best they could and the others formed a line to haul ammunition boxes up to the roof.

Shortly before 6 a.m. there was a sudden lull in the bedlam and little children appeared on the roofs of the town houses behind the Bat-house. Bob Bennett cupped his hands and shouted, 'Go down, go down.'

The two SAS machine-guns remained silent, not wishing to give away their position until a ground attack began. At exactly 6 a.m. all hell broke loose.

From shore to shore across the length of the wire the *adoo* opened up on the Mirbat defenders and, in groups of a dozen, their commandos began the assault. Using the still dim light, the clinging wraiths of mist and the broken ground for cover, they darted forward from rock to rock. They outnumbered the garrison by five to one and their fire-power was greatly superior.

On the rooftop Pete Winner waited behind his heavy machine-gun. Air-cooled and belt-fed, it could fire up to six hundred rounds a minute.

A few paces away Geoff Taylor, on loan to 8 Troop from G Squadron, adjusted the sights of the smaller 7.62 GPMG (General-Purpose Machine Gun) and prepared the feed belts with help from Roger Coles, a Bristol man built thin as a rake.

Mike felt the tension slacken in his stomach. He cleaned his spectacles with his shirt-tail and peered into the fog of dust and cordite. He forced down an appalling surge of fear.

Men were advancing on foot towards the perimeter wherever he looked. As they broke into a run, Mike turned and shouted, 'Open fire.'

Winner and Taylor were totally efficient with their weapons. The ground to the north of the wire was soon littered with *adoo* bodies shredded by heavy .50-calibre and high-velocity GPMG bullets.

The advancing PFLO lines continued, ignoring the screams of their dying. The wire was breached in places, and rocket launchers set up behind rocks. Soon the Dhofar Gendarmerie fort and the nearby gun pit shook to direct hits from Carl Gustav rockets. Gaping holes

appeared in the fort and bodies of dead gendarmes slumped over the wall embrasures.

The gun pit was undermanned but Laba worked like a demon to load and fire the Second World War relic over open sights and at point-blank range. His activities attracted a hail of bullets, one of which removed part of his chin.

Back at the Bat-house mortar pit 8 Troop's second Fijian, another giant, named Sekavesi, lost walkie-talkie contact with his friend and braved seven hundred yards of open ground under heavy fire in a dash from Bat-house to gun pit.

Roger Coles sneaked out of the Bat-house with a Sarbe ground-to-air beacon. He hoped to call a helicopter in from Salalah to evacuate the wounded. Choosing a suitable spot close to the beach, he signalled the machine, which came in low over the sea. Murderous enemy fire precluded any landing and the helicopter veered away into the mist. Coles was lucky to make it back to the Bat-house.

In the gun pit Sekavesi and the wounded Laba were working the twenty-five-pounder. Covered in blood, black cordite and sweat, burnt by the empty brass cases, they slammed round after round into the wire to their front. A 7.62 bullet entered Sekavesi's shoulder and lodged itself close to his spine. A second bullet cut a deep furrow along his skull. Blood cascaded down his face but, realizing the imminent danger of being overrun, he propped himself against a sandbag with his rifle and, wiping blood from his right eye, continued firing at the wire.

Laba limped across to a 60-mm mortar tube. A bullet penetrated his neck and the great Fijian fell dead. Beside him in the pit the Omani gunner lay writhing with a bullet in his guts. The big gun, of key importance to the defence of Mirbat, fell silent.

On the Bat-house roof Mike was deafened by the numbing roar of the battle but he sensed the sudden silence in the gun pit. Receiving no response to repeated calls with his walkie-talkie, he knew he must go to the pit without delay. Bullets were now passing over the Bat-house from the south as well as the north. This could only mean the *adoo* had outflanked the forts and were already into the village itself. Eight Troop were surrounded. Mike forced this unpleasant turn of events to the back of his mind. Bob, Pete and the others could hold the Bat-house; he must help the Fijians defend the northern perimeter at all costs. The thought of running the gauntlet from Bat-house to gun pit now that the *adoo* lined the perimeter wire with their full fire-

power, was to stare death in the face. Yet every man on the roof volunteered to go with Mike. He chose Tommy Tobin, the medical orderly. As he made to set out, Bob reminded him, 'You'll not get far in your flip-flops.'

Mike descended to his bed space and laced up his desert boots. Then the two men, edging around the mortar pit beside the Bathouse, sprinted to a low wadi bed and used its cover to advance a few hundred yards. They were halfway to the gun pit when the *adoo* spotted them and opened fire. With modern weapons, especially machine-guns, and at a range of one hundred yards, it is not at all difficult to hit a man-sized target. Fifty or sixty trained PFLO guerrillas now adjusted their weapon sights and concentrated their fire on Mike and Tommy.

Once clear of the wadi there was not a scrap of cover. Only speed and sheer luck preserved their lives during the four long minutes of their run to the gun pit. Mortar rounds exploded about them, burning tracer sighed above their bent backs and, ever closer, the ground beat of a chasing heavy-machine-gun pursued their path. From his rooftop Pete Winner spotted the *adoo* machine-gunner and, adjusting the sights of his Browning, blew the man apart. Mike and Tommy, lungs heaving and eyes blinded by sweat, flung themselves over the gunpit sandbags, Mike landing on the eviscerated stomach of a dead Dhofar Gendarme.

Mike summed up the position. In minutes they would be overrun. Only Sekavesi's rifle was still active in the pit and many *adoo* were already through the wire entanglements.

The Dhofar Gendarmerie fort close by was holed and silent. All *adoo* fire was now directed on the gun pit and its occupants. The gun's steel shield rattled and clanked as bullets struck its armour, direct hits slicing through and entering the pit behind. Tommy Tobin's jaw and one cheekbone were shot away from his face. He lay by Laba's body with blood pumping down his neck.

A group of *adoo* broke through the wire and rushed to the far wall of the fort. Creeping round to the corner closest to the gun pit, a mere fifteen yards away from Mike and Sekavesi, they unslung and primed their hand-grenades, closing in for the kill.

The endless hours of snap-shooting at targets back in Hereford in which both Mike and Sekavesi, like all SAS men, had been thoroughly schooled, now paid off. Ducking and weaving within their pit, Mike subjected everything that moved to the quick double-tap, two-shot

sequence that is the hallmark of Hereford training. He killed the first *adoo* just after he had unpinned a grenade. The man's own body covered the explosion.

A light machine-gunner targeted the two survivors and for a while movement was impossible within the gun pit. Unable to shoot at the approaching *adoo*, Mike failed to see a grenade land on the sandbag above his head. The explosion filled the air with sand, steel and a noise that seemed to crack his eardrums. Mike forced himself back up to his knees and then fully upright. Quickly he palmed dirt from his spectacles and, as he replaced them, saw the blurred image of an *adoo* immediately ahead and beneath the fortress wall. He fired twice and blew the back of the man's head on to the masonry.

A half dozen grenades arched out towards the gun pit. Most detonated against the outer sandbag wall but one rolled over the top of the sacks and dropped on to the body of the dead gendarme. Mike watched the smoke wisp away from the six-second fuse and braced himself for death.

The grenade failed to go off. Mike winged a prayer of thanks to God and began to wonder why he was still alive. He felt no fear any more. If he could survive this far, he was going to make it. A bullet passed through his hair and another fanned his cheek. He clearly saw an *adoo* aiming at him from beside the remnants of the perimeter fence. He killed the man and saw his Chinese field cap hooked up by the razor barbs of the wire.

Two BAC Strikemaster jets roared by, braving the near-impossible visibility. A curtain of *adoo* machine-gun fire rose to meet the planes and both were holed. They wheeled over the sea and Mike placed a fluorescent cloth panel on the floor of the pit as a guidance to the pilots.

The Strikemasters did what they could during the brief seconds of mist-free attack. Cannon fire and rockets racked the perimeter wire and gave the defenders of Mirbat a short but welcome respite.

Badly damaged, both jets limped away towards Salalah and the *adoo* attack resumed. Mike could now hear heavy firing from the seaward side of the gun pit and he called Bob Bennett to bring mortar fire down on the gun pit's immediate attackers. The SAS mortar man, Fuzz, jacked his tube up to maximum elevation but Mike was still not happy with the results.

'Get the bloody rounds *closer*,' he ordered.

'I can't,' Bob shouted at his walkie-talkie. 'They'll land right on top of you.'

'That's what I want,' was Mike's only reply.

Hearing Bob's relayed orders, Fuzz grinned and, lifting the weapon by its legs, hugged the tube to his chest. Aiming by trial and error, he sent bomb after bomb into the immediate vicinity of the gun pit.

Two more Strikemasters attacked the perimeter and at last the *adoo*, some five hours after the attack had started, began to retreat into the mist. To the south the sounds of battle mounted over a wide area and Mike was greatly relieved at a radio message announcing the arrival of G Squadron helicopter reinforcements. They had been called off a training exercise and fitted out for battle as quickly as possible. Within an hour the fresh SAS force had driven the remnants of the *adoo* into retreat.

Mike left Sekavesi in the pit and entered the shattered fort. Major Alistair Morrison of G Squadron found Mike there. In his subsequent report he wrote, 'I was speechless when I saw the area of the fort. There were pools of blood from the wounded, mortar holes, many rings from grenades and the twenty-five pounder itself was badly holed through its shield. The ground was scarred by the many grenades which had exploded. It was obvious that an extremely fierce close-quarter battle had been fought there. Each one of Captain Kealy's men made a point of telling me that he was the bravest man they had ever seen ... I believe his inspired leadership and bravery saved the lives of his men and the town from being captured.'

Amid the carnage and the body-bags, Labalaba was identified and taken a way by helicopter. Over a hundred of the PFLO attackers had been killed and many of the defenders were dead or dying. Bob and Mike sat together on the Bat-house roof feeling drained yet elated. Tommy Tobin was sent back to England to have his face rebuilt. Mike later visited him in the hospital in Aylesbury. A broken tooth had lodged in Tommy's chest and he died two months later.

Three days after the Mirbat attack Mike and his men returned to Britain on leave. Mike sat with his parents in their sitting room at Forge House in Ditchling, East Sussex. There had been no news coverage of the Mirbat event in Britain. Over supper and until 1 a.m., Mike unburdened himself to his parents.

'It was exactly like watching a film,' he told them, 'except that the dying really died. I thought I would be killed and I worried about

people coming here to the house to tell you I was dead ... it was very bloody ... I felt a great peace when it was over.'

Two years later Mike and Bob Bennett met at the SAS London headquarters and were shown an official painting commemorating the events of Mirbat. Their CO, Colonel Peter de la Billière, asked for their opinion on the painting's authenticity. Both men found their eyes pricking with the emotion of their memories.

Not until four years after the battle were details of it finally released to the general public, by which time the forces of the PFLO were on the retreat throughout Dhofar.

Mike Kealy was awarded the Distinguished Service Order by the Queen, a medal second in significance only to the Victoria Cross. He was the youngest Briton to receive the decoration since the Korean War. The only memento that he kept was the Chinese field cap he had retrieved from the perimeter wire before leaving Mirbat.

21

The River Wye passes by the villages of Fownhope and Mordiford on its way down to the Severn and, before entering the outskirts of Hereford, runs near the old-world pub, a place of log fires and genuine cartwheels, called the Bunch of Carrots. Until the late 1980s this was the acknowleged watering-hole of married members of the SAS Regiment, a fact that Davies discovered without difficulty in the first week of April 1978.

The Clinic had been busy in the USA throughout the past year. De Villiers had been paid promptly enough by Bakhait in Dubai. Sheikh Amr bin Issa's eldest son had left his school in England with two A levels and taken to the family business in a hands-on manner that would have been alien to his late father. He was totally uninterested in the matter of the *thaa'r*; indeed de Villiers had sensed a palpable hostility from the young Dhofari, who, as far as he could make out, hardly bothered to watch the Milling film before handing over the crisp Bank of Dubai cheque for one million dollars.

A temporary lull in new contract work had led de Villiers to dispatch Davies back on the trail of the Clinic's second Dhofar target.

The known facts were in this case quite helpful: Ali bin Amr Bait Jarboat had been killed on 19 July 1972 during an attack on the village of Mirbat. The detachment he had led was directly tasked with the capture of the British artillery gun and surviving members of his patrol had watched Ali shot down at close range by the foreigners in the gun pit.

Davies well remembered his previous attempts to elicit information from SAS personnel and knew that his task would not be easy. With patience, however, he was confident he would eventually identify the commander of the SAS Mirbat detachment.

He parked outside the Bunch of Carrots shortly after it opened and settled himself down in the Wheel Bar with a local newspaper and a pint of HP Bulmer's Strongbow cider. By 8 p.m. the pub was packed with drinkers and Davies made a mental list of likely SAS men. There were many obvious clues, from sun tans and hair cuts to 'brothel creepers', but Davies largely ignored these. Returnees from ambush duty in Northern Ireland or plainclothes terrorist-reaction duty at Heathrow would sport pale faces and, often enough, hippy-length hair. Desert boots worn in the UK had become as ostentatious to SAS men as old school ties to genuine Old Etonians, but men who are honed to a fine state of fitness and alertness, who prefer to observe and listen rather than swear and guffaw, develop their own stamp and mould.

Bob Bennett, on a local army course, was enjoying his usual evening drink in the Wheel Bar, accompanied by his wife Lyn and a number of his regimental colleagues. His eyes roamed the room as though they had a life of their own, missing nothing. Lyn often ribbed him, for she sometimes caught him at it when everyone else was engaged in the most intense of debates.

Not long after he had arrived and settled down in the larger lounge by the public bar, Bob spotted the Welshman. He positioned himself so that he could watch without being observed. He was in no doubt that this was the same man he had mentioned to Ken Borthwick the previous year. If he had been uncertain, the man's actions left no room for doubt. Over a two-hour period he moved between three groups of drinkers, keeping to the periphery, quick to laugh and offer a drink, never short of a grin or a nod. In two of the three groups targeted by the Welshman, Bennett spotted at least one SAS man that he recognized.

At 9.30 the Welshman returned from a visit to the lavatory and

came to a sudden halt as though confronted by a ghost. For a moment he stood transfixed and facing the wall, then immediately resumed his affable amble back to his latest drinking position. Ten minutes later, with a cheery wave at no one in particular, he donned a tweed cap and raincoat and left. Bob Bennett did not follow him because the last time he had contacted Ken Borthwick there had been no come-back: the man was obviously perfectly innocent, even if over-curious by nature.

Davies telephoned de Villiers with his discovery but was called away for eight months for a complicated job in Los Angeles. When he next returned to the Bunch of Carrots, in the first week of December 1978, there were a number of habitués from the SAS staff and a few ex-SAS men, including Bob Bennett, enjoying a pre-Christmas chat.

Having written the Welshman off as harmless, Bob no longer paid him much attention until the single word 'Mirbat' acted like a bullet in his ear and he tuned in to the Welshman's conversation with a group behind his back. 'I could swear the picture was on the wall right here,' the Welshman said, 'a small print it was, artist's impression of a battle and, like I say, I'm sure it had the word "Mirbat" printed below ... very powerful image, you know, stark fortress, smoking gun and bodies all over.'

'One of the lads put that up in the New Year,' someone offered, 'but Keith Grant moved it somewhere else last May when he did the alterations to the Wheel Bar.'

'Mirbat was quite an affair,' the Welshman pressed the point. 'I gather there were only a handful of your lads against a horde.'

'Aye, it was a right ding-dong,' a low Scots voice put in. 'Nigh on seven years ago now. It all came out in the papers a couple of years back. The boss there, Mike Kealy, got himself a gong. Deserved it by all counts.'

The conversation moved on, but Bob Bennett was alarmed. He had definitely been right in the first place. He waited until the Welshman took his leave, then he eased out of the pub's delivery door and took the details of the suspect's departing car. He did not attempt to follow, for he had no wish to disturb Lyn nor break up his party. He called Ken Borthwick. The police officer was out but Bennett left a message with his wife: 'The Welshman is back and his interest is still in Mirbat matters.' She assured him she would pass

the message to her husband on his return and, satisfied he could do no more, Bennett returned to the bar.

Early in the morning of Sunday 3 December 1978 the Committee met at 4 Somers Crescent, the London home of Colonel Macpherson. There was a full house, which was normal for winter meetings, especially when they were likely to prove punchy. Spike had convened the meeting at short notice, which meant something unusual was in the wind.

The colonel's wife was away at Balavil, the Macpherson family home in Kingussie, so Jane brought her coffee paraphernalia and the members sat in a cramped circle, as the sitting room was long and rather narrow. Bletchley was Chairman of the day and it was immediately clear that his mood was aggressive.

Spike was on about the Dhofar business once again and Bletchley was determined they should have nothing more to do with the wretched affair.

'No. No. No,' he thumped the side of his armchair. 'Don't you see that this is a departure from our very charter? The Founder and I' – he paused, then added with a venomous glance at Tommy Macpherson – 'and the Colonel, were in unanimous agreement when we first laid down the limitations to involvement. An important ruling was and, until last year, has always remained that we would never touch terrorist organizations. Not the IRA nor the Mafia nor lesser home-grown groupings. We are too small. We are unfunded and above all we are bound by the laws of the land.'

'Bletchley is right,' Macpherson interjected before the Chairman could continue. This was not difficult since Bletchley's sentences came in bursts of speed that often tailed away as though he had forgotten the direction of his flow. 'But we set out those ground rules many years ago now and no organization can survive or compete without adapting to changing circumstances.' He ran a hand through his short, wavy hair, a sign of exasperation that the Committee knew well. 'At the outset we designed our own suit of clothing in the fashion of the time but it has become a strait-jacket and we risk becoming castrated ... impotent. Let me suggest another Maoism, "A frog in a well says 'the sky is no bigger than the mouth of my well'." I believe the time has come to look closely at the Committee's well because we are here to protect our own *wherever* the threat comes from.'

Mike Panny's eyebrows rose. 'What aspects thereof?' He always

enjoyed seeing his name in the minutes as the instigator of penetrating questions and worthy new ideas.

'Any which reveal our outlook to be muffled by cobwebs. Exactly what activities should we become involved with? At what point should we tip off the police? How much force or coercion may our Locals use? To what extent must they feel bound by the letter of the law in cases where we know the law cannot help?'

'Not forgetting,' Panny added, 'the other side of the coin. I believe we should change the ground rules for the control of Locals. It cannot be right that only Spike knows the identity of our own men, that only he can contact them. I mean nothing personal, but I believe we should as a Committee have a much closer control over the Controller, be he Spike or some other person.'

Bletchley and Bob Mantell were nodding, Graves and the Twins shaking their heads and the Don airing a sardonic smile. Personal viewpoints were fairly evenly balanced on such topics. This was just as well since, far from being flexible, they were not far short of intractable.

'Chairman.' It was Macpherson again. 'This meeting has to end by 10 a.m., as you know. We are here to decide upon a single question. May I suggest we agree to a separate meeting to discuss general policy changes? This meeting must keep to specifics.'

'That's all very well,' said Mantell, filling the gap caused by an unexpected silence from the Chairman, who looked decidedly unwell: he appeared to lack tongue control and mopped sweat from his brow with his pocket handkerchief, 'but the Chairman is rightly concerned that any agreement to further activity on this specific matter involves a basic change of direction in our general policy. We therefore need to reassess the latter *before* we can address Spike's immediate needs.'

'Look, mate,' August Graves interrupted the excavation work of his little finger in his right ear to stab the air in Mantell's direction, 'wiv due respect to our Chairman, Spikey asked us 'ere to give 'im "yes" or "no" on the 'Ereford geezer. We all knew that when we turned up this mornin'. Right? Am I right? Course I am, so none of yer bleedin' moral yatter. I say put it to the vote and give the lad 'is answer one way or t'other.'

The Don shook his head in disbelief and said nothing. The Twins nodded as vigorously as their age and double chins permitted and Jane continued with her note-taking.

Bletchley found his voice. 'Since we are indeed pressed for time

we will vote on the immediate matter and at next month's meeting we will review the overall policy.' He nodded at Jane, who handled the agendas. 'I must again advise the Committee that in my opinion we should never have sanctioned last year's Oman operation. The pilot Milling had no connections at all with our interests and our man was of course unable to prove any links between his death and the Welshman we picked up in Hereford.' He turned to Mantell. 'That is correct, is it not?'

Mantell nodded, and answered, 'We passed the photographs to our friends in Scotland Yard. There was no record from their files nor those of the anti-terrorist branch. Immigration also drew a blank. None of the three men photographed by Spike's man in Oman have previous records on UK or Interpol computers.'

'There can be little point then, surely, in wasting further time on this Welshman. He may well be involved in skulduggery; in fact there can be no doubt of it, but the unfortunate Milling, I repeat, had nothing whatever to do with Mirbat nor with our people. My recommendation is that we direct Spike to leave the matter well alone and that you, Mantell, leak Friday's sighting of the Welshman in Hereford to the relevant police authorities.'

Mantell nodded. Spike raised his hand. 'The police can do nothing. They need proof and motives and names. We have none of these things. Either *we* follow up this new visit by the Welshman or no one does. If the latter, then it is my opinion that another death will result and almost certainly it will be one of the Mirbat survivors who dies.'

'Why so?' asked the Don, 'if Milling had nothing to do with Mirbat?'

'I don't know,' Spike said simply, 'but the Welshman who was last year linked to both Milling and Mirbat is now making fresh enquiries about Mirbat and is known to have located the names of those SAS men who fought there. There is, at the very least, a risk that he may try to kill one or more of them.' Spike looked around the room. 'This *is* clearly a direct threat to persons we are tasked by our Founder to protect. If one should die following our inaction, that will lie heavily on *my* conscience. I have no vote on the Committee but I strongly recommend that you direct me to have the Welshman found and followed immediately.'

Spike collected the nine sheets of A4 paper. Five were marked with a tick, four with a cross. Both Chairmen were permitted to vote

and Spike could guess which course each person, other than Jane and the Don, had supported. He was relieved. As he left the room he saw that Bletchley was sweating profusely and staring at the fireplace with an expression akin to despair.

They met halfway, at the Leigh Delamere service station, and Spike climbed into Darrell Hallett's Avenger in a corner of the busy car park. As usual the rear half of the car was stacked high with packs of Yorkie bars. Against the roar of the evening traffic on the M4 motorway, Spike gave Hallett his briefing.

Hallett studied the list of the seven Mirbat survivors, their addresses and known activities. Only three were currently in Britain and one of these was Captain Michael Kealy, still a serving officer in the British Army.

'I am working the central district at present,' Hallett said. 'I might as well concentrate on Bennett and Kealy since they will both be in Hereford. I have a colleague in Bristol who can keep tabs on the third guy.'

'Remember,' Spike emphasized, 'if you locate the Welshman, let me know as soon as he steps out of line in any way or if he meets either of the two in the photos. Have camera and recording kit ready for any meeting he's involved in. But *don't* get involved in any rough stuff unless he attacks you, Kealy or Bennett. As soon as you pick up any usable evidence we hand this one over to the boys in blue.'

22

Aware of the increasing sophistication of IRA active service units in mainland Britain, the Lord Chancellor issued on the 26 February 1982 a directive entitled 'Disclosure of Information from Personal Records'. From that date onwards no records could be divulged by the authorities without the specific permission of the servicemen involved.

On 4 December 1978 Davies had faced no such bureaucratic obstacles when he telephoned the Ministry of Defence Officers' Enquiries Department and asked for the current address of Captain Michael Kealy.

'May I ask your name?'

Davies gave a name.

'And the reason for your enquiry?'

'Yes, of course. I am sending out centenary details of Captain Kealy's old school, Eastbourne College.'

'I am afraid, in Captain Kealy's case, I am not at liberty to give you his address but I can give you that of his parents which you could, of course, also obtain through Directory Enquiries.'

'That would be most kind,' purred Davies.

The following day he was on the road before dawn in a Ford Escort from Tadnams. From London he followed the A23 as far as Albourne, then turned east to the sleepy village of Ditchling under the shadow of the South Downs.

Forge House was not difficult to find, being on the main road through the village and directly opposite the North Star pub. Davies parked in a side street and settled down to a cup of tea and fresh doughnut in the Tudor Bakery. Refreshed, he returned to the car and made ready his standard country gear consisting of basic bird-twitcher's ensemble, shooting stick, binoculars and a camera with an indecently long lens attached.

While parking by the North Star he noticed a blue Renault in the yard of Forge House whereas a green Mini that he had seen there earlier was gone. A jumble of items packed the rear shelf of the Renault and Davies picked out with his binoculars a seemingly innocuous pair of army puttees. These ankle wrappings, dating back to the First World War, are worn by many infantry units and are always khaki in colour with the sole exception of those of SAS officers. Theirs, like the pair Davies spotted in the Renault, are light beige.

Mike Kealy made his father a cup of tea and took it up to his room. The colonel hated illness and, confined to bed with influenza, he fretted to be out and about. Mike puffed up a pillow behind his father and sat on the end of the bed. He admired his father more than any man alive and was sorry he could not stay with him longer. His maternal grandmother had died ten days before and he had promised his mother he would be at the funeral in Frimley that afternoon.

A gentle reminder from his father sent Mike up to his room to shave. As he looked up and removed steam from the mirror, he saw

someone behind him. Without his spectacles he turned around. It was only the old bloodstained Chinese field cap that hung on the wall. He laughed. His aunt Olga had ticked him off only a week or two before about it.

'Get rid of that terrorist's hat,' she had said, 'it will bring you bad luck.' Mike took leave of his father and drove the Renault north. His mother had gone ahead in the Mini to prepare things. He would have spent a day or two in Ditchling to help her but he needed to be in Hereford to look after his wife Maggi.

They already had a daughter of three, Alice, and now Maggi was about to give birth to twins, so their doctor assured them. She had somehow contracted mumps with only two or three weeks to go, so Mike was treating her with kid gloves and felt uneasy to be away at all.

After a year with his parent regiment in Germany and Northern Ireland, he was overjoyed to be given command of an SAS squadron. His MFO crates containing his personal belongings had recently arrived from Werle in Germany at his new quarters in Hereford. Several days of DIY operations, in between nursing Maggi, stretched ahead of him.

He passed through Billingshurst and Loxwood. One thing that occupied his mind, apart from a natural worry about his adequacy to lead a squadron of Britain's finest fighting men, was the question of his physical fitness. His recent desk job had allowed him time for routine jogging, but Mike was used to being at peak performance. Few men could outpace him in the hills with a heavy rucksack and rough going and he believed he should take over D Squadron in top personal condition. As soon as Maggi was recovered he would settle into a strict training regime.

He arrived at St Peter's Church in Frimley at noon, just in time to join his mother in the front pew. After the service, with thirty or so relatives, they walked down the road to the White Hart pub for lunch. Later Mike drove to the nearby town of Chobham, where his father-in-law, the Reverend Acworth, was rector. After tea at the rectory he headed home with the gift of a corner cupboard protruding from the Renault's boot.

Where the A49 enters the suburbs of Hereford Mike turned right into Bradbury Lines, the Regiment's Headquarters and married-quarters area, and up Bullingham Lane. Number seventy-nine was fairly secluded, being set back from the road by a circular cul-de-sac.

When Mike needed to go into the main regimental compound he could either drive up the lane to the main gate and show his ID card, or walk to a side entrance in the security fence and enter with his electronic card.

Davies had long since drained his vacuum flask and the doughnut was a distant memory, so he was delighted when Kealy finally came home to roost. The fact that his married quarters were within SAS home territory did not please Davies at all and he left Bullingham Lane as soon as he had seen Kealy carry the corner cupboard into number seventy-nine and place newspaper over his front windscreen against overnight frost.

Leaving the Ford three streets away, Davies, complete with 'twitcher' gear and a torch, threaded his way through gorse and scrub to the rough ground immediately behind the Kealy's back garden. He noted a high water tower close by as a convenient marker and drove west to search for a suitable bed and breakfast. That night he settled for a retired couple in Stretton Sugwas. In December there were vacancies aplenty and he would change his base nightly as well as his identity.

Davies telephoned de Villiers in New York. 'I have located our person,' he said, 'and will need you here in a week.' He gave contact details and settled down to bore himself stiff with an old *Reader's Digest*. Tomorrow, with extreme caution, he would begin the search for a pattern to Kealy's lifestyle.

23

The long antiseptic corridors, as in all major hospitals, served as thoroughfares for two types of inmate: the sick and listless in pyjamas with too much time on their hands and the rushed-off-their-feet doctors and nursing staff for whom there were never enough hours in the day.

In the Maternity Ward of Hereford General Hospital a new doctor made his way, rather more slowly than most, from the staff toilets to the post-natal wing. There was a rapid turnover of doctors and

surgeons at the hospital and no identity check at the various hospital entrances.

Two years before, in Belfast's Catholic Mater Hospital, the MP Mrs Maive Drumm had been assassinated in her hospital bed by men wearing doctors' white coats. Since few hospital-based crime novels escape the cliché of criminals masquerading as medical staff, the trick might be considered dangerously overworked. But, if it works, why not use it? Davies certainly had no qualms about plagiarism. He approached a junior nurse in the reception of the Post-Natal Ward and learned both the location of Mrs Kealy's bed and the fact that she had produced twins the previous evening.

Maggi Kealy was awake and surrounded by flowers. Davies arrived with clipboard, stethoscope and wearing the ubiquitous white coat. He bent over the chart at the end of her bed and made an entry on his clipboard while attaching a small bug to the underside of the bed frame. The bug was fitted with a super-stick tab, not a magnetic clamp, to minimize transmission interference.

'All seems to be well, Mrs Kealy. Have a rest while you may.' He grinned and left her cubicle congratulating himself on his easy bedside manner. Following the copious array of signs, he made for the General Medical Ward and approached the Duty Sister there. He had come from the Geriatric Unit, he explained, and needed a supply of insulin and chlorpropamide. They had run short. Chlorpropamide is used by diabetics not requiring insulin.

He was given both drugs and signed two sets of forms to acknowledge receipt.

Three weeks of pussyfooting and freezing his toes off in the scrub behind Kealy's house had led Davies to the firm conclusion that Kealy could never be dealt with inside the SAS citadel of Hereford. Twice Kealy and his wife had spent some time in their back garden, and on each occasion they were nursing a sick rabbit. Kealy had been complaining that he never had time to keep fit and that, once the babies were born, he would spend more time on the Brecon Beacons. Hills that Davies also knew well, these were the main SAS training grounds where a small number of unfortunates had over the years died of exposure in their keenness to pass SAS selection. Davies had formulated a simple plan to put before de Villiers on his arrival.

Darrell Hallett failed to find any trace of the Welshman in the many hotels, motels and guest-houses he visited around and about Hereford,

despite his photographs of Davies by the Gulf Hotel swimming pool. Eventually he had given up and set about shadowing the postman Bob Bennett. Again nothing. Only an Afghan hound had shown any untoward interest in Bennett. So he switched to Kealy.

At 4 p.m. on Boxing Day Kealy, carrying his young daughter Alice, arrived at Maggi's bedside. Hallett parked two ranks away from Kealy's Renault and settled down to watch for anyone with an unhealthy interest in Kealy or his car.

Twenty minutes passed and Hallett found his attention continually drawn to the occupant of a Ford Escort four cars away from and parallel with his own. The man wore a doctor's coat but what niggled Hallett were the earphones and something about his profile. It came to him in a while that the Escort had a perfectly good radio aerial, so why the headphones? Furthermore, Mason's excellent telephoto lens had obtained first-class side views of the Welshman and, apart from the fact that the man with headphones was balding, he was the spitting image of Hallett's quarry.

Determined to check out this coincidence, Hallett quietly reversed his car, circled the car park, which was full to capacity, and drew up again facing the Escort from two car spaces away. He watched the man through his binoculars, then glanced at the Muscat photograph. He felt excitement mounting. It could *not* be a mere coincidence. This *was* the Welshman.

Davies must have sensed rather than seen Hallett's interest in him, for he was engrossed in the conversation between the Kealys. He realized he was glimpsing a world of tender togetherness, of selfless love between two humans that he would never know for himself. His eyes were focused in the middle distance, his mind far away, when that sixth sense possessed by many people who live on the edge, swung his gaze to the car that had moved around from behind to opposite him and from which no driver had emerged.

To Davies, Hallett's binoculars might just as well have been a gun. He tore off the earplugs, started the car and screeched into reverse. Hallett was faster still. The two cars made for the exit but Hallett swung his Avenger violently across the path of the Escort. Yorkie bars cascaded forward on to him. Davies, fearing a police ambush, decided escape was more likely on foot. He dashed for a side door in the nearest hospital block, with Hallett, unencumbered by coat and suit, gaining ground fast.

Davies came to bay in a first-floor lavatory. He was out of breath.

Hallett, a street fighter since childhood, automatically assumed a boxer's stance. Davies kicked out and contacted Hallett's kneecap. Hallett's guard dropped briefly and Davies lanced a direct blow, straight as a snooker stroke, at Hallett's neck with the handle of a broom he had snatched up. Hallett snarled in pain but resisted the urge to finger his neck. His boxer's straight right caught Davies in the nose and mouth, splitting his upper lip. As he closed in, the door opened and two cleaning women with buckets entered. Both screamed and Davies knocked them out of the way as he lurched from the room.

Hallett tried to talk to the women but his throat felt mangled. To swallow was excruciating. He followed the Welshman as best he could but the corridors were thronged with merry people involved in a Boxing Day party. By the time Hallett reached the car park there was no sign of the Escort. He rang Spike's number and croaked his report to the answering machine. Kealy was definitely at risk. He should be given closer protection at once.

De Villiers and Meier were ill at ease. Davies's description of his attacker at the hospital did not tally with their idea of police surveillance. Yet, if not from the security services, who was the man? Was he from the same stable as the tall man in the Sumail *falaj*?

De Villiers had sent Davies back to the USA. He would now be a liability in Britain and might lead the unknown hunters to Tadnams or the Clinic. All the same, Davies had done well and de Villiers quite liked the method that he had suggested, and for which he had begun to prepare.

The hospital tapes confirmed Davies's opinion. Mike Kealy had told his wife that the regiment wanted him in Belfast for a week's introduction to the work he and his new squadron would be doing there. Once he returned, there would be a week or two before he started his Irish tour of duty. 'I must get some more hill training in before then,' he told his wife.

'But you're super-fit already, my love,' she said.

He shook his head. 'No, that's sadly not so, but I'll up the daily training and then do a couple more weekends in the Brecons. If I round that off with an endurance march with the selection students, I should be back on course and fit for Armagh or wherever.'

His wife knew better than to argue. Mike had always been a fitness

fanatic. He bounced Alice on his knees and they talked about the twins and the future.

The Clinic listened carefully to the tapes and looked at the many photographs Davies had taken of the Kealys, their home in Hereford, their car, the two main entrances to the SAS barracks, and even Forge House in Ditchling. Davies's written report was efficient and thorough. His conclusion was to the point. Major Kealy could not safely be terminated at his place of work nor in his home. There remained his stated intention to train on the Brecon Beacons. Davies's method was based on his knowledge of those hills during the winter months.

24

Hallett eased through the dark jungle of the shrubbery without a sound. He wore a green track suit and a grey scarf wrapped around his swollen throat. The wind was bitter and ice covered the nearby pond.

Rhododendrons crowded the house itself, a two-storey 1930s building wedged between the road and the railway some two miles out of Hereford. Captain Tony Shaw of the SAS and his family were quartered there and Hallett watched their New Year celebrations with the Kealys fully aware that, unarmed as he was, he could do little but provide a warning if the Welshman and his colleagues decided to attack Kealy at this isolated spot.

A week later, on 14 January, gaunt from lack of sleep, Hallett took yet another cup of black coffee from his vacuum flask. He was parked outside the Rectory, observing the guests at the retirement party of the Rector of Chobham. Everyone enjoyed themselves. Maggi Kealy's father, the Reverend Roney Acworth, made a fine speech and Hallett signed off. With the best will in the world and unswerving loyalty to Spike Allen, he simply had to get back to work or Rowntree would sack him.

'No one has shown the least interest in Kealy or his family,' he assured Spike, 'since I met the Welshman at the hospital. My own

opinion is that he, and any boyos with him, have been frightened off.'

Reluctantly Spike agreed. He was fully aware that Kealy might still be in danger but his Locals did not grow on trees. Weeks spent alternating between their normal employment and long hours in the cold watching strangers for Spike did not endear the cause to them.

With a sigh, Spike telephoned Wallace, a farmer from Malvern who had alternated the Kealy watch with Hallett, and stood him down.

Their heavy bergen rucksacks on the back seat, the two SAS officers drove down the A465 to Abergavenny and, via Llangynidr, to the dam of Talybont Reservoir. Parking the Renault close by the weirs, they donned lightweight SAS combat jackets, DMS boots and their thirty-five-pound rucksacks. They made off, with the long, easy strides of the experienced mountain men that they were, up the Tarthwynni Valley.

From a telephone a mile away in the village of Aber, Meier called de Villiers, who, with three regular Tadnams men, was parked beside the public call box close to the Storey Arms Outdoor Centre on the other side of the Beacons.

Meier returned to the Talybont weirs and clamped a bug beneath the dashboard of the Renault. The passenger's window had been left slightly open but, even if all the windows had been closed, Meier would still have been inside the car in less than two minutes, leaving no signs of entry.

Before leaving Britain, Davies had marked an Ordnance Survey map with the detailed route of the SAS 'endurance march', with highlights where the track bottlenecked in especially remote reaches.

Midweek, midwinter and during the hours of darkness it was safe to count on very few hill walkers being abroad on the Beacons. Such were the conditions required by Davies's plan.

Well after dark Meier watched the two men arrive back at the Renault. Neither showed signs of exhaustion. As they took off their boots and rucksacks their conversation centred on the Shah's flight from Iran the previous week.

As Kealy closed the boot on their wet equipment he said to his companion, 'Well, that wasn't so bad. We should give the selection lads a good run for their money on Thursday.'

'What time does it start?' the other SAS man asked.

'The three-tonners leave Hereford at 1.30 a.m. and the first walkers set out from here around 3 a.m.'

'The forecast is lousy.'

'I know but that's unlikely to stop play.'

'What's the standard weight these days?'

'Same as always,' said Kealy, 'fifty-five pounds all-up.'

'And the course?'

'Still forty-one miles to be done in a maximum of seventeen hours.'

As the Renault departed the sound in Meier's earphones faded and quickly disappeared. He switched off the receiver, for he had no need to hear more.

Over the next three days of deteriorating weather, the Clinic and their helpers familiarized themselves with the misty heights of the barren Brecon Beacons.

De Villiers had purchased his clothing and equipment from a government-surplus shop in the Strand. The owner had explained the various army-surplus items: Denison camouflage smock, OG trousers, KF shirt, khaki puttees, DMS boots and a Royal Engineers' badge fitted to a standard black beret. Ancillaries included a poncho groundsheet, hexamin stove with fuel blocks, 57-pattern webbed belt with pouches, three plastic water bottles, mess tins, eating irons and a large rucksack of the type known to airborne soldiers as a bergen.

With his hair cut short, army-style, de Villiers parked himself and his bergen on one of the wooden benches at Hereford railway station. The London train was due in twenty minutes. He opened a pack of Players No. 6 and offered a cigarette to the tall man in blue jeans and leather jacket slumped dejectedly beside him. De Villiers had selected him from among some twenty others over the past two days.

'Don't mind if I do,' was the only response.

De Villiers produced a Ronson Storm lighter and lit their cigarettes. 'Haven't seen you around,' said de Villiers, glancing sideways at the man. 'What went wrong?'

'One of their bastard staff,' the soldier grunted, 'thought I swore at him yesterday on the Fan.'

'Did you?'

The man gave a half-smile. 'Maybe. I felt more knackered than I thought was possible on the second time round. All my blisters burst. Maybe it's all for the best but I hate the thought of the lads back in

Catterick. They'll take the mickey something awful for months. I was so *sure* I'd make it. What about you?'

De Villiers was as charming as only he knew how, and as convincing. They travelled to Paddington together, and exchanged cap badges, and by the time they went their separate ways there was little de Villiers had not learnt about the SAS selection course to date and the expected horrors to come.

At 11.45 p.m. on the night of 31 January and in heavy rain, a Ford Transit van in its GPO livery backed up briefly against the perimeter fence to the rear of the SAS officers' mess. From its roof de Villiers threw down his bergen and dropped down over the high fence, breaking his landing with a standard parachute roll.

Within seconds he was hidden behind the dark walls of the NAAFI, adjacent to the regimental cookhouse. With an hour or so to wait, he settled back under a shrub, his poncho drawn over his beret. Even if Meier failed, the first stage of the evening's plans were under way and the weather forecast was hopeful: severe gales and snow on high ground.

Meier had tried to woo one of the Army Catering Corps cooks but was foiled by SAS Security. His plan had been simple: identify one of the white uniformed chefs by the bins at the rear of the cookhouse. Not difficult with binoculars from his car in Bullingham Lane. Track the man to his drinking spot in the evenings and bribe him, as part of a wager, to let a fellow soldier, Meier himself, into the camp in his company and wearing 'whites'. But, as Meier learned when he befriended a pimply ACC youngster, the SAS forbade the cookhouse personnel ever to leave camp in their uniforms. Instead there was a changing room within the cookhouse and any unrecognized cook entering the main gate would be challenged by the MOD Police to show his ID card. Furthermore, Pimples informed Meier that Scouse, the chief SAS cook, who had been there twenty years, was a terror who kept close tabs on all his staff however temporary their posting. One of his rulings was 'no strangers behind the hotplate'.

Meier racked his brains but non-technical improvisation was not his forte and when, by 10.30 p.m. that Thursday night, he had no safe means of entry to the camp, he left the matter to de Villiers's skill and drove south to Talybont.

Forty-five minutes after midnight, with the rain still drumming down,

de Villiers recognized Mike Kealy emerging from the shadows to the right-hand side of the HQ block, the direction of the officers' mess. Kealy was fully kitted out but moved quietly and easily.

De Villiers swung his bergen over his back and followed Kealy to the nearby cookhouse. He climbed the four stone steps immediately behind him and they entered together. Inside the well-lit, L-shaped room thirty or forty students and selection staff were already seated and stuffing themselves with food. There was little chatter or cama-raderie, for this was the final test of Selection Week, a milestone in the careers of the lucky few.

De Villiers kept his belt kit on. He dumped his bergen beside Kealy's and slipped a tiny radio bleeper into one of its side pockets. He joined the food queue at the hotplate, where the duty cook soon helped him to a large plate of mixed grill and a mug of hot tea. He had watched Kealy pass by the table where the instructing staff sat; the only animated group. The senior instructor, a giant of a man, greeted the captain with a smile.

'Hallo, Lofty,' Kealy smiled and took a seat at one of the tables reserved for the students.

De Villiers, careful to avoid any eye contact with students or staff, sat close to Kealy and when the latter went off to fetch a spoon, he reached across for sugar and palmed the contents of a packet of white powder into Kealy's tea.

The powder, ground down from four 250 mg tablets of chlor-propamide, would not have an immediate or predictable effect. After an hour or two Kealy would begin to feel sweaty, weak and increas-ingly disorientated, for chlorpropamide is a drug that promotes the action of insulin within the body. Kealy's blood sugar would slowly fall below a tolerable level and would leave him dangerously vul-nerable to the elements. The effects of hypoglycaemia would steadily increase to a peak, or from Kealy's point of view a nadir, somewhere between three and six hours after ingestion.

Many of the students were loners. Some were veteran sergeants, even sergeant-majors, from airborne units with years of service behind them. If these men passed into the SAS they would enter as mere troopers and take their chances of promotion alongside far younger and less experienced soldiers.

Initially over a hundred and fifty soldiers from throughout the British Army had signed on for selection. After a week's introduction to navigation and other basic skills, they were subjected to three

weeks of softening up with ever-increasing grades of difficulty. They had fallen like flies, for the SAS selection staff watched every move and circled vulture-like to pounce on the merest whiff of weakness. The unfortunates found themselves waiting on Hereford station with a one-way ticket back to their own regiment.

The fifth and last week had been a killer and, for the forty weary and blistered survivors now congregated in the cookhouse, this was the final act. Known simply as 'Endurance', the test involved each individual travelling alone over forty-one miles of difficult terrain with fifty-five pounds of equipment. Seventeen hours was the maximum time allowed but even if a man completed the course far more quickly he might still fail selection – with no reason ever given. Courses of over a hundred and sixty selectees had ended without a single man entering the SAS. No wonder then that the trainees gulped down their food in an introspective mood, paying little attention to one another. De Villiers felt happier when the instructors, saying nothing, rose from their table and the students followed suit.

Outside in the semi-darkness de Villiers kept close to Kealy. When the two three-ton Bedford lorries stopped by the Guard Room, the trainees collected their rifles and then mounted up with their bergens. De Villiers, in the rain and the shadows, moved around but did not enter the Guard Room.

The chief instructor rode in the cab of the leading lorry. Kealy, apparently keen to be treated no differently to the trainees during his self-imposed fitness jaunt, climbed into the back along with nineteen others, including de Villiers.

The vehicles whined their way through the outskirts of Hereford, dodging heaps of litter caused by the national strike.

'Guess who's joining the strike tomorrow?'

Disembodied voices in the back of de Villiers's lorry.

'I didn't know anyone was still at work.'

'Yeah, well, the gravediggers are all out as from tonight. Die now and yer old lady'll have to clear a space in the deep freeze.'

'Not in Hereford,' said a Welsh voice. 'All our diggers are part-time. Most of them are the local fire service laddies.'

By the time they reached Pontrilas at the eastern edge of the Brecon Beacons National Park most of the passengers had fallen silent in the canopied darkness. A mile from the Talybont Reservoir's dam and close to the northern rim of Talybont Forest, the Training Sergeant-Major halted the lorries in a car park beside Tarthwynni

river. There was no shouting of orders. Each man had received his detailed instructions back in Hereford. The bergens were weighed on spring scales and Lofty, the Training Sergeant Major, waved the trainees off one by one into the night.

De Villiers moved into the bushes and, when Kealy set out, one of the first to go, he followed some fifteen yards behind. He did not switch on his tracker unit for the bleeper but kept in touch with Kealy's outline, different from the students' because of his old-fashioned bergen. Most of the students also sported Denison cam-smocks but Kealy wore the shorter SAS windproof. With only a fifteen-pound bergen load and, fit though he undoubtedly was, de Villiers still found it hard work to keep up.

All the trainees carried three-quarter-length foul-weather coats made of plastic-coated nylon. 'Don't ever march in 'em,' was the Training Sergeant-Major's advice. 'You'll get as wet from your own sweat as you ever will from the rain. Then, next day, any downwind opposition will smell you a mile off. Just use them when you're leaguered up and it's pissing down.'

Although few of the remaining trainees knew one another by name, some had become aware of Kealy's identity. He had joined in their hill-slogging tests on two previous occasions and the word had spread that he was a regular SAS officer with a remarkable record. Kealy kept himself to himself. The muted adulation of the trainees, the sidelong glances and whispered comments as the news spread of a hero in their midst, made him feel awkward and embarrassed. Even so the advantages of training alongside these eager 'wannabees' outweighed the niggles because they were at peak fitness and many were ten years his junior. He knew that, by measuring his own performance directly against theirs, he would be sure that he could match the stamina of any man in the squadron he was about to command.

For two hours Kealy went well despite the darkness, driving rain, a steep climb of two thousand feet over broken ground and areas where the snow lay knee-deep.

Towards 5.30 a.m., nearing the summit plateau of Waun Rydd, de Villiers noticed with satisfaction that Kealy's gait showed signs of weakening. For a while he would climb steadily with a deliberate step, then follow a zigzag course for a period, then once again head directly west as though on a bearing to some point just visible to his front.

As Kealy's speed lessened, lone trainees began to catch up, and when they reached the plateau, marked by the cairns of Carn Pica, there were five or six soldiers huddled together and shouting against the shriek of a sleet-laden south-westerly with gusts up to seventy knots. De Villiers squatted by his bergen some distance upwind as Kealy reached the group of trainees. He concentrated on remaining out of sight of the soldiers without losing touch with Kealy.

Approaching the students at the cairns, Kealy exhorted them to carry on west but most were already shivering and fearful of exposure. Two decided to head north to seek shelter in the valleys of Nantlannerch and the others headed south for the Neuadd reservoirs. Kealy shrugged and took a compass bearing due west. He knew the subtle symptoms of hypothermia only too well. He had taught many a young soldier how to recognize the dangers of exposure. He also knew how to avoid its onset despite the very worst conditions. Rule one was to realize that, no matter how clever a man may be at spotting others becoming hypothermic, *no one* can be sure of recognizing his own deterioration, simply because, as the body core temperature drops, the body draws heat from the head. The brain begins to slow down, taking away the normal state of awareness and the will needed for self-preservation.

An undrugged Kealy would have had no trouble with the simple eight-hour slog from Talybont to the Storey Arms. The weather was atrocious and he wore light clothing as was his custom and that of many other SAS mountain troop veterans. With heavy pack, rifle and cotton clothing, Kealy had many times completed far longer marches in more dangerous conditions. He knew every step of the route and, unlike many others that night, he never lost his way. Physically in fine shape, for he jogged daily when involved in desk work, he had recently joined the SAS trainees on two snow-bound forced marches and showed himself to be as fit or fitter than the best of them.

Kealy knew that trained airborne troops can travel, at temperatures below minus fifty degrees centigrade with blizzards producing a chill factor of minus seventy degrees centigrade, for many miles carrying heavy packs day after day, and wearing only breathable cotton clothes. Thoroughly soaked with sweat, 'body-thin' from *weeks* of inadequate rations and lack of sleep, they nevertheless avoid hypothermia so long as they keep moving fast enough to maintain their body core temperature above thirty-three degrees centigrade.

He knew that he was in a far superior state to such a scenario

because, far from body-thin, he was well fed and his metabolism was acting like a factory, pumping out heat from the large breakfast he was still digesting. Even without the Mars bars that he ate whenever he felt his energy flag slightly, he would, if unaffected by the drug, have been more than capable of dealing with the conditions. Severe they certainly were from a standard mountain-walker's point of view, but not from Kealy's. At worst the wind strength gusted to seventy knots and the air temperature was as low as minus nine degrees centigrade, but this merely produced a chill factor of minus fifty degrees centigrade – no problem as long as he kept moving.

Kealy knew all this and was fully aware that he must not stop. The curious state of lassitude and the overwhelming desire to rest that he was so unexpectedly experiencing must, he determined, be a temporary setback. Something he had eaten perhaps, a chill on the stomach, or a bug? He fought doggedly against the inertia and, luckily, the worst conditions were, after Carn Pica, all behind him.

It was getting lighter. The going was flat in place of the tortuous climbing to date. There was now a well-used hilltop path underfoot from which most of the snow had been blown. Previously he had struggled up a steep, tussocked hillside through knee-deep drifts. The path was one he had often used and led west along the ridge of the Brecons, dropping into a sheltered pass at Bwlch y Fan. He had only to continue at a pace consistent with maintaining his body heat and all would soon be well.

'Fight the drowsiness ... All will soon be well.' He repeated this to himself and concentrated on the track to his immediate front. 'Always a little further ... Always a little further.'

A few other students still persevered and, over the next hour, two or three noticed Kealy's stumbling westerly progress. Knowing who he was, their own flagging morale was greatly boosted. If Major Kealy DSO, SAS veteran and hero, was finding the going hard then *they* must be pretty damn tough to be *en route* still. One or two offered him help, gloves, a foul-weather jacket. He tripped on a rock and bruised his knees slightly. After a short rest to recover, he shook himself and carried on. He was damned if he would give in or accept help. He flung away the spare gloves and the jacket.

If things *did* get too bad he would remove one or two of the bricks that he carried to make up the statutory fifty-five-pound bergen weight. But he was sure he would get his second wind back before such a step became necessary. He estimated that some one thousand

yards up the track, which headed WNW, he would slow down to negotiate the ridgeline bottleneck of the Bwlch y Ddwyallt and join the well-trodden tourist path from the Pentwyn Rescue Post.

By 8 a.m. he felt the leaden weight of inertia begin to lighten and slowly, as his blood-sugar level eased back to normal, his brain was again fed with the sugar it required.

The wind howled by in powerful, horizontal waves but Kealy knew he would be fine *unless* he stopped to rest. He jammed his cloth hat down, its flaps covering his ears. His bergen covered his back and his waist. Things were on the up.

As Kealy passed by two small ponds, de Villiers glimpsed through the hood of his heavy windproof a solitary Dayglo-tipped metal pole propped up by a pile of loose rocks. Reaching into his inner pocket, he produced a compact Motorola walkie-talkie. He estimated arrival within the next twenty minutes. At 8.30 a.m., in conditions of mist and lashing sleet, Kealy was halted by a large man in an orange cagoule. Standing astride the track, the man shouted, 'Please help, my wife is dying. She is blue with cold.'

The one thing Kealy had no desire to do was to stop, even briefly. He was going well now, savouring the gradual withdrawal of the leaden miasma he had fought against since Carn Pica. But he was at heart quite unable to turn down a cry for help. Swearing to himself, he nodded to the man and gestured for him to lead on.

Some thirty yards through the mist to the side of the track and half hidden by a shallow depression, was a four-man igloo tent in army camouflage colours. Here the man stopped. Kealy shrugged off his bergen, automatically feeling for the first-aid pouch that hung over his backside between the water-bottle containers. In the dim light of the tent Kealy perceived two men sitting back with orange cagoules. Both smiled at him. The man who had stopped him outside was bent over a fourth person inside a sleeping bag.

As Kealy carefully wiped his eyes with his hands, for he still had trouble with his contact lenses, he felt a hardness pressed against the small of his back.

'Do nothing stupid, Major Kealy. We are armed and you are in no fit state to cause trouble. Simply lie back against the wall of the tent and look into the light.'

Kealy did as he was told, half wondering if Lofty and his staff had added a new and unexpected twist to the trainees' endurance test. He screwed up his eyes against the bright light that shone in his face.

He heard a soft, mechanical whirr as of a cine camera.

After the accusations were over, along with Kealy's bemused denials, his arms were pinioned, his shirt and windproof peeled back and a hypodermic needle inserted into the fold of soft skin under his armpit. Within seconds he lost consciousness as the insulin surged through his veins, and the Tadnams men, helped by de Villiers, eased his body out of the tent.

Taking great care with their footprints, de Villiers and one other carried Kealy to the side of the track and manoeuvred his limp arms into the bergen's shoulder straps. Propping him into a half-sitting, half-lying position against the bergen, they removed his hat and placed his rifle some distance away as though discarded. The other two men removed the bleeper, packed up the tent, leaving no signs of its presence, and all four then headed along the footpath to Pencelli.

Now that Kealy was motionless, his body began to lose heat rapidly through convection, conduction, radiation and evaporation. Quite when he died is open to doubt.

At close on 9 a.m. two trainees found his body. One, a captain, thought he felt a faint pulse but could not be certain. They did the best they could and Signaller Simon Maylor spent many hours pressed body to body against Kealy inside a survival bag within a hastily fashioned snow-hole.

Twenty hours later improved conditions allowed a helicopter to land. Kealy's body was airlifted to Brecon Hospital Mortuary for an autopsy. All signs of chlorpropamide and excess insulin had long since dispersed within his bloodstream.

There were those among Kealy's friends who found it hard to believe that a fit and experienced mountain man, such as he, could have died in such circumstances but, since there was no other possible explanation, even the canniest of SAS staffers agreed that 'anyone can die of hypothermia in such conditions'. That was the obvious answer. There could have been no foul play, for there was no one with any motive. Far from it, Kealy was a friend to all who knew him.

The Brecon coroner, Trevor Evans, discussed the matter with the Chief Constable of the South Powys Division and reiterated on several occasions that he felt the SAS should be more careful with their trainees.

Mike Kealy's grieving parents remained baffled. They knew their son, a man of enormous common sense and practicality, would have

removed bricks from his bergen long before he reached the stage of lying down and giving up. 'Anyone can die of hypothermia,' they were told by sympathetic old friends. But they knew Mike was not 'anyone'.

The media learned of the tragedy and the angle they took to explain the conundrum of so experienced a man simply lying down to die was as unfortunate as it was sensational.

Sun:	'SAS hero Major Mike Kealy lost his last battle ... a desperate attempt to show he was still as tough as his young recruits.'
Western Mail:	'SAS Major died trying to outdo recruits.'
Daily Telegraph:	'SAS hero died in snow trying to prove fitness.'

Kealy's close friend Major Tony Shaw concluded, 'He was an experienced hill-walker who knew the risks well. He had instructed soldiers and knew the effects of hypothermia and how to avoid them. He looked at this test purely in subjective but positive terms: he wore light clothes to avoid overheating and to increase his speed. When he realized he had miscalculated it was too late, but he could not give up and walk off the hill. Once he had decided to undertake the task, it was in his nature that nothing would be allowed to stop him.'

The greatest irony was that Mike Kealy did *not* lose his last battle against the elements. He won because of his doggedness and lost his life because of his innate kindness.

Major Kealy's obituary appeared in the *Daily Telegraph (The Times* was on strike) on 6 February 1979. Tony Shaw wrote of him, 'He stands as a memorial to all that is courageous and honest. We do not often see his like. He will be sadly missed.'

25

... For ten years they had seen each other well away from Tokai and in between Anne's regular visits to her husband's hospital bed. Their love matured and gradually impinged upon de Villiers's innermost psyche. Then, suddenly, Jan Fontaine contracted jaundice at the hospital and died. His unexpected death forced de Villiers to confront an issue he had studiously avoided. He knew that he resented, even hated, Fontaine, but he never for a moment considered the easy solution of a hospital accident. That would be murder, not impersonal business and would sully the pure and solid core of his love. Likewise he knew he could never propose marriage while he was still earning his living by killing.

He lived by the unwritten but rigid law of the contract killer. If he took on a job, he would see it through to the end. He would complete those contracts still in hand but he would take on no new work.

In the African winter of 1986, two months after the death of Jan Fontaine, de Villiers flew with Anne to Pietersburg and hired a Land Rover. Unhampered by time limitations, they wandered the Transvaal, camping among the quiet pools and mist-laden hills of Magoebaskloef, to the night calls of Samango monkeys. Then, high in the Woodbush Mountains, they backpacked through forests of kiepersol and cabbage trees, gazing up at giant ironwoods alive with birdsong.

Further north they crossed the Soutpansberg range and the Limpopo river into Zimbabwe. De Villiers took local advice to find the most famous of the giant baobabs, over a thousand years old, that tower over the thorn and mopane trees of the savannah. Ignoring ant bites, he clambered about with his camera in search of weird angles.

The best of South Africa's many wild game parks was undoubtedly the Kruger National in Eastern Transvaal, so they recrossed the Limpopo and entered the lush riverine forests to the south of Phalaborwa.

Along the Wolhuter Trail they spotted oribi, sable and white

rhinos and, resting a while in quiet shade beside a game pool, de Villiers asked Anne whether she would say yes if ever he asked her to marry him. She answered with a question.

'I know you cannot talk about your work. I have always known not to pester you with my curiosity. But, if we become as one, will you trust me enough to confide in me?'

De Villiers looked down at his hands and spoke slowly. 'My life with you is a million miles from my business activities. They are incompatible and I have decided, now you are free, to change my job. This will take a little while because there are things which I am bound to see through. When I leave you next month I shall deal with the outstanding business as quickly as possible.'

'And then?'

'Then I will settle in the Cape. I will find work with animal photography and wait for your answer.'

Somewhere north of the Malelane Gate to the park a wildebeest crashed out on to the red-dirt *murrim* track ahead of the Land Rover. De Villiers swerved and, by misfortune, one wheel struck a sharp rock. The vehicle careered into a boulder and de Villiers was knocked unconscious.

When he came to his senses he found that Anne was in pain. Her safety-belt had saved her face but her legs had been driven backwards and he suspected internal injuries. After giving her painkilling pills, he made for the Malelane Gate, thumbing a lift from a passing truck to the nearest telephone. An ambulance took them to Nelspruit Hospital but de Villiers was adamant that she must have only the best treatment and, against the doctors' advice, flew with her from Nelspruit to Johannesburg, having caught the daily plane by the skin of their teeth.

That evening Anne was sweating, her pulse racing, and she was in shock. The doctor carefully lifted her legs one by one. As her right leg moved, she screamed. Her blood pressure was low. After blood tests and a cross-match she was given a Dextran drip and an X-ray. Within minutes another doctor cheerfully announced to de Villiers that Anne had broken her pelvis: nothing that a simple operation would not fix, but the immediate problem, rendered critical by the delay before hospitalization, was internal loss of blood. Once the cross-match results were available, at least four pints would be replaced.

While de Villiers's own cuts were being cleaned up more

thoroughly than at Nelspruit, bottles of the correct blood group were removed from the hospital blood bank, warmed up and given to Anne via the drip.

The operation went smoothly and three months later Anne was well enough to ride again at La Pergole ...

26

Davies sensed an urgency, an impatience quite at odds with the cool deliberation of the de Villiers that he knew, to nail down the last two Dhofar targets. For the past seven years the Clinic had kept busy enough, achieving some spectacular successes, and their reputation within the contract world was as high as ever.

Three million dollars was not a sum to be sneezed at but, since the late Sheikh Amr's son Bakhait was still not chivvying the Clinic to complete the *thaa'r*, they had continued to postpone further research work into identifying the remaining targets.

They knew from the data originally furnished by Sheikh Amr that the targets were thought to be Sultanate soldiers, not SAS men. This information revealed that Mahad, Amr's second son by his first wife, was killed in the early stages of an operation on 4 January 1975 close to the communist base of Sherishitti. He was killed by heavy mortar fire from the SAF position on the twin-headed mountain overlooking Sherishitti. Tama'an, Amr's second son by his second wife, had fought with the Bin Dhahaib unit and was killed on 19 September 1975 at the close-quarter battle of Zakhir by a shell from an armoured car.

The records of both relevant army actions were held inside Oman by the regiments involved at the time, with some files in general records in the Bayt al Falaj Headquarters. To identify the officers or NCOs responsible for killing the sheikh's sons required access to those records.

Despite the Clinic's achievement of official No Foul Play verdicts with both Milling and Kealy, there had been in each case ominous signs of official awareness from some unidentifiable quarter. Davies was no longer willing to risk his neck anywhere near Hereford and the three members of the Clinic were in all likelihood logged on the

immigration files of the Omani Police. It would be at best foolish for any of them to risk putting their heads into the Omani noose again. With virtually no tourists coming into that country, the police were able to scrutinize each and every new entrant by the No Objection Certificate method. So, year after year, the risk had remained too great, despite the potential reward, at least while the Clinic had ample work elsewhere.

Since neither the Hereford nor the Oman dangers had diminished, Davies did not find de Villiers's new enthusiasm remotely appealing. He said as much but de Villiers remained obdurate.

'We must approach from a different angle.'

'We could send someone else,' Davies suggested hopefully. 'The agency have suitable people.'

'You and Meier would be happy with a thirty percent cut in the fee? That is what we would agree to, should we subcontract any part of the identity-locating process. Never mind our reputation for self-sufficiency.'

'Are you saying *we* must re-enter Oman?'

'Negative,' de Villiers thought aloud. 'We need information *without* going in there. Someone already in Oman must work for us ... Why not that old brigadier, the friend of the sultan? He was very helpful before ... He may remember me.'

'You mean Brigadier Maxwell. He *will* remember you,' Davies expostulated. 'Too right. He will associate you directly with Milling's death,' added Meier.

De Villiers shook his head. 'That is an assumption. Maybe you are right: maybe not. We do not know that he ever connected the enquiries of two harmless American historians with Milling's subsequent accidental death. It is possible the police did not make enquiries and never even questioned the Brigadier.'

'But the man who followed us, the Sultanate officer, possibly Omani Intelligence Service, what of him? If OIS knew about us they are bound to have traced back our visit to the Brigadier. They will know he gave us Milling's name.'

'Perhaps not. I say it is worth trying since nothing is lost if the brigadier proves to be suspicious, unhelpful and tells Omani security about our call. On the other hand, if he merely remembers us as diligent researchers, with no sinister connections, he may well tell us who was in command of the Armoured Car Squadron at Zakhir on 19 September 1975. After all he is the official biographer of the

Sultan's Armed Forces. If he doesn't know, no one will.'

The brigadier had not been well for some time and was recuperating in his new home at Sidab, a gift from the Sultan, when de Villiers finally made telephone contact. Maxwell's old retainer Darwish answered and reluctantly fetched him from his afternoon siesta. The brigadier's arthritis was causing him a great deal of discomfort in addition to the effects of a more serious illness, but his brain was as keen as ever and his great warmth of character was evident even over the telephone. Of course he remembered their meeting at Bayt al Falaj. He would be only too happy to help with any further enquiries.

De Villiers, confident that Maxwell was genuinely keen to help and harboured no suspicions due to the Milling affair, decided not to say how sorry he was about the helicopter pilot's accident. He merely launched straight into his questions.

'In September 1975 ...'

'Yes, yes,' said Maxwell, 'the closing stages of the war.'

'There was a battle between communists and the sultan's armoured cars in a place called Zakhir.'

'Not Zakhir,' the brigadier chuckled. 'No, my friend. The region is known as Defa but there is a solitary tree called the Zakhir Tree and, for reasons of local geography, there were a number of bitter engagements there over the years.'

'Would you have any detailed accounts of that particular period in '75?'

'Absolutely. No problem at all. Since we last spoke there have been two or three excellent books. All obtainable through the book trade.'

He gave de Villiers three titles with the publishers' details. 'I feel sure you will find all the data you need in these works but, if you still lack information, let me know.'

De Villiers was effusive in his thanks. 'One more question, Brigadier, who was the commander of the Armoured Car Squadron at that time? Perhaps I could get accurate details from him.'

'Yes, indeed.' Maxwell thought this was an excellent idea. 'It was Patrick Brook, a cavalry man, of course, and ... no, wait a minute. Patrick left us in early '75, so it must have been his successor, another donkey-walloper, as we call them, named Mike Marman. Bit of a wild character but an excellent officer — 9th/12th Lancers as I recall. He'll tell you all about the Zakhir Tree contact.'

'Is he in Oman still?' de Villiers prompted.

'Gracious no. Left long ago. Most chaps only serve for two or three years over here. I expect he's back in Britain or Germany. You should contact the Anglo-Omani Society or the SAF Association in London. They keep the addresses of all ex-Sultan's Armed Forces people.'

De Villiers thanked the brigadier again and promised he would send him a copy of the finished history on its publication.

In the autumn Davies began full-time work on the Zakhir research. That October he attended the monthly lecture meeting of the Anglo-Omani Society at their usual venue, Bury House, 33 Bury Street in St James's. Wearing a city suit and his old Parachute Regiment tie, Davies turned up at 6.30 p.m. and joined a dribble of single men and married couples, who ascended to the upstairs meeting room without any form of identity or ticket check.

He found some forty chairs lined in rows opposite a small screen and a dozen or so guests being helped to sherry and cocktail biscuits by a friendly waitress. One or two solitary figures stood around looking awkward, and Davies moved in. Two of the men he approached, an oilman from Petroleum Development Oman and an ex-Scots Guards NCO, had not been in Oman in 1975 but a third, an engineer specializing in water drilling equipment and an obvious extrovert, had worked in Dhofar on and off from 1974 until 1977. He knew many SAF officers and was an avid reader of anything and everything to do with the Dhofar Campaign.

Davies steered the conversation round to the Zakhir event and listened to a flow of enthusiastic comment from the engineer. No, Zakhir had not been a SAF operation. The SAS were the main combatants and they had indeed received vital support from the Armoured Cars. A cavalry officer named Simon Marriott had distinguished himself but he was not the Armoured Car Squadron boss. That had been Mike Marman, a splendid fellow, well known for shooting up an SAF officers' mess with a Kalashnikov assault rifle during a well-lubricated celebration.

'Is Marman here today?' Davies asked.

'No, I've never seen him at one of these meetings,' the engineer said, 'but then I only come infrequently as a guest. I'm not a member of the Society. If you want to contact Marman, or any ex-SAF chap, just ask the Secretary for the members' address list. Give me your

address and I will let you know if I come across Marman's where-abouts.'

Davies left him one of the Tadnams postbox addresses. He was now certain that Marman was their man but he double checked all the same, obtaining back copies of the Regimental Journal of Marman's unit, the 9th/12th Royal Lancers. In their 1976 magazine he found a short article written by Marman that gave graphic detail of various actions fought by Marman in Dhofar from October 1974 until mid 1976. It clearly stated that he had taken command of the Armoured Car Squadron in January 1975. Now Davies had only to find the man.

He was unable to obtain an address from the Anglo-Omani Society but a phone call to the SAF Association's Secretary elicited a forwarding address via Lloyds Bank in Reading. Subsequent ferreting traced the elusive major to his most recent domicile, a tiny house in Clapham.

Orders to Middle East bookshops unearthed, at outrageous prices, the three books Colin Maxwell had recommended. *Who Dares Wins* by Tony Geraghty did not mention the Zakhir event, but *We Won a War* by John Akehurst provided Davies with an excellent photograph of Marman's face, and *SAS: Operation Oman* by Tony Jeapes gave an account of the Zakhir Tree fighting and the key involvement of 'a troop of Saladin armoured cars from Defa'.

On 15 September 1975 *The Times* reported that a priceless Rembrandt had been slashed by a nutter, a national steel strike was imminent, the Prince of Wales was in Papua, the price of cigarettes had risen to forty-five pence a packet, a bilingual secretary in London now earned three thousand pounds a year, Henry Fonda had opened a one-man show in Piccadilly and *Fawlty Towers* had had its first showing on television. There was, of course, no mention of Dhofar, a country whose existence was unknown to the vast majority of Westerners. At dawn that day an SAS troop in western Dhofar planned an attack on the communist guerrillas known to use the region of the Zakhir Tree as a base for Katyusha rocket launchers. The SAS troop included a tough bunch of individualists, Sergeant Rover Slatting, his close friend Danny, Wee Grumpy, Matt and the muscle-bound Tony Fleming.

From their SAF base at Defa, thirteen SAS men set out with two ex-PFLO guides. The ground was sodden and a clinging mist

compounded the darkness of the night. The guides failed to find the Zakhir Tree and, shortly before dawn, the SAS men split into two groups, the better to find their target. Danny, a corporal, moved ahead with one guide and finally located the tree. He also spotted many fresh bootprints and smelled smoke-dried meat. On his way back to Sergeant Slatting's SAS group he glimpsed an *adoo* patrol through the mist. All hell broke loose. The SAS killed three guerrillas, and their own man, Geordie Small, died of blood loss from the femoral artery. Heavily outgunned, and without the benefit of the surprise they had sought, Slatting's group of seven men lay low in the mire of wet clay amid a jungle of thorn bushes.

Tony Fleming was shot through the spine and lost the use of his legs. Two men dragged him to the centre of their hide and, as they did so, a guerrilla leapt up some ten paces behind them. Slatting turned and killed him.

A murderous crackle of bullets hid the noise of *adoo* with AK47s and grenades belly-crawling from bush to bush towards the SAS survivors. Branches snapped and broke all around, torn away by high-velocity bullets. To stand up was to invite instant death. The conditions of mist and thick scrub demanded instant reaction to any hostile movement. The *adoo* closed in with cunning and patience.

Slatting and Danny between them accounted for four more of the guerrillas with their skilled sharpshooting. Beside them the fifteen-stone Tony Fleming lay white and still. They knew that to attempt a withdrawal, to move him, would kill him. Slatting radioed his officer. He and his men would stay where they were until they were overrun or until the SAF back-up group could reach the Zakhir Tree.

One of his men nudged Slatting. The SAF group *had* already arrived. Through a gap in the mist they could be seen advancing down the opposite side of the valley and directly towards their position. A 'British' officer, fair-skinned and peak-capped, led the assault, his men stretched out on either side in their green uniforms and *shemaghs*. A feeling of relief swept the beleaguered SAS but was dashed when the 'US Cavalry' turned out to be regular Yemeni troops from South Yemen in support of the *adoo*. Their fire was intense and within minutes every one of the SAS men was hit.

A bullet passed through Slatting's neck and knocked him down. He staggered to his knees but was wounded twice more. Unable to move, he lay listening to his comrades announcing their own injuries.

All around them the *adoo* crawled closer. Some were already a mere twenty yards from the thorny SAS redoubt.

Danny saw a movement and blasted an *adoo* from his cover with an M79 grenade. A minute later an *adoo* grenade exploded by Danny's side but the shrapnel miraculously scythed by above him. The SAS medic crawled among the wounded, applying dressings and morphine-laden syrettes. SAS counter-fire began to slacken and the *adoo*, encouraged, closed in. Slatting was struck by a fourth bullet but remained conscious.

At 8.30 a.m. the Armoured Cars and an SAF platoon under Captain Alistair Laurie Walker managed to work their way forward to a position overlooking the *adoo* and raked them with 76-mm shell fire, killing many regular People's Democratic Republic of Yemen troops and PFLO guerrillas, including Tama'an bin Amr.

By 9 a.m. only the melancholy chime of the thornbird and the occasional low curse of tired soldiers sounded through the mist below the Zakhir Tree. The bodies of the guerrilla dead and dying remained among the bushes long after the armoured cars had withdrawn to their Defa stronghold with the SAS wounded stretched across their engine decks.

27

... Tree-lined Silom Road is the business heart of Bangkok but, behind the high walls that skirt one section of its rod-straight length, a seminary of nuns inhabit a strict Carmelite convent and it is this building that serves as a convenient marker for the entrance to the sex capital of the world, two great parallel roads, Patpong One and Two.

Brothels are forbidden by Thai law but nine hundred and fifty, describing themselves as bars or clubs, thrive in Bangkok alone, with names such as Pussy Galore or Purple Pleasure. For gay visitors, Pretty Boy Lounge, the Golden Cock and many others await their patronage. The bustling pavements throng with pimps of both sexes trawling for clients. Inside the cramped neon dens their sharp-end colleagues, clad only in high-heeled shoes, hypnotize with oiled

buttock and sequinned nipple. Most are under eighteen, many far younger and, unlike the majority of their European counterparts, they sport firm, lithe bodies that would cause lip-tremble in the most elderly of monks. They pose and pout from revolving carousels, or upturned fruit boxes, so that their shaven crotches gyrate at nose level to their audience.

The *farangs*, foreigners, flock to 'Sin City' in their hundreds of thousands, AIDS notwithstanding, for where else could they find such abundance of youth and beauty cheaply available and amenable to every conceivable deviance?

Meier indulged in an annual tour of Far Eastern sex cities and seldom omitted a Bangkok visit, usually for a four-day stint. Giving himself wholly to the cause of sensual gratification from 5.30 p.m. until 2 a.m., he would sleep soundly for eight hours in his fifth-floor executive suite at the Bangkok Hilton. After breakfast in bed he would pass the day by the hotel's spacious figure-of-eight outdoor pool with a supply of subscription magazines that were his greatest joy: hi-tech electrical and mechanical engineering titles and a medley of publications for model cars and aircraft enthusiasts.

On his first evening in Bangkok, Meier normally took in a sex show to stimulate the level of his prurience. This invariably consisted of pretty pubescents in the act and ladies with acrobatic genitalia opening Pepsi bottles, fire-eating and causing bananas or ping-pong balls to disappear.

October was the end of the rainy season, averaging eighty-four degrees Fahrenheit of clammy humidity. Meier liked to be driven around town in the early evening like some fat vulture, beak a-dribble with anticipation, circling fields of carcasses before descent and satiation.

For five hundred *baht*, on the second evening of his 1986 visit, Meier found an air-conditioned Mercedes with plastic flowers around its steering wheel and a less than normally talkative driver.

But for the girls of the New Petchburi and Sukumvit Road area the tour was unimpressive. Straight streets, crazy cat's cradles of overhead wires, smog from diesel pollution, a fetid river stench from the Chao Phraya and everywhere giant hoardings advertising Marlboro, Seiko and Sony. Young Thai bodies in their thousands nightly welcomed the humping *farangs*, Meier chuckled to himself, in order to balance the huge Thai import bill with their vital contribution to the nation's invisible exports.

The Mercedes dropped Meier at the *soi*, or small street, close to his hotel and in front of the Cleopatra Massage Parlor. Joining a small throng of tourists, he put on his spectacles and peered into a brilliantly lit auditorium in which sat a hundred or more bikini-clad Thai girls. Later there would be two or three hundred of them but now, at 5.45 p.m., business was just beginning. Meier liked this best as he knew the girls were at their cleanest. He called for the General Manager and asked for his favourite girl of the previous year. She had gone away, beamed the Thai flesh-keeper, but he would happily make recommendations.

Meier settled on number 89, Voraluk, and her younger friend Tui. All the girls in the dazzling goldfish bowl sported hand-held number plates to facilitate selection, and the pair gave beaming smiles when hailed to Meier's side.

The three took coffee together in a nearby lounge. Meier made no attempt to talk and merely sat with his coffee mentally devouring the girls. They did not mind and chattered merrily enough. When Meier rose, straightening the front of his safari jacket to cover any visible sign of his state of mind, the girls took his hands and, giggling, led him to the lift and thence to an upstairs room, on the way collecting condoms, key and hygiene items from a fat floor lady.

The room was plush with sofa, bed, bath and, on a section of tiled floor, an outsize air-bed. Tui explored Meier's mouth with her tongue while Voraluk undressed all three of them and bathed Meier thoroughly.

With a sweet-smelling unguent, Tui anointed the air-bed and her own body. Meier was laid on the bed and the girls alternately massaged his body with great care and total intimacy. Voraluk lay beneath and facing Meier while the lighter Tui snaked her oiled body up and down over his back in the time-honoured fashion of the Thai body-body massage. Her pubic mound, her stomach and breasts took over the work of the hands of a European masseuse. In a while the wonderful movement from above caused Meier to penetrate Voraluk but Tui seemed to sense the event. She rose, disengaged them and turned Meier around. Then, with Voraluk still below him, continued her massage for a further ten minutes. Her expertise lay in keeping her client at the very brink of release.

The two girls dried Meier down, led him to the bed to attend his instructions and afterwards showered him before returning him to the General Manager's office. He paid six thousand *baht* and praised

his host for the continued excellence of the Cleopatra.

Tui reappeared in a smart blouse and skirt and drove Meier in her own Toyota to the Fish Supermarket in Sukumvit Road. With a trolley, they plundered displays of red mullet, snapper, grouper, sea bass and many other species. A uniformed attendant cooked the fish on the spot and they drank their meal down with glasses of local *sanuk* amid a bustle of *farangs*. Meier took his leave of Tui, for the urge was again upon him, and summoned a three-wheel *tuk-tuk* to take him to the Grace Hotel, locally known as the Pussy Supermarket. This adjoins the Arab ghetto in Soi Nana Nua, an ugly block of dirty skyscrapers sprinkled at base level with a smatter of mosques and pseudo-minarets.

Meier passed through the dingy lobby of the Grace wrinkling his nose at the shish kebab and curry odours from the adjacent Arab restaurant, a place of rice and belly dancers. He descended a staircase and entered a dimly lit basement lined with a long, narrow bar and prowled by over two hundred freelance prostitutes.

Every manner of client dallied at the bar, drank in the many small booths or propped up the pillars that gave the Coffee Shop its aspect of subterranean nastiness. Cigar smoke swirled around these pillars like fingers of mist about stalagmites, and everywhere were hungry eyes and stiffened loins. It was the sort of noisome chamber of erotica Meier loved. He took a whisky to a vacant booth and let the atmosphere sink in.

The low, predatory babble of Western businessmen and robed Arabs was punctured from time to time by the crude shouting of British, Dutch or German yobs and crescendos of 'yeah, yeah' from the jukebox.

Lone druggies and alcoholics were out of place, for this was the court of the sex goddess. Tarts of every age and background were on offer, slowly sweeping the cavern for business. Many were part-timers moonlighting for extra cash, to buy a car perhaps, or new clothes for their children. In Bangkok there are over two hundred thousand girls and an unknown number of boys living wholly or partly by sex earnings. Since an income from prostitution can be ten times that of a standard city job, small wonder many succumb to the temptation despite the dangers.

For an hour Meier turned down the callers at his booth, narrowly eliminating a dark thirty-year-old with large firm breasts and wasp-waist clad in a crocodile jumpsuit. He settled for an elfin-featured

thirteen-year-old in a school uniform. She led him to a tiny room, some blocks away from the Grace Hotel, where she kept a baby in a brightly coloured cot.

Meier stayed until 1 a.m. and marvelled at her skill. She spoke passable American English in her sing-song way and told him he was big. Many *farangs*, she said, were smelly, and Japanese so small she had to use a special small condom like a finger-stall; normal-sized ones, she said, just slid off.

Back at the Hilton, Meier was welcomed by the General Manager, a charming man who had recently moved from a major Hong Kong hotel that he had run for many years. Meier ordered a Mercedes for the morrow to take him to Pattaya Beach, down the coast of the Gulf of Siam: a place of sun and sand as well as sex.

At 10.30 a.m. he was woken with breakfast and the *Bangkok Post*. He was especially interested in the London kidnapping of Israeli nuclear technician Mordechai Vanunu and extremely annoyed when a loud knocking on the door of his suite turned out to be an unexpected call by de Villiers.

'Try to look happy to see me.'

Meier grunted and wiped crumbs from his lips.

'To what do I owe this enormous pleasure?'

De Villiers, it transpired, had been at work in Melbourne when a call had come through from Davies. He had decided to fly via Bangkok just in case Meier proved reluctant to withdraw from his Thai pursuits, as had happened on previous occasions.

'We leave for London on this evening's flight.'

Meier cancelled his Mercedes, silently cursing both Davies and de Villiers...

28

Douggie Walker had managed the Antelope pub for a good many years. Like his soppy black labrador, Sam, who loved the clamour and life of the main downstairs bar, Douggie was a large and amiable figure. The Antelope's clientele, on the evening of Thursday 30 October 1986 was as rowdy as ever, a mix of all backgrounds, with always a good many strangers to add to the atmosphere.

At the bar Douggie recognized a gang of ex-army regulars and accepted the offer of a pint from Keith Ryde, one of several Oman Army officers who used the pub as a rendezvous, usually at lunchtime.

The talk was of a yuppy named Jeremy Bamber who two days earlier had been jailed for life for the callous murder of five members of his own family. Hoping to inherit a fortune, he had intended that his sister be blamed. A heated conversation developed on the topic. Douggie, Ryde, 'Smash' Smith-Piggott and Jackson could be counted on, under the gentle influence of Benskin's draught bitter, to escalate the most unlikely of subjects into a major debate. Mike Marman was normally in the thick of it all but that evening he felt a touch subdued and decided to go home for a quiet read and an early night.

On the wrong side of forty and unemployed, he was temporarily feeling a touch sorry for himself. His mood probably stemmed from his last meeting with his fiery but beautiful ex-wife, Rose May. The previous weekend he had called at her Kensington flat to take their sons out for the day. There had been a fierce argument that still tasted bitter to him. Sometimes they seemed to hate each other but then he would notice afresh her blonde hair and goddess-like figure, her classic Slav features and those lovely, far-away eyes and wonder how he and Rose May had ever grown apart.

She was born Rose May Cassel-Kokczynska, of a Swedish mother and a dashing Polish officer who had taken part in the last recorded cavalry charge against German tanks in 1939, spent the war years in Soviet camps, then settled in England, where Rose May was born. When Mike met her, on holiday in Sardinia, she was head teacher at her own Montessori school in Kensington.

(photograph by kind permission of Soldier 'I')

Mirbat.

David Mason in the Middle East in 1977.

Darrell Hallett in Berkshire in 1979.

(photograph by kind permission of Jock Logan)

Left to right: Barry and Meryl Davies, Rose and Jock Logan, Pauline and 'Mac' in the Crystal Room, Hereford.

He was at first everything that Rose May had dreamed of: a charming, handsome cavalry officer, regimental skier, communist-fighter and an unashamed lover of the good life. When she knew him better she found he needed mothering and this was doubly attractive.

Marman looked about the Antelope, searching for he knew not what. I should not have left the army, he thought; that was when things started to go seriously wrong between us. He looked at his watch: 6.15 p.m. He would have to hurry if he was to make it back for his favourite part of the day: a hot bath listening to Radio 4. He took his leave of the others and left.

At the door to the pub, Marman was suddenly aware of a brawl going on fifty yards down Eaton Terrace and right beside his pride and joy, a brand-new, red and black Citroën 2CV. Two men were slugging it out on the narrow pavement, right against his car. Breaking into a run and ignoring the huddle of jeering bystanders, Marman found his car key and got in. He would be bloody annoyed if there were any dents. The 2CV might look like an upturned bucket but it was highly economical and that was increasingly important after six months without a job. One of the combatants, a black man with a bald and bleeding skull, bounced back against the passenger door as Marman, swearing, pulled away and accelerated out of Eaton Terrace, vaguely aware of blue lights flashing to his rear.

Past Battersea and well into Clapham, he turned into Blandfield Road. Since his divorce three years ago, he had grown close to a lovely girl named Julia, but they lived their separate lives and Marman had purchased his Clapham terraced house with his army savings. There were usually a couple of art students renting a bedroom, but that evening his only current tenant was out on the town, so he had the house to himself.

Marman's house was directly opposite the shop of a friendly greengrocer who often looked after his keys and mail. Marman parked as close to home as he could and let himself in. He flung his blazer and tie on to the sitting-room table, poured himself a whisky and rushed upstairs. As usual, he left the front door ajar, for he was a sociable sort and few days passed by without some friend or other dropping in. Marman was not worried by security. As he often said, 'There's nothing worth stealing, bar my radio, and if they want to get in, a lock won't stop 'em.' Within minutes Marman was in a foaming Badedas bath with his drink beside him and the radio drowning out all other sounds.

Meier double-parked immediately outside 9 Blandfield Road and, at 7.05 p.m., as soon as the signature tune of *The Archers* began, he nodded. 'Davies says Marman never misses the programme and likes to listen in his bath. The door is half-open. The camera is all set.'

De Villiers carried two plastic salesman's bags, one containing brochures about life assurance. Once in the sitting room, he went directly to the blazer. Davies had assured him that Marman's black *Economist* diary was normally kept inside the inner pocket. De Villiers swore silently after glancing at the handwriting; it was too small for the 1600 ASA film in the Olympus XA4 to cope with without using a tripod or flash. The result might prove too grainy, when enlarged, to be legible. Better to play safe, especially as there was little danger of interruption. Meier, in the car outside, would find a pretext to stall any visitor and they knew only Marman was at home.

From one of the bags de Villiers took out Meier's custom-made foldaway frame. He placed the diary on the table, ensuring that its open pages were kept flat by the strip of piano wire that stretched between the legs of the frame. Next he slotted the Nikon F2 camera into place, pointing down and some seventeen inches above the open diary. Meier had selected a slow, fine grain film in conjunction with a flash attachment and manually set the optimum exposure. De Villiers pressed the plunger of the cable release and took a single photograph of each set of pages for the month of November. Six minutes later he was once again with Meier and the diary was back in Marman's blazer pocket.

29

The surveillance period was the key to success. In Marman's case Davies had been patient and professional from the outset. After three weeks, still without a hit plan, he had given de Villiers his considered advice. Go for Marman's diary, for he keeps it with him and uses it like a yuppy does a Filofax. From his forward planner pick a date when he is out of London and alone in his car, and fix a road accident.

Davies also recommended that they fudge the warning film. Since the days of Kealy, video cameras had become widely available

and video film easily edited. In Marman's case it would be almost impossible to serve him notice of pending death without building a major embuggerance factor into any subsequent accident plan.

The problem with Marman was his unpredictability and his almost obsessive love of human company. He was hardly ever alone. His girlfriend Julia was with him on and off much of the time after she finished her daily job at J & B Whisky, his art student very often spent all day and night at 9 Blandfield Road and a constant stream of friends, mostly ex-army, kept dropping in to yarn over stiff drinks.

When Marman went out, there was absolutely no pattern to his movements. Job-hunting appeared to be the motive of some of his calls but more often he went instinctively to one of half a dozen pubs, such as the Antelope, where he knew his friends would be. He would join them on extended tours between various 'in' watering-holes, until a party was mentioned, whereupon the whole group would head off to change for dinner if applicable, or straight to the flat of the party-giver, not returning home until the early hours.

Since the Clinic never reacted to mere happenstance, de Villiers had agreed with Davies and gone for the Marman diary.

At a Tadnams safe house in Trebovir Road, a grotty basement next to a Slav-owned hotel, the photographed pages of Marman's diary were studied in detail.

'On Saturday he will spend the day wine-tasting at the Hurlingham Club,' Meier observed.

'His girl works there, so she is likely to be with him,' said de Villiers dismissively.

'But afterwards,' Meier's finger stabbed at photographs, 'he goes for drinks with Poppo. Saturday night is always good for us. Who is this Poppo?'

'Forget it.' De Villiers flicked to another sheet. 'We have only three suitable events in the whole month and all are out of London. He will travel alone in his Citroën. We *know* that. We have the timings and the routes will be obvious from any road-map. I say we con-centrate on these and forget his London life.'

There was no further discussion of the diary entries and Meier began to look like a cat anticipating a bowl of cream.

De Villiers pinned a map of England to the wall. 'Marman will be making four specific journeys over a three-week period. Two in the west of the country, one to Suffolk and one to Rugby. The most detailed is down here,' he said, indicating the general area of Salisbury

Plain. 'We know exactly when Marman will be travelling between two known points ... Meier,' he looked up at the Belgian, 'what are your thoughts?'

The response was immediate.

'The "Boston Brakes". It must be. It cannot fail yet nobody will ever suspect sabotage.'

Davies was shaking his head. 'It failed in Boston, boyo, so why not here?'

'It did not *fail*,' Meier snapped. 'You know that. Circumstances in Boston changed at the last minute so we abandoned my method. But everything was ready and would have worked. I rehearsed for two months on the old airstrip with the Tighe brothers in the stock-cars. I could take over control at five hundred yards and by the end I had one hundred percent success. One hundred percent. That is not failure ... *boyo!*'

De Villiers raised his hand. 'OK, OK, keep your skin on, my friend. I have every faith in your brilliance but what if we go ahead with your Boston Brakes on his Salisbury journey and it does fail?'

Meier nodded violently. 'In the impossible event of failure there, I move the equipment to the car of another suitable third party and we catch him later up here.' He indicated Suffolk. 'But I tell you for sure: it *cannot* fail if I am on the controls.'

De Villiers was pensive. 'Certainly we need to ensure total lack of suspicion at this stage to avoid any interested party connecting Marman with Kealy and Milling. There can be no doubt that the Boston Brakes is perfect from that point of view.'

'If you are both dead set on it,' Davies sighed, 'as I can see is the case, then we'd be better off down south. We know some of the coastal geography, at least.'

The previous summer the Clinic had worked for a Paris-based agency that used them from time to time. De Villiers suspected that the client was a drug baron, controlling the Channel route into Britain from Deauville, and wanting a rival group wiped off the map without creating ripples. Although gang warfare was not exactly the Clinic's field, the fee was good.

Davies had pinpointed the target's landing and hand-over spot as a desolate stretch of Pagham Harbour Nature Reserve to the north of Church Norton, in West Sussex. Having observed two previous hand-over ceremonies, he decided that a seaborne attack by Tadnams heavies in the narrow harbour, or a land attack as the French

rendezvoused with their reception party, would both lead to major mayhem. To achieve a surprise attack, the Clinic had obtained through a Saudi purchasing agency a twelve-seater, 40-mph hovercraft with a quiet engine and twenty inches of obstacle clearance. The Tadnams group had approached over mud-flats, done away with the four-man French crew using silenced HK53 sub-machine-guns, and towed their boat out to sea without reaction from the land-based reception party. They failed to locate the heroin but sank the trawler in forty feet of water before hovering back to the mainland.

'Marman's Wiltshire return journey is scheduled for the afternoon of Tuesday 11 November. Is ten days sufficient time for you, Meier?'

'I will start collecting the gear together immediately with help from the agency. I can see no problem on that score. The difficulty will, of course, be finding a suitable proxy.'

De Villiers did not hesitate. 'Marman will be at home this evening, so Davies and I will pay him a visit with the video. You go ahead with a full proposal for Wiltshire on the eleventh that we can decide upon tomorrow.'

Had Meier objected to the timetable, he would have done himself a favour, but his brilliance did not extend to seeing into the future.

30

The door of Marman's house was ajar on the evening of Monday 3 November. Inside, oblivious to the draught, he was entertaining an old friend from his days in Dhofar. The two men occasionally met for a drink and to set the world to rights.

'I could always tell he was a chancer,' Marman exclaimed, commenting on the recent resignation of Jeffrey Archer, Deputy Chairman of the Conservative Party, following accusations of involvement in a sex scandal. 'That lewd smirk gives him away.'

'You are quite wrong,' said his guest. 'I have it on the best information that the woman was put up to it. A prime case of carefully planted disinformation. Once the smear has been disseminated, especially when the dirt is fairly credible, the victim will never live it down. Archer will be tarnished in the minds of the majority long

after they have forgotten the actual details of the supposed scandal' — he knocked cigar ash on to the carpet — 'and in this case the timing is excellent. The accusation was published on the twenty-sixth in the knowledge that Archer would reply the very next day ... and what happens on the twenty-seventh ... the Big Bang, of course, the City's greatest event in decades. Not much space left in the daily rags for Archer's repudiations at the time when he most needed to scream them far and wide.'

Marman nodded. 'His wife's a good-looker. I could do more than sketch her if she gets fed up with hubby.'

'Not bad, your latest offerings, Mike. Where did you do them?'

The offerings in question were a handful of pencil and charcoal sketches of nudes, mostly reclining on a beach or emerging from the sea.

'Ah yes, did I not tell you? Had an excellent sailing holiday in the Med. It helped me to sort myself out and think positively about life. Indeed a great time was had by all. That lass actually had her bikini on at the time I sketched her, sad to relate.'

'You're very good at it, you know.'

'Stripping girls in my head, you mean ... Thanks,' he laughed. 'I do feel much better for the time away. I was beginning to be very down in the dumps after months of negative responses to my job-hunting. Makes you feel you're over the hill, a has-been with no prospects but the dole.'

He rose to fill their glasses. 'To employment,' he said, and they toasted his prospects. 'Next week I've a couple of good meetings lined up. You'll remember Searby, Brook and Amoore, all good lads in Oman. Well, they're helping out with likely leads.'

'How's Rose May these days?'

'I see her most weekends when I collect the lads.' He was silent for a while, slowly turning his glass about. 'I miss her, you know. Julia's a very good friend, an angel, and Gillie, just up the road, is like a sister to me. But it's not the same. The loneliness, the regrets, what could have been. Footloose and fancy-free sounds good but it's not for me.'

'I wouldn't call you footloose. What about this place?'

Marman's rather lugubrious expression lightened. 'Yes, it's a life-saver. That was dear Gillie, of course. It was her suggestion to get in on the property market, and my God she's proved right. What with the hugely increased value of the investment and the rental

income, it's been a boon. But I still need a job. Two sons at Bousefield's and I do want to do my best by them. Rose May's a good mum but everyone needs a father.'

Marman's own father, a brave RAF pilot in his day, had emigrated to Australia in 1962 when Michael was seventeen and determined to become a cavalry officer. When his family had departed, Michael stayed with his grandparents in Kingston. A quarter of a century later, apart from one brother in the RAF, he seldom saw his family. The 9th/12th Lancers had given him the best years of his life. They had been his home but now he was on his own, a fish out of water. Never mind. He was a fighter. He would start a new life ...

Marman realized he was in danger of appearing morbid. Boring hosts and party-poopers were anathema to him. He changed the subject to that of mutual friends and was soon back to his normal, cheery form.

There was a heavy knocking at the door and Marman's friend rose to depart. 'I'd better be going, Mike, or Monique will be wondering where I am. I'll probably drop in for a dram next week sometime.'

At the door he was confronted by two plainclothes police officers. One, holding an identity badge, addressed him with obvious deference.

'Mr Marman, sir, could we trouble you briefly?' He introduced himself and his colleague.

'No. I am just leaving. This is Mike Marman. Been up to some naughtiness, has he?'

He left and Marman ushered in the unexpected visitors. They accepted the offer of tea and while Marman fixed the kettle they sat down so that Davies was able to position correctly the briefcase that concealed a Sony video camera with a wide-angle lens.

Marman, they suggested, had, at 6.40 p.m. on Thursday 30 October, been in a brawl outside the Antelope public house, 22 Eaton Terrace, which had upset members of the public. His own car had been reported by two bystanders as having fled the scene on the arrival of the police. Marman vehemently denied any involvement in the fracas.

David Mason was annoyed. He prided himself on his memory for faces yet he could not place the policemen at Marman's house. The fawn Range Rover, a manual 1985 model, sped up the M40 and A40 to Oxford and then Eynsham, as Mason niggled away at the recesses

of his mind, attempting to match the two faces to an associated event. Eventually, not far from home, it came to him in a rush and the Range Rover accelerated, gravel flying, as Mason realized the full implications of his blunder.

Running into Scott's House, he located the keys and let himself into the gun-room. Inside one of the inner document safes he located a green folder and withdrew a sheaf of photographs, the Sumail pictures of Milling's killers that he had taken ten years earlier. There could be no mistaking the two men. The colleagues of Floppy Hat had called on Michael Marman that evening. They might conceivably still be there.

Mason telephoned at once and was greatly relieved when Marman answered. 'No. They have gone. They were only here for twenty minutes. Something to do with a street fight at the Antelope. Thought I was involved but I soon put them right and they apologized. Why do you ask?'

'Listen, Mike,' Mason said with deliberate intensity, for he knew Marman took most things in life with a pinch of salt, 'those men were *not* policemen. They are dangerous and you should avoid them like the plague. I will be with you as soon as I can tomorrow to explain.'

After a good deal of amused cajoling, Marman promised that he would at least lock his doors and windows that night, if only to humour Mason.

Mason then called Spike Allen, who was in and agreed to contact the Feather Men immediately.

31

Colonel Tommy Macpherson believed that British citizens exposed, in the 1980s, as wartime Nazi killers and torturers should not receive a free pardon merely because they had outwitted justice for forty years. He also believed that the hunt for the killers of Milling and Kealy should continue until they were caught. When Spike Allen called him, some nine years after Kealy's death, to say his assassins

were again at large, Macpherson's immediate reaction was 'Excellent. This time they will not slip through the net.'

He agreed to a Committee meeting the next morning despite an unavoidable early date with the New Zealand billionaire Ron Brierley at the London flat of an Irish entrepreneur.

Since the 1970s Macpherson's life had become very full and, in four weeks' time, he was due to submit to the Secretary of State for Defence a full report, called for by Prime Minister Margaret Thatcher, on employment and other problems effecting the efficiency of Britain's Territorial Army and other volunteer reserves.

Two years earlier, Macpherson, a senior non-executive director of the National Coal Board and the close confidant and adviser of Ian MacGregor, the NCB Chairman, had performed two roles that were to prove critical in the defeat of the miners' leader, Arthur Scargill. First, he persuaded Ian MacGregor to limit his appearances on television and to let the more subtle and down-to-earth Michael Eaton become the visible face of the NCB. Second, he urged the formation of British Coal Enterprises with the specific and enormous task of finding new work for the miners that MacGregor had to render redundant.

Additionally Macpherson had chaired the London Chamber of Commerce, the British National Chamber of Commerce, the CBI's London and South-Eastern branch, Birmid Qualcast, Webb-Brown International and the Mallinson-Denny Group.

Even when the Founder of the Feather Men had initially checked out the young Tommy Macpherson in the early fifties, his record had been impressive. Educated at Fettes College (of which he was now Governor) and Trinity College, Oxford, he was a First Open Classical Scholar, an Athletics Blue and Scottish International. He also played rugby and hockey for Oxford. Soon after the outbreak of war he joined the Scottish Commando from the Queen's Own Cameron Highlanders, became a POW in November 1941 but escaped late in 1943 and served in the Special Forces with the French and the Italian Resistance. He received the Military Cross with two Bars, the Légion d'Honneur, the Croix de Guerre and various other honours.

By the winter of 1986 Tommy Macpherson was as busy as he had ever been, but on the morning of Tuesday 4 November he hurried through his meeting with Ron Brierley and Tony O'Reilly, the Chairman of Heinz International, and arrived only minutes late for the Committee meeting of the Feather Men. Bletchley was in the

chair and Macpherson was shocked at the look of him. Thin and gaunt to the point of emaciation, he seemed to have lost interest in his appearance. His collar was awry and food stains were clearly evident on his poorly adjusted tie. A recent minor road accident, when his foot had applied pressure to his Audi's accelerator instead of the brake, had left contusions and cuts on his forehead, eyebrows and nose. All in all he was a sorry sight and Jane, seated close beside him with her notes, was obviously giving him the mother-hen treatment.

Macpherson nodded his apologies to the Chair and Spike Allen spoke. 'The Chairman allowed me to wait for your arrival, Colonel, before bringing up the specific matter which is the reason for today's unscheduled meeting.'

Macpherson nodded.

The Don smiled to himself. Spike had fought Bletchley hard to delay things for Macpherson's benefit.

Apart from Macpherson, nobody was aware of the reason for Spike's sudden call. Their interest was aroused. The Twins had long since retired, replaced by two fifty-year-olds with excellent Home Office connections. Both had been put forward by Mantell and seconded by Bletchley. August Graves had dubbed them the 'little grey men'.

'Most of you,' Spike's voice was toneless, 'will remember that in 1976 the Committee sanctioned one of our Locals to follow a suspect to Arabia. The Local identified this man's intended target but, unfortunately, the wrong target. An ex-Marine helicopter pilot was killed and the three Europeans involved were photographed but not identified.'

Spike looked around. As he later commented to Macpherson, 'You could hear a flea fart, they were so attentive.' Bletchley had begun to sweat profusely and his shoulder moved with a furtive tic as though some manikin was trying to burst out of his collar-bone.

'A year later,' Spike continued, 'one of Bob Mantell's sources in the Worcester police gave us another lead to the same suspect. This time our Locals identified the correct target but their watch was called off when, after a three-week period, the suspect appeared to have been frightened off by one of them. Sadly this second target, an SAS officer, was killed and no additional information was obtained about the assassins.'

'A pretty abysmal record by all counts,' muttered Mike Panny.

Spike ignored him and continued. 'A great deal of water has passed under the bridge since then but yesterday, a veteran Local recognized the same suspect who was implicated in both previous murders, at the house of a Major Michael Marman in Clapham. The suspect posed as a policeman and was accompanied by a second colleague whom our man also recognized from the 1977 Milling affair. The reason for their visit to Marman's home seems to have been familiarization with his house and circumstances.'

'What has Marman to do with the two previous targets?' Mantell asked.

'That is *not* the point,' Bletchley burst out. White in the face and shaking as though from St Vitus's Dance, he hammered his fist on his papers. 'The question should be: "What has any of this to do with *us?*" ' For a minute or more, words seemed to fail him. He leant forward, jerking at the neck, and Jane placed her hands anxiously around him. His eyes stood out and he stared at her, gulping as though for air. Believing Bletchley was having a stroke, Macpherson was about to suggest an immediate journey to hospital when Bletchley recovered both his voice and his composure.

'Before I make further comment,' he said to Spike, 'have you finished your report?'

Spike shook his head. 'I believe the suspects intend to kill Major Marman. He served in Dhofar with the Sultan's Armed Forces as did the other two officers. The motive may lie in some knowledge possessed by all three targets. It may even have to do with revenge or blackmail. I ask that the Committee sanction an immediate and close watch over Marman until such time as we have enough evidence of intent to murder or I am proved to be wrong.' Spike sat back and several people spoke at once.

As Bletchley was again gripped by a palsied shuddering, Bob Mantell became his mouthpiece.

'As the Chairman noted and I repeat, "This has nothing to do with us." May I remind you all that my friends at the Yard looked very closely at the Kealy case. They found absolutely no evidence of foul play and the South Powys police have closed the matter for good. I must remind you further that a majority of this Committee agreed at that time to have nothing further to do with the Dhofar Connection, as the Don insisted on calling the two killings.'

Mantell paused, shifting his gammy hip, before continuing on a new tack. 'I also have to ask you ... does this Marman have any link

with our flock? Should we feel motivated in any way to protect him? What I am querying is: did he or did he not serve with an SAS unit?'

'Negative,' said Spike, 'but he is our only link with the men who killed Kealy, and therefore our only chance of obtaining justice for the killing of an SAS officer.'

'With due respect to our Regular brethren,' Mantell countered, 'we exist to look after living individuals with SAS histories and their families. The pursuit of justice for Kealy's killers, though laudable, is not our concern. The Marman case is outside our terms of reference and purely a matter for the police.'

'We have been though all this before.' Macpherson's voice was low and controlled, but Spike, who knew him better than the others did, could see that he was angry. 'Since Mantell has engaged in repeating the rationale for inaction, let me remind old members, and suggest to our newer colleagues, that the police simply cannot act upon vague threats, with no known motivation, to non-VIP members of the public and by unidentified persons. Therefore, if we have good reason to believe Major Marman's life is in danger, we should help him. No one else will. Major Kealy was a very brave SAS officer and I do believe we should extend our activities to putting his killers where they belong, should they again fall into our laps.'

''Ere, 'ere,' shouted Graves, who had become very hard of hearing. 'We can't just let these greasy buggers slip through our 'ands.'

'May I speak, Mr Chairman?' The more pallid and elongated of the two grey men looked up from behind rimless half spectacles and Bletchley mouthed an affirmative.

'The Police Commissioner, Sir Kenneth Newman, only last month gave official warning that he had instigated new moves to clamp down on what he called "private security organizations operating at the very frontiers of official tolerance".'

'He was talking about the registered groups, not us,' Macpherson interrupted. 'Our existence remains unknown to the Commissioner.'

'Yes, but the burgeoning of semi-clandestine security outfits is causing growing alarm to Special Branch. Blue-chip companies have begun to hire hi-tech spies from these firms to check up on each other *inside* the UK. As the Cold War recedes, unethical home-based organizations will find themselves more and more under the official searchlight. Signs of this have already begun. The Home Office last year authorized significantly fewer phone taps and mail intercepts against left-wing subversive suspects and a correspondingly greater

number against certain domestic elements worrisome to Special Branch.'

Mike Panny decided not to be outdone in the field of in-depth know-how. 'I agree. These security mobs are now so numerous and their activities so questionable, that a clampdown is inevitable. In London alone we now have the KMS "Keeny-Meenies", Alistair Morrison's Defence Systems, Control Risks, Winguard, DSI, Saladin, Lawnwest, Cornhill Management, SCI, Paladin, Argen, Delta and of course the grandmother of them all, active since 1967, Watchguard.' He waved an admonitory finger around the table. 'Mark my words, although many of them take care to stay legit, not all can effectively leash their hounds. Scandals will result.'

Macpherson had recognized a growing tendency in some of the longer-serving Committee members to fight shy of any course of action that might conceivably backfire on their personal reputations. This applied especially to Bletchley. Like Macpherson, he had become a senior player in the City with a string of prestigious non-executive directorships, various high-profile charity presidencies and, until he was recently curtailed by his strange indisposition, rode an exacting social merry-go-round with the highest in the land. It was apparent to Macpherson that Panny, the Don and Mantell were suffering on a lower plane from the same aversion to the sanctioning of any course of action by the Feather Men that carried a risk of publicity that might compromise their untarnished reputations. All had much to lose and little to gain, a very different situation to that which had existed at the time of their induction to the Committee all those years ago.

Only Spike, August and Jane remained largely unaltered by the passage of time, by changing circumstances and fashions, Macpherson thought. Maybe it was time for a spring clean. Even as the idea crossed his mind, it was discounted. The Founder, a man of intense loyalty to old friends, would never sanction it. The Founder was himself none too well these days and Macpherson would not willingly approach him with contentious points unless there was no alternative.

The matter of Marman was thrashed out and put to the vote with an inconclusive result.

'On a decision which involves life or death, I exercise my right to request that we reconvene with the full Committee tomorrow.' Macpherson made his move as soon as the tied vote was announced.

He had been expecting it and had reluctantly made up his mind to bring out his only trump card.

The absent Founder's casting vote in favour of the Marman-watch was implemented at the next meeting, a perfectly correct procedure, and the word went out immediately to John Smythe and five other Locals in the South-East. Spike was taking no chances this time.

32

Meier's technical brilliance was an undeniable money-earner for the Clinic. The agencies they used were aware for instance that he had designed a sleeper bomb of the type used to attack the Conservative Party Conference in Brighton in 1984. This he could pre-set to go off a year after he had planted it. With quartz chronometers, standard VCRs and long-delay batteries linked in tandem, he could place the bomb kit during the dismantlement by contractors of the grandstand of some annual royal event. Without any further action, he could be certain that the explosion would detonate a year later to within a minute of a pre-set time and date.

In Boston in 1974, Meier had spent three months planning a staged road accident by an ingenious 'third party' method that became known within the Clinic as the 'Boston Brakes' and which, after rehearsals had honed it to perfection, was aborted, much to Meier's frustration. Now that he had the chance to resurrect the system, he was full of the joys of life.

'This is Jake, who was worked with Tadnams for four years. Though I say so myself he is a genius with cars. He designs transmissions and is not put off by unethical improvisation. He is at home with what you' — Meier looked at de Villiers — 'would describe as the Rube Goldberg factor and our Welsh colleague might scornfully call Heath Robinson.'

Jake, a weedy fellow with etiolated complexion and bad teeth, played with his hands, twining the long and surprisingly powerful-looking fingers about one another as though embarrassed by praise from a maestro.

'Glad to have you with us,' said de Villiers. Then, changing the

topic, 'The video is fine. After some hours in the dubbing studio, we have it so the sheikh will suspect nothing. The film shows me accusing Marman of the killing at Zakhir and he denies it hotly. It looks real good. All we need now is to nail this guy in such a way that there is a hundred percent absence of suspicious circumstances.'

'Two hundred percent,' Meier retorted. 'Let me take you step by step.'

'You normally do,' Davies said, slumping back in his chair with an exaggerated sigh.

Outside in Trebovir Road the street resounded to gunfire and Meier looked up, startled. Davies chuckled at his discomfiture. 'Ever heard of Guy Fawkes? You should have ... he was your alter ego but for the one-year fuse delay.'

'Mercedes,' Meier recited, 'has a training workshop in Unter-türkheim which, since 1916, has turned out apprentices that later advanced the world of engineering in many amazing ways. Jake here received three years' training there and later achieved the diploma of master mechanic from the West German Chamber of Handicraft. He has studied my Boston system and is impressed. We will be working together until completion.'

Meier moved to the central table, on which he had laid out a road map of southern England. 'First,' he said. 'We have Davies's report on the target. The man is *macho cojones*, a real swordsman or, as Davies puts it, very free with his whatsit. In practice this means he enjoys female company and is seldom alone. We are all agreed that the best scenario, to catch him alone, is out on the road.'

Jake put in his oar, his voice as cadaverous as his face. 'We are lucky this man has a Citroën 2CV. Very feeble machine. Cracks easy like an eggshell. The driver has no *Unterschied*, no protection.'

Meier nodded at his acolyte. 'This is correct, quite so, but to continue, having established that the action will be on the road, we ask ourselves: why no bomb? Why no sabotage? Why not make the brakes fail and hope for a fatal result?' He paused. 'Because with all such events the police conduct an immediate forensic study and even I could not get away with a No Foul Play verdict.'

Davies coughed. 'Get on with it.'

'Again, if we should have a Tadnams heavy in a reinforced car ram into the 2CV or drive Marman off the road, it will be obvious foul play. So what can we do? Of course, we need a *random* third party to collide head-on with his car at more than thirty miles an

hour. This will certainly be fatal to Marman and the police will never even contemplate premeditation.' Meier beamed. 'The Boston Brakes will achieve all this for us.'

Davies cut in. 'In principle maybe, but I don't see your third-party random drivers rushing in to volunteer their services as guided missiles.'

Meier ignored him. 'The theory is very simple. We find someone who we know will drive on the same road at the same time as Marman but in the opposite direction. I follow behind this chosen and doctored car with Jake driving me. You follow behind the 2CV and we keep in radio contact so that I know exactly when and where the cars will approach each other. Depending on the aggregate speeds, but at a likely distance of five hundred yards prior to the projected passing point, I take radio control of the random car and steer it to a head-on collision with Marman.'

'What if they happen to meet in a traffic jam, or at a roundabout, or on opposite sides of a steel crash barrier?' It was Davies again.

'Of course, that is possible. But with a country road like the A303, the odds against not meeting on the open road and at high speeds are greater than nine to one.'

'But still possible?' Davies persisted.

'Yes, and that is why our device will be detachable. We know from the diary that we have two other chances. Jake and I would simply transfer the device to another proxy car in readiness for another known Marman journey.'

'OK, OK,' de Villiers was unconvinced, 'but how the hell do you select a suitable proxy?'

'This we have already done.' Meier's voice was sugary and conspiratorial. 'Come, look at the map here.' He indicated the region between London and the south coast. Two red Chinagraph marks indicated Marman's Clapham house and the Wiltshire village of Steeple Langford.

'The target will lunch at the village here, departing at 3.15 p.m. in order to return to Clapham in time to make job-hunting phone calls. Then he goes round to his girlfriend, Julia, in Brook Green. We give him an average speed on a clear dual carriageway of fifty-five miles per hour and a simple mathematical process tells us he will at 3.45 p.m., even allowing fifteen minutes and ten miles per hour overall differences to the planned parameters, be somewhere between Winterbourne Stoke and Popham on the A303, a stretch of over thirty

miles of fast road. All we need now is to find a driver who is scheduled to be heading west in the opposite direction, along that same twenty-mile stretch at 3.45 p.m.'

'That,' said Davies, 'is where you come unstuck.'

'Not at all,' Meier responded. 'Look at the map here and you can clearly see that the A303 is a main arterial road between London and such towns as Exeter and Plymouth. What sort of person needs to drive that route frequently? A representative of a company with offices in both places. Naturally the city of Plymouth brought to my mind the hovercraft we used to such good effect last summer. That was a Slingsby SAH2200 model originating from a manufacturing group named ML Holdings with a subsidiary based in Plymouth. Tadnams quickly rustled up, from an acquisitions research company, the necessary background data on ML, Shorts of Belfast and five other firms with London and Plymouth units.'

De Villiers was nodding quietly, with growing enthusiasm.

'What clinched the selection process was that ML Holdings are due to hold a Main Board meeting in Plymouth on the morning of 12 November. Any London-based directors will need to be in Plymouth the preceding night which, if they are to dine on expenses at a good Plymouth hotel, will mean their passing down the A303 mid-afternoon on the eleventh, D-Day.'

He paused to let the point sink in, then continued. 'We forgot about the sales force at this point and concentrated on the senior staff and non-executive directors who would have to attend their Board Meeting. We are now in the process, with full support from Tadnams, of narrowing down a list of fourteen likely characters.'

'Narrowing down?' nudged de Villiers.

'Checking out which executives will be heading west at any point on our key stretch of the A303 at 3.45 p.m. in six days' time. Meanwhile, Jake will have the equipment ready tomorrow evening and we will commence rehearsals with four stock cars at the Tadnams airstrip in Kent on the seventh. I will not have lost my touch with the control system but, as always, practice makes perfect.'

Davies studied the road-map and avoided the smug, sideways glance of his technical colleague.

33

During the evening of Friday 7 November, Meier stopped the car at a garage in Stockbridge and asked the elderly attendant for the best route to Exeter.

'Well, my friend, I can tell you which way *not* to go, and that's by the A30. It may look more direct, but what with its traffic problems and all, you'd be a fool to take it. Go along the A303 as far as you can, close to Honiton, then join the A30. That's what the folks round here all does.'

Two miles south of Stockbridge, Meier and Jake left their car by the roadside on the outskirts of the village of Houghton. The previous night they had visited the houses of three ML executives on the short list. Men from Tadnams had broken into other offices and homes and now the process was being repeated for the last of the listed men. After Houghton, Meier and Jake had two further calls to complete, at the homes of ML executive Pollock and another non-executive director, Sebire.

There were two key items to find and in the case of Sir Peter Horsley, the non-executive director of ML Holdings, both would have to be at his home in Houghton, a fine Victorian house called Park Court, since he worked from there and not in London. The only reason he had been included on the list was that he was as likely to use the A303 to go to Plymouth as were his London-based colleagues. Tadnams had included a copy of the *Who's Who* entry for Horsley, which indicated that he was a man of considerable distinction: ' ... 1940 Fighter Command ... Commands No. 9 and No. 29 Squadrons ... Equerry to Princess Elizabeth and the Duke of Edinburgh 1942–1952, Equerry to the Queen 1952–1953, Equerry to the Duke of Edinburgh 1953–1956 ... Deputy C-in-C Strike Command 1973–1975 ...'. Numerous other achievements were also catalogued and Meier could only hope that, as a retired Air Marshal, Horsley did not warrant government security cover.

Leftover fireworks crackled and fizzed intermittently around the

little village and Horsley's dogs, a Dalmatian and a large Münster-lander, were decidedly edgy.

Meier and Jake, with a duffle bag, skirted the front drive with its deep gravel noise-trap and, from the magnificent rear garden, spotted Sir Peter in the kitchen with his dogs. His wife was nowhere to be seen.

'Keeps the dogs in there all night,' whispered Meier. 'Got their baskets, rugs and foodbowls by the Aga and no dog-flaps. We're in luck.'

Since Sir Peter's diary was liable to be downstairs they decided to wait until he moved upstairs to bed. Meanwhile they moved to the spacious double garage, built as an attractive and entirely separate two-storey unit, some distance from the main house.

The garage swing doors were up and open. One car space was empty. The other was occupied by a shiny BMW Series 7.

'Nip upstairs, Jake,' Meier ordered. 'Check there's no one up there. I'll get the machine's vital statistics.'

Meier opened the duffle bag and slipped into a boiler suit. He disappeared between the front wheels of the BMW with the bag. In a short while he was interrupted by Jake.

'I think we have luck with this man.' He held out a black desk diary.

Meier took off his gloves and the light from his head-band torch lit up the diary's pages. 'Where did you get this?'

Jake explained. He had mounted the stairs on the outside of the garage and, on the upper floor, entered an open-plan office by way of an unlocked door. There was obviously a noteworthy lack of crime in Houghton. Three large desks occupied the office above the garage and Jake discovered that Sir Peter, his secretary and his wife all worked there. He could find no diary anywhere in, or on, the first two desks but Lady Horsley kept hers open on her blotter, and Jake's optimism was prompted by two of the entries, one for Monday 10 November: 'Depart for Ma's'; and one for Tuesday 11 November: 'P. leaves at 3 p.m. Yelverton by 6 p.m.'

'Looking *very* good.' Meier nodded and laid a hand on Jake's shoulder. 'Well done indeed. Take a note of all the entries from today until 13 November, then replace the diary. I am nearly finished.'

Meier noted that with the swing doors closed, and black-out cloth taped over the windows, the place would be light-proof. The walls were of solid brick but a sound-baffle was needed to line the inside

of the swing doors. He checked the power points and the BMW's own jack-set. They would need Tadnams men on outside watch and a mechanic to help with the work. He noted what he could see of the brake system, the Michelin XVS tyres, forty thousand miles on the clock, registration 3545 PH, car type BMW 728i automatic.

Meier and Jake finished their further ML executive check-ups at 5 a.m. and, by noon on 8 November, de Villiers was able to select the file on Sir Peter Horsley from thirteen others. He was by far the most suitable.

All equipment and tools were centralized at the Kent airstrip, a BMW 728i automatic with ABS braking system was purchased along with two 'target practice' cars, and the fitting and control rehearsals began in earnest with two days in hand. Meier and Jake, seemingly tireless, were in their element.

Early on Sunday morning Spike received a routine call from John Smythe, who was controlling the three-man Marman watch. There had been no sign of the Welshman nor of any other outside interest in their charge. 'Keep at it,' Spike had told him.

Smythe was a quiet, reliable sort and particularly appropriate for the work since he had followed the Welshman to London some nine years before. Still unmarried and self-employed, Smythe had become one of Spike's key Locals in the South-East, after moving to Reading in the early eighties.

Mike Marman, after a late night following drinks with his friend Poppo Tomlinson, had intended to spend that morning doing nothing very much with Julia. He surprised them both with a last-minute decision to go to church because it was Remembrance Sunday. They drove the 2CV to the Guards Chapel in Whitehall and joined a full and enthusiastically lugubrious congregation.

Like many of his old army friends, also at the service, Mike had pinned his three medals to his overcoat and wore them with pride. He should have had a fourth, the Distinguished Service Medal, but for the decidedly cold shoulder the authorities had shown him ever since his shooting up of the Midway officers' mess in Dhofar. He chuckled to himself at the memory. Wall plaques, bottles and glasses had smashed into splinters. Officers and staff had jumped for their lives as Major Marman, with a wild yell, had sprayed the main bar with his Kalashnikov assault rifle set to fully automatic. A glorious memory. He had always hated overbearing senior officers and that

episode had given quite a few of them something to think about.

Although Mike had listened in amazement to David Mason's warning and his remarkable story about the killing of John Milling and Mike Kealy, both of whom he had known, he was not convinced. It was inconceivable that anyone could actually be plotting to kill *him*. Somehow David had got things wrong. Nevertheless Marman's grin faded as he thought about it. Mason had asked him to mention the threat to nobody and he had agreed not to.

During the sermon, Marman found his thoughts dwelling on death. So many of his best muckers from army days were dead, killed in the war or in peacetime soldiering. Charles Stopford had recently crashed his Beaver plane into a hilltop at Dummer, the home village of Sarah Ferguson. Then, last weekend, he had called at Rose May's and only one of his sons had come away with him. The elder son, Alistair, had stayed to comfort his mother. Rose May's fiancé, Alan Stewart, had been killed earlier that week. A talented Thames TV news producer, on his last day's coverage of the famine in southern Sudan, he had driven over a mine and died of the injuries.

Rose May had said to Marman, 'How strange life is. My peace-loving Alan is dead, yet you, after all your years of wars and bloodshed, are still alive and totally unscathed.'

34

On Monday 10 November five men arrived at Park Court soon after midnight, having parked the dark-blue Volvo estate car in a field at the northern end of the village. They carried tools and equipment in easily portable containers, apart from the pressurized diver's bottle, which was slung over de Villiers's shoulder, and the bulky curtains, which the two Tadnams men carried between them. They moved at well-spaced intervals, ready to fade into the shadows, but nothing and no one disturbed their progress to Sir Peter's outhouse garage.

Meier sprayed WD40 lubricant on the moving parts of the sliding doors before attempting to close them. The Tadnams men confirmed that Horsley and his dogs were asleep, then remained outside to keep watch and to warn against any noise coming from the garage.

ROAD ACCIDENT ON 11 NOVEMBER 1986

1984 model BMW 728i, Reg No 3545 PH (46,678 miles at time of accident)

DIAGRAM #2: MODIFIED BRAKING SYSTEM

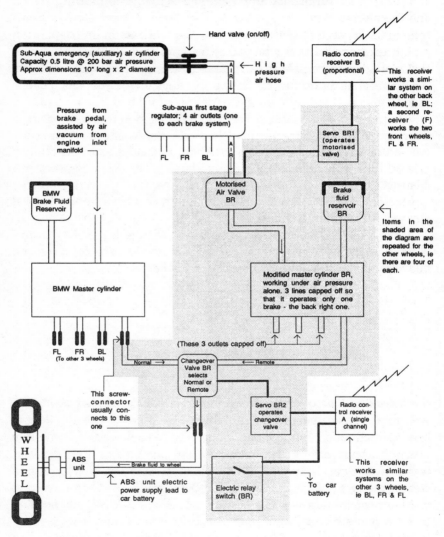

Meier and Jake had twice attached and removed the equipment using their rehearsal BMW 728i automatic. De Villiers had come along to help Meier and, perhaps, to reassure himself that the plan really was as sound as Meier had painted it.

With the sound-baffle curtains in place against the sliding doors and the black-out blinds taped to the windows, Meier assembled the thirty-two separate, labelled units together with the wires, cable and piping to connect them, while Jake laid out the tools and positioned the spotlights to be powered from one of the garage's wall sockets.

'You are sure you can detach everything afterwards?' de Villiers asked.

'No problem at all,' Meier replied, 'but you don't have to worry. Even if we cannot retrieve the device for some unforeseen reason, we can quickly prepare other sets. If the police should find all this *in situ*, they will merely conclude somebody is after Horsley, not Marman.'

De Villiers murmured, 'Would it not be easier to override Horsley's steering rather than his brakes?'

Meier nodded. 'Easier when it comes to the action phase but not practical to install given our particular needs. We would require heavier gear and a lot more time. Then again Horsley, if he survives the impact, must be confused, not suspicious, about what went wrong. To fiddle with the steering will not achieve this. Obviously, when the brakes on a wheel lock up and the car goes into a skid, the steering will not work properly. Afterwards the driver will not be able to explain what went amiss. He will be confused and uncertain. Was there a brake failure or some other malfunction? He cannot tell.'

Meier gestured at the equipment line. 'The beauty of controlling the brakes is that, if Horsley survives, he will remember perfectly well that the car deliberately disobeyed the steering wheel. He will be mystified, of course, but not suspicious. Remember, also, that the gear must be as easy as possible to *remove* quietly and by torchlight tomorrow night. That would not be so were we to doctor the steering.'

Meier squatted down by his pre-fabricated devices. 'If all this had to be mounted as a single unit, it simply would not fit under the bonnet. We attach everything in nooks and crannies. Even if Horsley should lift the bonnet, say to check the oil, he would notice nothing.'

De Villiers could see that Meier was already convinced that success was the only possible outcome.

'The difficulty with my system is the unpredictable behaviour of the four individual brakes. I have used radio control with model cars, boats and aeroplanes of my own design, some scaled to half life size, but nothing has required as much practice to perfect as this system. This week, in Kent, we have rehearsed on tarmac and on uneven grass, and I can now predict the reaction of most drivers to the sudden realization of an imminent collision. I should also stress that we can abort right up until the last moment if the actual meeting point is marred by any form of obstacle, static or moving, between the two cars.'

'Exactly what is your plan in layman's terms?' De Villiers was keen to comprehend as much as possible and Meier was delighted to expound.

'You will maintain permanent radio contact with me as you travel east behind Marman's car. You will keep me informed of his exact position as he continues to come closer to Horsley. Jake will drive me in the Volvo and ensure that, at the moment when I take over control from Horsley, our Volvo has a clear, uninterrupted view of the BMW. I will then steer the BMW to head-on impact with Marman's Citroën.'

Meier removed a notebook and pen from his black boiler suit and drew a diagram of a standard braking system. 'We assume that this model may have anti-lock ABS brakes since they were developed as an option in 1978. Because of its personalized registration plate, we have no idea of its year of manufacture. Therefore my system can cope with ABS or non-ABS models. Very few British drivers chose the ABS option but Horsley may just be one of them.'

Meier ran his finger along his diagram. 'The key part of a braking system is the master cylinder, full of brake fluid and connected to a brake-fluid reservoir, so it is always topped up. When you press the brake pedal, that pressure, assisted by an air vacuum from the engine inlet manifold, forces the fluid out of the cylinder, down a narrow pipe and against a piston that in turn forces the brake pads to clamp on to the brake disc. This is of course repeated down three other pipes to the three other discs. Release the brake pedal and the fluid is allowed back into the cylinder.

'If ABS units are fitted, they are positioned between master cylinder and piston and powered by an electrical supply from the car battery. Since we will not want the ABS to work when I take control I will,

by radio control, cut the electrical supply to the ABS unit. What do you know about radio control?'

'Nothing,' said de Villiers.

'The key kit is a "servo" motor or actuator which, on receiving a signal from a small radio receiver, will cause a lever to move through ninety or even a hundred and eighty degrees and mechanically turn a valve, or a switch, on or off. So the actuator is controlled by the receiver, which in turn receives its orders from a transmitter up to several hundred yards away. My transmitter consists of a board with four joysticks to control each of the BMW's four brakes. As I pull at a particular stick, the corresponding brake is applied as hard as I wish. This is achieved by two "proportional" control transmitters, but I will also use a "single channel" transmitter to activate my entire system and to deactivate the ABS system if we find there is one. The latter transmitter is capable of operating several actuators and relays all at once ... All understood?'

De Villiers nodded. 'Clear as Mississippi mud.'

'In that case,' Meier said, 'you will have no problem with *my* braking system.' He rapidly sketched a more complex diagram on to a fresh page of his notebook. 'The source of power I will use to substitute the pressure from Horsley's foot is this little air cylinder, ten inches long by two and a third inches in diameter. It is a standard retail item as used by experienced scuba divers and contains half a litre of compressed air pressurized to 200 bar for emergency use.'

Meier's index finger moved down his diagram. 'Next we have another item of scuba equipment, a "first stage regulator", which is a device for distributing air at different pressures to different parts of a diver's paraphernalia. We will be using it to split the air four ways, each to a separate system for each brake. From each outlet in this regulator, air will flow into a separate motorized air valve, whenever I cause its tap to open. When I close the tap, by a movement on a joystick, air will escape and the brake will be released as much or as little as I wish.'

De Villiers seemed to be happy so Meier continued. 'For each wheel there is then my own design of master cylinder, which I have modified by capping off three outlets and using just one to channel brake fluid to the brakes. A more complex modification, achieved by the excellent Jake, has been to enable the cylinders to operate on air pressure alone, without either mechanical pressure or normal vacuum

assistance. Each of my cylinders is topped up by its own brake fluid reservoir.'

Meier picked up one of four small valves. 'These are critical to my system. A simple change-over valve which, at the switch of a lever, will divert brake fluid from one routing to another. When on "Normal" the BMW's master cylinder will relay Horsley's foot pressure to the brakes, but when I switch it to "Remote" *my* system will take over. On my control board I have a single masterswitch transmitter that will, at the chosen moment, change the four valves to "Remote" and, as appropriate, isolate all four ABS systems. From that moment, I will be in control of each of the four brakes.'

The three men set to work to the pattern pre-established by Meier and Jake. There was little noise and no unanticipated problems.

The brake fluid was drained into a drip tray and the brake lines, disconnected from the master cylinder, were connected to outlets from the change-over valves. These last were pre-connected to the modified cylinders and to their servo motors. The wiring to the receivers was also already in place.

Separate lines from the change-over valves, labelled 'Normal', were connected back to the BMW's master cylinder. Then came the fiddly job of tracing the positive wires from each ABS system and fitting the electric relays in series for connection to the single channel receiver. Using specialist tapes, Meier and Jake clamped the many new units firmly in place and, via a voltage transformer, affixed the receivers and servo motors to the car battery. The system and the five reservoirs were then topped up with brake fluid when set both at 'Normal' and at 'Remote'.

With the car's own jack in position and one wheel off the ground, de Villiers spun the wheel manually. Meier, as though by magic, then stopped the rotation by touching a temporary remote transmitter control. All four wheels were tested in this manner and the air cylinder then topped up to 200 bar from the fully pressurized fifteen-litre diver's bottle.

Meier then set the system to 'Normal', the three remote transmitters to 'Off', the three receivers to 'On' and the air cylinder's hand valve to fully open. The system was primed.

By the time every visible sign of their presence was removed and the swing doors were open again, the only trace of the eight-hour visit was a faint smell of brake fluid mingled with sweat, and even that had dissipated by dawn.

35

John Smythe had no dependents and lived easily on his means as a freelance photographer. He was never happier than when doing a job for Spike. He remembered Mantell, who first recruited him, but Spike epitomized the sort of person he would himself like to be. He never considered the possibility of being paid for his time and seldom passed his expenses to Spike. Smythe hero-worshipped his Nottingham coal-miner father, and knew he would have approved, if he were still alive, of everything Spike stood for. He felt he was doing his bit for Blighty, for the well-being of his fellow citizens and, as Spike had once put it, acting as a freelance ferret-man to seek out those vermin the official gamekeepers do not catch.

He was slightly uneasy about the day ahead since none of the four Locals cooperating over the Marman watch could help out until the evening, so he was entirely alone for the day. To follow a mobile 'mark' without being spotted requires great concentration and quick reactions; a far more demanding task than can be imagined by someone who has not tried it.

Marman had left Blandfield Road at 11.05 a.m., filled up the 2CV with 3-Star leaded petrol at a fuel station on the M3, and arrived at Steeple Langford in Wiltshire's Wylye Valley at 12.45 p.m. Smythe parked well away from the entrance to the drive of Manor House and sat himself down at the upper rim of a cow field. There was a blustery autumn wind but he wore a battered Barbour jacket and tweed cap. He had, as always on jobs for Spike, an old gas-mask carrier containing coffee flask, cheese sandwiches and his late father's binoculars.

Mike Marman was in a very fine mood because Rose May had telephoned him the previous evening to say her father had agreed to pay for their son's private education costs; an enormous load off Marman's shoulders. He was also happy to be seeing his hosts, General Robin Brockbank and his wife Gillie. The general, now colonel of Marman's old regiment, had also been its commanding officer at the time Marman joined up.

The Brockbanks were full of advice and information to help Marman find civilian employment and he much enjoyed the meal with them. He drank only a gin and tonic and a glass of wine because he was driving and felt pleasantly relaxed when he took his leave at 3.15p.m., with ample time to get back to Clapham during office working hours.

Smythe found that he could not tail the 2CV quite as he would have liked, due to the presence of a white Ford Escort that kept to the same route as, and some distance behind, the Marman car.

As his wife was away visiting her mother in the north, Sir Peter rose early and worked with his secretary, Mrs Bromley, in the outhouse office until lunchtime on his Board papers and the agenda for the following day. He planned to arrive at the Moorland Links Hotel in Yelverton, near Plymouth, by 6.00 p.m., in plenty of time for the Board dinner that evening.

After a leisurely lunch he reversed the BMW out on to the drive and switched on the car radio to keep him company on the long drive down the A303.

Meier nodded to Jake. The Volvo nudged away from the kerb in the centre of Houghton and a stone's throw from Park Court.

Some twenty minutes later, at 3.25 p.m., as the Volvo passed the Bulford turning off the A303, heading west, de Villiers's voice came over Meier's CB radio. 'Two CV doing seventy miles per hour. Just crossed the A360 turn-off. Out.'

Meier's fingers flickered on his calculator. He muttered to Jake, 'Marman will reach the big roundabout in three minutes. We will be there in one and a half minutes. Horsley *must* keep his speed up so we meet well clear of the far side of the roundabout.'

De Villiers's voice again: 'At the Stonehenge fork now. One and a half miles to the roundabout. Still seventy miles per hour. One car behind me. All clear ahead of Marman. Out.'

Meier's veins stood out on his forehead. His knuckles were white as he clutched at the control board strapped to his left thigh. 'Dammit. *Geh schnell, mach schnell, man.*'

But Sir Peter was in no hurry. A Bedford horsebox with a woman driver was already on the roundabout and using the same exit lane. Sir Peter slowed down and only began to overtake when clear of the roundabout.

De Villiers's voice cut through the babble of Meier's cursing. 'Two

CV still seventy miles per hour. Last stretch to the roundabout. Still no cars ahead of Marman. Out.'

'No good,' yelled Meier at Jake. 'The horsebox is in the way ... quick, overtake, overtake ... No, the horsebox driver will suspect. You must get past Horsley too ... go on, go on ... I can operate OK looking back.'

The road was almost dry, the sky overcast but visibility excellent. The dual carriageway climbed gently to the west with an almost imperceptible leftwards curve.

Sir Peter had overtaken the horsebox at sixty-five miles per hour and was intending to return to the inside lane. He glanced in his mirror to check that all was clear behind him in that lane and, accelerating gently to seventy, he was halfway back across the central broken white lines when a large car overtook him at speed.

At this point the nightmare began. The BMW appeared to yaw violently and Sir Peter's heart missed a beat as he clearly felt the car's rear end lurch sideways. A burst tyre? He could not be certain but what was increasingly clear, as he struggled to control the now wildly snaking vehicle, was that neither the steering nor the braking system was having any effect on the chaotic course of his maverick car. It was as though the car had developed a mind of its own. It swerved to the right and struck the kerb of the central grass reservation.

Sir Peter sensed the red blur of an approaching car before the actual impact. The 2CV, travelling at seventy miles per hours, struck the BMW head-on and Marman was killed instantly, his skull fractured. His car spun away to the very edge of a sheer forty-foot embankment.

Jake was cheering. 'Perfect ... *ausgezeichnet* ... You are a genius.' He had seen the crash in his mirror. 'Nobody could survive. The 2CV is like a concertina.'

But Meier was shaking. He switched the BMW back to 'Normal' and shouted at Jake. 'Stop, stop. We must be sure the job is done.' As Jake slowed, Meier released his pent-up emotions. 'That was very, very bad. *Never* have I had such trouble in our practice in Boston and Kent. The bloody horsebox ... I am first from the side, then from the front, but all our practice was from behind.'

He wiped his damp forehead and removed his spectacles. 'It would not go straight. Did you not see? I could not get the angle right. So, knowing all was lost if I continued to try for the optimum angle, I slewed it round ... My last chance ... You see, I was too late to crash

into Marman. My only sure chance was for Marman to crash into the BMW.'

'Never mind, you did good. It is finished. Forget the problems.'

Meier reached for the radio and tried de Villiers's call-sign. Silence, but then they had agreed on strict radio silence afterwards.

They were five hundred yards past the scene of the crash. Already, closer to the scene, cars were stopped on both sides of the dual carriageway. Both men grabbed for their binoculars.

John Smythe was horrified. He had used the Ford Escort as a shield all the way from Steeple Langford, keeping well behind, for he was aware of Marman's programme and so was not worried about losing sight of the 2CV. He had begun to nurture suspicions about the driver of the Ford.

When the crash occurred the Escort had gone on past the accident site and out of Smythe's view. He pulled to the side some three hundred yards short of the BMW's resting place. The 2CV was out of sight, down the bank. Smythe was mystified. He was certain he had witnessed a planned murder but who and where was the guilty party?

He reached for his binoculars and scrutinized the occupants of the stationary vehicles as well as the small group of people gathering by the crashed cars. All seemed innocent. Back behind him the road was empty but for moving traffic. However, some two hundred yards away, on the far verge of the dual carriageway, he saw the Volvo and, refocusing his binoculars, felt his skin prickle at the back of his neck. He had studied the Sumail photos long and hard and he had an excellent memory. One of the two men in the Volvo was definitely the man in the floppy hat. The chin, the nose line and the general set of the lower features were identical.

Smythe had no alternative choice of action. When he found a telephone he would give Spike the sad news but, meanwhile, he would gently check out what he fully realized might turn out to be merely an embarrassing coincidence. As he pondered his move, it came to him that *both* Volvo occupants had used binoculars. Bird-watchers or racegoers perhaps? Perhaps not. He decided to avoid any risk of losing them. Instead of turning around at the distant roundabout, he would cross the central reservation. Finding a gap in the traffic, both ways, he did just that.

As Smythe's Morris Marina TC Coupé jolted on to the eastern carriageway, Meier took alarm. This was his undoing, for it served

to confirm Smythe's suspicions. He gave open chase as the Volvo accelerated away. Jake took the Stonehenge Fork and at Tilshead, in the centre of Salisbury Plain, veered east on to West Down. Smythe kept close but, on a minor dirt track, found himself confronted at a sharp bend by the halted Volvo and one of its passengers pointing a gun at his windscreen.

Too close to reverse and unarmed, Smythe knew he stood a good chance of dealing with both men if only he could just get within kicking range of the gun. He could kick more quickly than the gunman could squeeze his trigger. This was not conceit: it was standard knowledge to thousands of karate practitioners everywhere.

Smythe raised his hands and stepped out of the Marina. As Meier moved to frisk him he made his move. The gun, a .44 Magnum Blackhawk, flew to the ground but Meier eluded the follow-up blow and closed in a bear-hug with Smythe.

Jake, having retrieved the revolver, moved behind Smythe and shot him through the back of the neck. This was an error, but Jake was a mechanic, not a gunman, and for a moment he could not comprehend why Meier and Smythe *both* fell to the ground and lay still. He felt a sharp pain in his wrist from the kick of the heavy revolver and his ears rang. Brain, blood and bone splinters from Smythe added to the mess that was Meier's face.

Jake crossed himself instinctively and dragged both bodies into the Volvo's spacious rear compartment. He covered them with the sound-baffle and drove to the agreed rendezvous with de Villiers in Andover.

De Villiers showed no visible distress at the news of Meier's death and accepted without question Jake's explanation of the accident. He phoned a Tadnams number and, three hours later, two men arrived in a Volkswagen Polo. Jake placed some tools and a brake-fluid container in two carrier bags and transferred them to the Polo. They did not see the Volvo again.

De Villiers had watched Sir Peter Horsley being taken off to hospital with head lacerations but otherwise seemingly unhurt. The two wrecked cars were transported to a garage in nearby Amesbury, Panelcraft Motors, which de Villiers had studied carefully before coming to the rendezvous.

At 2 a.m. that night, the two men broke into the garage without difficulty and leaving no signs of their visit. By torchlight they removed all the parasite components, reconnected the brake lines,

bled the brakes and refilled the system with fluid. They were clear of the building by 4 a.m. but the police accident inspector did not arrive until after 11 a.m. and his necessarily rather limited check revealed nothing suspicious.

Three weeks later Sir Peter Horsley was warned that the police were considering a charge against him of causing death by reckless driving. Sir Peter hired a private investigator and, the following April, his name was completely cleared at an inquest in Salisbury. The key factor was evidence from witnesses, such as Mrs Elspeth Allen, the horsebox driver, that Sir Peter's car began to swerve when driving smoothly in the middle of the road and *not*, as the police had suggested, following tyre contact with the kerbside.

The coroner, Mr John Elgar, recorded a verdict of misadventure and concluded, 'Sir Peter's vehicle was seen to snake along the A303 for some reason which we will never know, then crossed the central reservation and came into violent collision with the other vehicle.'

In late November 1986 Davies showed a letter, addressed to him at one of the Tadnam's postal addresses, to de Villiers. The water engineer whom Davies had met at the Anglo-Omani Society's meeting the previous October had written to say how sorry he had been to read of Major Mike Marman's death and that, incidentally, he had been wrong as regards the Zakhir action. Marman had not after all been in the armoured cars on that occasion. The relevant officer had been Captain Simon Marriott, one of the Marman's Troop Leaders in Dhofar.

Both surviving members of the Clinic agreed they would say nothing about this to the sheikh, since Marman remained, by wider definition, responsible for the action. They had acted in good faith and had already received his cheque in return for the film taken in Blandfield Road, newspaper evidence of the ensuing accident and their file on Marman's apparent responsibility for the death of Tama'an bin Amr.

Part 4

36

Epilepsy is common. Five hundred thousand people in Britain alone are epileptics. The disorder can attack anyone, at any time, sometimes developing in old age. Genetic factors are often responsible but, as in Mac's case, an accident can cause structural abnormality to the brain and bring on 'secondary' epilepsy. Anti-convulsant pills usually help epileptics to lead a normal life but there are often side-effects such as nausea, hair loss, coarsening of the features, drowsiness, double vision and disturbing nightmares.

Mac had served with distinction in the SAS until, when he was driving a Land Rover over the Dhofar *jebel* in 1975, a land-mine had blown him into the windscreen. His skull was driven inwards, impacting his brain. Mac had suffered intermittent epileptic fits ever since. His eleven-year-old daughter, Lucia, was a plucky, loving girl who had never known a time when daddy did not have fits. She knew about the recovery position, the dangers of choking and had coped all alone on occasions when she was back from school but her mother was still at work.

Mac never remembered anything about his attacks. But many of his dreams recurred so often that they lingered etched in vivid colours in his waking mind. Most were corrupted regurgitations of his past but, obedient to no normal chronology, they unfolded in a weird disorder as though conjured into being by a madman. Mac was able to repeat every facet of the dreams to Pauline; not that she was able to draw much meaning from them. He would see himself plucking chickens at the factory the previous week then, in an instant, playing children's games with his brother on the hills above Cork away back in the forties.

The war dreams came often and with particular clarity. One began at Windsor Castle with Mac in the dress uniform of the Grenadier Guards. The drill parade passed directly through a wall and entered the dripping woods of the wadi Naheez. Now the other men were

in sweat-streaked camouflage, SAS comrades bearing heavy bergens, their wary eyes darting sideways through dense groves of *habok*, the euphorbia used to treat camel mange. A huge bird alighted and the men, all but Mac and a Hadr tribesman, were gone. Mac loved all living things. He knew the bird was a sacred ibis from the sea-*khors*, or creek. From the *habok* there now issued other wonders, Tristram's grackle, great white pelicans, shrike and sunbird, yellow-vented bulbul, kingfisher and Paradise flycatcher.

The Hadr led Mac into a fluted limestone cavern where together they took combs of light honey from the bees' nests. They sat on a rock and ate the honey unharmed by the angry bees.

'With many others,' said the Hadr, 'I fled from the Yemen to avoid death by *thaa'r*. Everywhere the blood is spilled to avenge previous killings. There can be no end to it.'

Mac's honeycomb became a packet of army hard-tack biscuits. As he crouched low among the boulders, sweat ran down into his eyes. A spider crawled over the back of his neck: he flicked out with repulsion but it was only the parachute-cord necklace to which he had taped his morphine syrettes, wristwatch and identity discs.

Jock Logan tapped him on the shoulder and nodded. The advance was on. The 'Duke' was there, Major Richard Pirie, dead now but always in the dreams. And the CO, Johnnie Watts, with his great wide grin and enormous confidence. G Squadron SAS. Jebel Samhan, Dhofar. Mac, the mortar expert, was part of the heavy gun troop, each man burdened by a hundred and twenty pounds of weaponry, ammunition and water ration: in that heat a crippling load.

Up ahead the ex-communist *firqat* group began to crouch as they advanced, a sheepdog-like lowering of their backs as though sensing some alien presence close by. Mac knew that they could smell the enemy.

An Englishman, Kenneth Edwards, led the *firqat*, the Khalid bin Walid band, and Mac saw him bring up his rifle. Suddenly immediately below them and dead ahead, Mac saw thirty or forty heavily armed *adoo*. Their Kalashnikov assault rifles indicated hard-core guerrillas; the *adoo* militia toted semi-automatic Simonovs. Smoke curled from cook fires. For once the *adoo* had been caught napping.

Max and his group opened fire. Jock Logan, Barrie Davies and Ian Winstone sent a hail of GPMG bullets and 66-mm LAW rockets into the midst of the *adoo*. They charged down, blood-lust up, fear and

heavy loads forgotten. Dead and wounded from both sides soon littered the dustbowl.

In the dream Mac felt again the unbelievable heat, smelled the cordite, heard the buzz of the flies.

They ran short of ammunition and enemy guns from surrounding ridges began to pick them off.

The scene switched to the wadi Adonib in February 1975 with three G Squadron troops 'beating' the forested wadi floor. Mac was halfway up one flanking hill and on a smoke signal from the squadron boss, a peer of the realm, he brought his deadly 60-mm mortar into play with backing from his team, Mick and Ginge. The second round targeted an *adoo* patrol and, when the SAS beaters arrived, nothing was left but a leg and a pair of rubber flip-flops.

Now Mac sat at the long narrow saloon of Chancers Wine Bar with Tosh Ash, as witty as ever, and drinking like there was no tomorrow. Tosh had been one of the lads and fit as fit. Now a pub-keeper and *bon viveur*, his face was florid, unhealthy. They drank to Mac, Callsign Five, Mortar Man Extraordinary. It was one of the better dreams.

On 28 November 1987, thirteen years after the end of their time in Dhofar, Jock Logan and Barry Davies met in Hereford, as was often their wont, and walked together along Hampton Park Road to see their old friend. There were those who no longer visited Mac, perhaps because they had seen him on a bad day when the mood was on him, perhaps merely because their friendship had dissolved with time as is the way of life. But Jock and Barry shared with Mac moments and memories that each of them savoured and knew could never again be matched for sheer intensity of feeling.

Jock had with him a fat and well-thumbed album of photographs, not just of Oman days, but going back to the sixties, when he and Mac and Frank Bilcliff were at the forefront of Britain's rock-climbers. Among many other feats their group had been the first army men ever to scale the Old Man of Hoy's crumbling flanks. Since Dhofar days, Jock had married a pretty lass who had worked at the Bunch of Grapes from 1967 to 1971. They had a lovely daughter now who was the best of friends with Mac's daughter, Lucia, and Jock had been Mac's best man. Jock's home was in Aberdeen, where he thrived at his job as salesman for a drill-bit manufacturer servicing the flourishing oil industry.

Barry Davies was a salesman for Cardiff-based BCB, manufacturers and retailers of survival equipment. He had had his first book published earlier that year, a best-selling manual on survival techniques. Ten years earlier Barry had received the British Empire Medal for his part in an SAS operation sanctioned jointly by Prime Minister Jim Callaghan and Chancellor Helmut Schmidt.

In October 1977 four Palestinian terrorists hijacked a Lufthansa airliner. They were acting in support of the Baader-Meinhof gang and demanded release of the gang's leaders from German jails. A German commando unit from GSG-9 was tasked to release the Lufthansa hostages with help from an SAS officer, Major Alistair Morrison. (Morrison had relieved Kealy's group at Mirbat five years before and in 1979 he was one of the first to learn of Kealy's death on the Brecon Beacons.) Barry, then a sergeant, was tasked to accompany Major Morrison with a supply of special SAS flash-grenades. The hijackers led the Anglo-German team a merry dance and in Aden they murdered the airliner's pilot. Flying on to Mogadishu in Somalia, they dumped the body on the runway, ending any remaining chances of negotiation. Morrison and Davies then led in the highly successful attack by GSG-9 and both men were later decorated for their courage.

Barry was well respected in the SAS but he was by nature an entrepreneur and had for a long while been interested in the housing market inside Hereford. In the late sixties he found an excellent house in a suburb of Hereford for his friend Mac and soon afterwards introduced him to a lovely girl named Pauline, who became Mac's lodger and later his wife.

The two men turned into Salisbury Avenue. It was Saturday. Pauline was at work in town but they had called at her shop, Chelsea Girl, to collect the house keys.

'Pauline says the fits are slowly getting worse despite Mac's medication. His dark moods come more frequently. It must be very difficult for Pauline.'

Jock nodded. 'He's a lucky man having those lassies for wife and daughter. They will stand by him to the end.'

After medication Mac slept for nine hours uninterrupted by the dreams. He awoke refreshed and looking forward to the visit from his friends. He was a quiet, proud and very private man. So long as he was employed in honest work he could keep his head up, no matter how bad the fits. Unfortunately this caused something of a vicious circle since hard work quickly made him exhausted and prone to worse attacks. To fend them off he would increase the tablets, which in turn made him drowsy and brought on the dark, destructive moods.

Mac hated the moods and the way he behaved when under their influence. He wished above all to be the best possible husband, father and friend and he hated feeling exhausted. But, to give up his job, to be unemployed and dependent entirely on Pauline's work, would be more than his personal pride could bear.

During these run-up weeks to Christmas he had to work twice as hard at Sun Valley Poultry, for the chicken orders came thick and fast and everyone was on overtime. He earned a hundred and sixty pounds a week, Monday to Friday, and, despite the fits, had held the job down for several months. Sun Valley was on the far side of town and Mac travelled by bicycle. The pills often affected his balance and made him wobbly. Pauline, he knew, was increasingly worried, especially since a recent incident when a passing van had knocked him off his bicycle on a roundabout.

He fussed around the sitting room and puffed up the cushions. There was little to do as Pauline kept the place immaculate. Lucia was away at a ballet class in Church Road.

Jock and Barry arrived and Mac soon forgot his worries. They spent a merry afternoon in reminiscence, laughing over once shared hardships and recalling long-forgotten faces brought alive by Jock's photographs.

After tea, Mac began to show signs of tiredness and Barry discreetly suggested it was time to leave. Jock promised to return the following day to collect his album and, when they were gone, Mac

sat alone with a lager and thumbed slowly through the pages. He stopped at a photo captioned 'Operation Dharab, January 1975'. The two men with an 81-mm mortar tube were shirtless, bronzed and lean. Mac and Tosh Ash in their prime on the day both were wounded by the same bullet. That day Mac unknowingly became a marked man.

Operation Dharab was planned as the biggest army offensive of the five-year war against the communists, an attempt to attack the guerrilla stores centre of Sherishitti, a complex of caves deep in guerrilla-held mountains. First an army force of six hundred and fifty men would seize the ridgeline position of Defa, then advance into the beginning of the densely foliated zone that began two miles to the south, and on to a pair of bald hilltops known as Point 980. This position overlooked the valley of the caves, two and a half miles to the east. From Point 980 the final advance would be launched at Sherishitti.

The main army force was Jebel Regiment (JR), John Milling's old unit, supported by Red Company of Desert Regiment (DR), whose second-in-command was Captain David Mason. Each of the four companies would have *firqat* guides and SAS liaison men attached. Two SAS troops and a strong *firqat* contingent would lead the advance under the command of SAS Major Arish Trant. Mac, Tosh Ash and their mortars would accompany this group.

On 4 January the Defa position was secured and the advance began. The SAS, after heavy fighting, secured an advanced position and finally Point 980. As over five hundred soldiers arrived at this feature, the SAS moved on to another hill, coded Point 604. As they prepared for the night a small group went forward to lay trip wires and claymore mines just ahead of their position. Tony Shaw, close friend to Mike Kealy and about to take over the SAS squadron in Dhofar, was the point-man and leader of the mine-layers. An *adoo* patrol attacked them and there were casualties on both sides.

A great deal of confusion and indecision held up the advance the following day and the overall Dhofar commander, Brigadier John Akehurst, summarily removed the officer in charge and replaced him with Major Patrick Brook, Mike Marman's predecessor as Armoured Car Squadron leader.

Patrick Brook and the SAS major sent three of the companies east through dense scrub to gain positions above the caves before a final attack on Sherishitti. This move began on the morning of 6 January

but the lead unit, Red Company DR, went a little too far south, a fact they recognized once they reached the wide, open valley that led to the caves. Their company commander, Major Roger King, suggested holding their position along the edge of the great clearing in order to give cover to a further advance by 2 Company JR across the open ground.

Two Company's acting commander, Captain Nigel Loring, arrived and surveyed the wide valley ahead. His *firqat* liaison man, an experienced SAS sergeant, advised him, 'Don't go across. It will be suicide. Go *around* the clearing.' But Loring could see that the open area was well covered from two sides by men of Red Company and, knowing that speed was of the essence, he stood up and led his men out into the sunny clearing, overlooked on the far side by the rocky hillside that was his objective.

When Loring and his lead platoon were well into the open the *adoo* sprang their trap. The far slope exploded with sound. There was no cover, so wounded men were hit again and again until they lay still. Captain Ian MacLucas was hit by seven bullets. Nigel Loring was killed. The killing ground echoed with the groans and the entreaties of the dying. To break cover and enter the valley from either side would require an act of great courage.

The Red Company soldiers and the SAS returned fire as best they could and certain individuals risked all in a crazy attempt to rescue the wounded. One of these was Sekavesi, the giant Fijian who had been with Mike Kealy at Mirbat. Another was Captain David Mason of Red Company, who, weaving from side to side, forced himself through the maelstrom of bullets, rockets and mortar explosions and spent two hours under fire to succour and rally the wounded. He finally staggered back with his friend, the wounded MacLucas. His escape unscathed was miraculous. Within months he was awarded the Sultan's Bravery Medal.

When all their wounded were retrieved, and only the dead left behind, the Sultan's force withdrew to Point 980. Behind them they heard the single shots of the *adoo* firing into the bodies in the clearing.

Jebel Regiment had suffered thirteen dead and twenty-two wounded. Ian MacLucas, saved by David Mason, was still a paraplegic in 1991. Many *adoo*, mostly of the Bin Dhahaib unit, were killed in Operation Dharab. One was Mahad bin Amr bait Anta'ash, the second son of Sheikh Amr's first wife. He was ripped apart by mortar fire from the SAS mortar position.

Mac and Tosh Ash of the G Squadron SAS mortar group were both wounded by the same *adoo* bullet and evacuated by helicopter. Barry Davies was pulled back to take over command of the mortars.

Mac felt a wave of tiredness and carefully laid the album down on the carpet. He was asleep, so Pauline answered the door the next morning when Jock called in, before returning to Aberdeen, to collect his photographs.

As Jock left he noticed, as he had the previous evening, a black Volkswagen Polo parked close by the bus stop opposite Mac's house. The driver, a woman in dark glasses, was reading a magazine and did not appear at all bothered when Jock walked purposefully in her direction.

'Could you tell me the time?' He leaned over so that his face was close to hers.

She smiled and wound down the window. 'Nine fifteen,' she said and returned to the pages of *Cosmopolitan*.

Jock thanked her and returned to his car. The accent was Midlands with no foreign inflection, but that was no guarantee. Why was she there; had been there the previous day? Only a keen, suspicious eye would have picked up any significance in her presence, only somebody who knew of Mac's uniquely hazardous status. Knowing the various terrorist organizations who might have good reason to fear and therefore to hate the SAS, Jock was fully aware that a man with Mac's history and health would be a prime target for any of these groups.

Distinctly uneasy, Jock stopped off at a pay phone in town and called his old comrade-in-arms and long-time friend Detective Constable Ken Borthwick of the Worcester Police. He would know whom to alert.

38

They met on a bench overlooking the Serpentine and surrounded by noisy Canada geese. Spike had not been in touch with Mason for almost a year and the latter was pleased at the short-notice summons.

'Do you remember the events of January, February and March 1975 on the Dhofar *jebel*?'

Mason was surprised by the question but he had good reason to recall the period with clarity.

'I lost some good friends at the time. Do you want a potted history?'

Spike nodded.

'I was attached to Jebel Regiment for the disastrous attack on Sherishitti, an *adoo* weapons store, and I worked closely with their officers. Later, in mid February, at a base called Hagaif, the soldiers from one of the companies involved at Sherishitti mutinied against their major and forced him to leave by night alone in his Land Rover into enemy territory. Three weeks later, two of the remaining Hagaif officers and the pilot of their helicopter were shot down and killed. I knew all of them well.'

Mason paused to light a cigar.

'Four days after the Hagaif mutiny, at my own base close to the Yemen border, I spent the hairiest night of my life. Seven men from another company set out on a patrol via a narrow track below a cliff face. The *adoo* had sewn the track with PMN plastic mines and three of the men were hurt, two losing feet and a great deal of blood. A second group were sent to help but they too ran into mines and only added to the casualties. With another officer, I took a small unit out around midnight and carefully made it some seven hundred feet down the cliff to the first wounded man. There was little we could do but haul the mine victims up on stretchers. One died just before dawn. When I came to one of the wounded he held up the remains of his leg for me to dress. All he said was, "*Al lahham, al qadam, kull khallas*" (The meat, the foot, all finished). At every step we knew

that our own feet might be blown into fragments. A bad night to remember.'

Mason looked up and saw that Spike was waiting. 'That was it. A period of setbacks or so it seemed at the time. Soon after my friends crashed at Hagaif, two other Bells were shot out of the sky with further fatalities and an SAS Land Rover was destroyed east of Hagaif by a land-mine.'

'Did you know the occupants?'

'Of the Land Rover? ... Yes, probably, but not well enough to remember their names.'

'Well, the driver was the finest mortar man in the regiment.' Spike took a sheet of A4 from his briefcase and scanned it. He put on spectacles to do so. Anno Domini, Mason thought wryly. 'You will find his full name and personal details in a file I will give you.' Spike tapped his case. 'When the Land Rover was blown up, he was thrown forwards and badly injured. At the FST unit in Salalah the surgeon diagnosed that the part of his brain controlling his character had been damaged. I will call him Mac, the nickname used by his friends then and now. He appeared to recover very quickly and was soon able to rejoin his squadron out in Belize, sent there to counter the Guatemalan threat. He was promoted to sergeant but had increasing problems with concentration. His attention simply wandered from the job in hand.'

Spike handed the file to Mason and continued. 'About a year after the mine injury, the SAS were forced to retire Mac. He received a handsome army pension and continued treatment by the very best military medicos. A rehabilitation course – he chose welding – was not a success and Mac retired to his home in Hereford and a succession of local jobs. His condition has slowly deteriorated but he still holds down a job and lives with his family and may well continue to do so for years to come.'

Spike swivelled on the bench, looking directly at Mason. 'As an Irishman, Mac is careful to keep a low profile – ex-directory and so on. I was called on Saturday night with a warning that somebody is having Mac watched. The police have checked that there is no evidence of known terrorist involvement, so they are not interested.'

Mason was nodding. 'You think it's our friends again?'

Spike gazed out over the water. 'Milling ... Kealy ... Marman ... all dead ... Smythe missing. This *may* be our chance to catch the people responsible. Maybe not, but it is worth an effort.'

Mason agreed and Spike promised him the support of three other Locals, including Hallett. He told Mason to warn Mac without alarming him unduly; also to give him an ankle-buzzer, a single-frequency alarm transmitter, which Spike handed to Mason in an envelope.

'Search the local hotels for the Sumail men. The old photos may be a bit out of date but better than nothing.'

When Mason left, Spike remained with the geese. The Committee, he knew, would not approve. They would veto any further action involving the Dhofar-connected killings. That was why he had not asked them. For the first time he had instigated action by Locals without Committee approval or even awareness. If they should find out, Spike realized, there would be a move to get rid of him. But they need never know and he was damned if he would miss out on this chance to catch the killers.

39

In November 1986 Sheikh Bakhait received a video and file on the death of Major Michael Marman. A cheque for one million dollars was paid to de Villiers, who passed on an appropriate amount to Davies.

Meier's death caused neither man undue concern but they were baffled by the origins of Smythe. His car, his clothing and his behaviour had shed no light on his identity. The binoculars that he carried were almost antique, certainly not equipment on issue to field agents of Special Branch or the Secret Intelligence Service. They agreed that the two men who had previously crossed their path, during work on the sheikh's contract, had been similarly difficult to classify.

De Villiers shrugged. 'We will get nowhere hypothesizing. Whoever they are, they cannot know our identities and they have only one more chance to intercept us.'

De Villiers returned to Anne at La Pergole, tasking Davies to concentrate on locating the sheikh's fourth man to the exclusion of all other work. This Davies proceeded to do with the utmost care.

Not one but two million dollars were at stake for the completion of the sheikh's contract. Even so, Davies was thoroughly wary.

He spent an unprecedented amount of time in Cardiff with his wife and, since this frustrated her normal philandering, he found her difficult to please without maintaining a shower of expensive gifts, weekend flights to exotic spots and healthy cheques for the business. In between bouts of wife-cossetting, Davies rented a small flat in Hereford and, over a five-month period, frequented a number of local pubs known to be haunts of the SAS. He perpetuated his standard cover as an insurance salesman and became known as a congenial divorcee who liked nothing better than to dispense alcoholic largesse and enjoy good company. Determined to raise no suspicions, Davies asked no questions and merely bided his time, listening and waiting for the right contact.

Sheikh Amr had been specific. His son had died fighting Sultanate troops near Sherishitti on that fatal day in January 1975. Together with two other *jebalis* of the Bin Dhahaib unit he had been killed by a mortar barrage from the army position on the twin bald hills to the east of Zakhir. De Villiers's discovery of the book *SAS Operation Oman* had revealed that the man in charge of the mortars on that day was not, as they had thought, a Sultan's Forces soldier but rather an SAS mortar controller.

In May 1987 Davies joined two of his Hereford pub acquaintances for a meal at a fish and chip shop called Chancers. He was introduced to the owner, a friendly, hard-drinking fellow, who also owned an adjacent wine bar and upstairs restaurant. Davies became a regular patron of the wine bar and a confidant of its owner, Tosh Ash, ex-member of G Squadron SAS.

Tosh and his wife had in 1986 purchased the Golden Galleon fish and chip shop and the adjoining premises. They had worked hard to convert the site and lived in a comfortable flat above the restaurant. By the following spring the place was a proper little gold-mine and the wine bar attracted many of the older SAS men of Tosh's generation, who enjoyed the atmosphere of the long, narrow bar, audio-visual jukebox and ceiling-suspended monitor screens, as well as palatable plonk at good prices.

Despite Davies's growing friendship with Tosh and the fact that he was not after information that could conceivably be described as classified, let alone secret, the months passed by with no sign of progress. Davies knew that, to an SAS man, secrecy is a fetish. All

his careful preparations would be wasted were he to ask a single question out of place. So, he kept his patience and explained the delay as best he could when de Villiers made enquiring phone calls.

One cold autumn evening Tosh asked Davies up for a drink in his flat above the restaurant. Over a stiff whisky Tosh poured out his woes. Life was a bastard. His health was giving out and the wife was being awkward, very awkward. Davies, having listened to local gossip, thought there might be good reason for such awkwardness but he said nothing. Tosh became maudlin. Without prompting from Davies, he began to reminisce about the army. The finest days of his life. How he wished he was back. He mentioned many weird names in various parts of the world that meant nothing to Davies until the word Sherishitti dropped from heaven into his lap. He was ready for it. 'That was where you attacked the cave system, wasn't it Tosh?'

Tosh was surprised. Did Davies know about Sherishitti?

Davies laughed. 'Your memory is going. You told me all about the event a month ago.' To prove it he reeled off all that he knew by heart from many readings of the Jeapes and Akehurst accounts of the action. 'I think,' he ended, 'that you said you were controlling the mortars on hill 985.'

'No, no, no,' Tosh exclaimed. 'That was poor old Mac, the best mortar-man in the British Army. I was with him' — he subconsciously felt for the old wound in his wrist — 'and we were both hit by the same bullet. But he was the boss with the tube, not me.'

'Why *poor* Mac? Did he die?'

Tosh shook his head.

'No, though sometimes I think he wishes that he had. His skull was damaged some weeks after Sherishitti and he's never been the same since. A proud man, Mac, still keeps a job down, over at Sun Valley Poultry, however sick he's feeling.'

Tosh filled their glasses and they drank to Mac and other absent friends. 'He comes in here from time to time. You've probably seen him.' Tosh reached for a black book entitled *This is the SAS*, by Tony Geraghty, and thumbed through it. 'That's Mac.' He indicated a photograph of Prince Charles inspecting four SAS soldiers back in 1970. 'The fellow on the right with the sharp nose.' Tosh chuckled to himself, his mood beginning to lift as his domestic worries receded. 'You should have seen old Mac with a mortar. He could aim by sheer instinct, ignoring the aiming marker, and I never saw him miss a target.'

Tosh sighed and stood up. 'Give either of us a mortar nowadays and we'd be hard pushed to hit an advancing regiment. You ought to see poor Mac on his bike. Wobbles all over the place. Bloody lethal to himself and everyone else. Mind you some days he's quite OK; it all depends on his pills. Up at the factory they say he gets so drowsy sometimes, the other lads have to cover up for him.'

Davies told Tosh he was unlikely to call again for a while owing to pressure of work. That night he called de Villiers to come at once.

Three days of observation outside Sun Valley Poultry revealed nine possible Macs but only one whose features tallied with Tosh's photograph. Davies followed the man to Salisbury Avenue and, on the third day, noticed the cyclist's problems with balance. Outside the factory that evening Davies heard the words, 'See you tomorrow, Mac', shouted by a colleague and knew he had his man. The watch of the Salisbury Avenue house was maintained by the Tadnams people, allowing Davies to establish the movements of Mac, his wife, his daughter and all callers to the house.

In the last week of November, soon after the arrival of de Villiers, a car with a doctor's sign on the rear window parked outside Mac's house and Davies followed the driver back to Sarum House Surgery in Ethelburt Street. At 2 a.m. on Wednesday 2 December de Villiers let himself quietly into the surgery, leaving no trace of entry. There was only one 'Mac' with the correct address in Salisbury Avenue and de Villiers photographed the relevant details on his medical file.

'He has epilepsy,' he told Davies back in their car. 'He may die in a few days or after many years.'

'Are you saying we'd better hurry?' Davies asked.

De Villiers ignored the question. 'What's the prognosis, to date?' continued Davies.

'Easy. He spends many weekends at home and often alone. The best time is Saturday morning at 8.15 a.m. The wife will have gone to work and the daughter to ride her pony. The only other possibility is on his bicycle, but that is a definite second best as he usually travels at the busiest times of day.'

De Villiers drove to London to collect the necessary equipment.

Davies never returned to Chancers. Tosh Ash died eight months later. His body was found by the seaside in Spain. It seemed that he had taken his dog for a coastal walk and, when another dog attacked his, he died of a heart attack.

40

Early in December David Mason's other commitments forced him to withdraw from the Salisbury Avenue watch. Darrell Hallett met him in a tea-room in Ross and took over the operation. Mason had already visited a number of hotels and bed and breakfast houses asking for help to trace the men in the Sumail photographs. There had been no response despite the paucity of out-of-season tourists and Mason's two Mac-watchers had seen no sign of outside interest in the house or the man.

Hallett was no longer selling Yorkie bars. After his twelve years of faithful service, his employers had put pressure on him and others to resign as they wanted to reduce their sales force in South Wales. With free help from two ex-SAS officers, one a city barrister, Hallett had fought for his rights and, on 28 March 1985 at the Cardiff Industrial Tribunal, he had won £3,500 in an out-of-court settlement from Rowntree in respect of his claim of unfair dismissal. By dint of hard work, he had begun to build a new career with one of the major life-assurance groups and found it increasingly difficult to take time off for Spike. Wild horses, however, would not keep him from another chance of meeting up with the elusive Welshman.

Mason explained the VHF pocket receiver, which would bleep should Mac press his ankle-buzzer — an action easily and unobtrusively carried out even at gunpoint.

'How long does Spike want Mac covered?' Hallett asked.

'For as long as the two of us are game.'

'D'you realize this thing has been going on for nearly ten years and we're still none the wiser as to the motives of the opposition.'

Mason stubbed out his cigar, ignoring the glare of the elderly waitress, who instantly removed the evil-smelling ashtray. 'You say ten years, Darrell, but we don't know that we were in at the beginning. Milling may not have been their first target. Nor do we have any idea how many more people they are after.'

'Why do you give up valuable time for Spike?'

Mason smiled. 'I like the man. I believe there is a need for us. We

harm nobody but characters who would, without us, continue to harm others. What about you?'

'I'm Welsh,' Hallett mused. 'I like to see fair play and, in this particular case, the boyo you followed to Muscat once gave me a very stiff neck.'

'Charles Bronson and his *Death Wish* films have done us no big favour,' said Mason. 'No member of the public would be seen dead condoning vigilantism and that is how our activities, if revealed, might be classified. The silent majority might approve but most would never admit it. Just listen to the shrill squeals directed at the very idea of Guardian Angels on the London Underground. Everyone knows there are not enough Transport Police to protect the passengers yet few approve of the thought of red-bereted patrols.'

'I can think of nobody,' Hallett interrupted, 'who would not support the Angels when saved from yobbos or rapists on a dark and lonely Tube platform.'

'Too right,' said Mason, 'but the fools who denounce our existence do not stop to think of the lives we have saved and the fears we have eased.'

'Ah well,' said Hallett, paying the bill, 'I am proud to have worked with Spike and you and the others. To hell with the righteous bloody Pharisees. My conscience is clear and that's what I have to live with.'

'Are you happy with everything?' Mason asked, handing Hallett the receiver.

Hallett smiled. 'If they show their faces, they'll regret it.'

41

Both men wore dinner jackets but the soles of their patent-leather shoes were rubber. It was their custom, when walking in cities at night, to dress in the manner least likely to alert the suspicions of patrolling policemen. People in smart dinner jackets are seldom involved in the pursuit of physical crimes. Davies carried a briefcase.

At 3 a.m. de Villiers and Davies donned thin leather gloves and entered the shrub garden to the immediate right of Mac's house. The

previous night Davies had used a silenced .22 to shatter the lamp of an unwelcome street light in Salisbury Avenue.

Once within the darkness of Mac's rear garden the two men placed triangles of black cloth over their necks. These covered the whiteness of their dress shirts and they moved like shadows into the gloom of an adjacent garden. It was possible that some busybody insomniac might have seen them enter the premises and called the police. If so, they could expect a visit during the next hour and would evade any front-and-rear police approach.

After an hour, damp and cold, de Villiers deemed it safe and they entered Mac's garage, which functioned only as a storage shed, to wait out the early hours.

At 6.30, well before dawn, they slipped across the big, open garden to the rear of the house. Both men were agile and Davies had previously checked all relevant details. Mac always kept his bedroom window wide open, appeared to sleep soundly, probably because of his medication, and apart from caged hamsters there were no animals or birds kept as pets. All windows were hinged, not sash-operated, with firm, ample outer sills.

Standing on the window-sill of the dining room, de Villiers reached up and soundlessly raised himself up to and through Mac's open window. Davies followed. Deep breathing indicated an undisturbed Mac, so both men entered the large double wardrobe at the far side of the bed, and settled down for a further wait.

At 7.30 Pauline and Lucia rose, washed and ate breakfast. Pauline normally worked on Saturdays and, before leaving the house, would say goodbye to Mac, who had the weekends off. That morning, shortly before 8 o'clock, she popped her head around the landing door to his bedroom and saw that he was sleeping soundly. Closing the door quietly, she left for the bus stop, a stone's throw from the house.

'What about the daughter?' de Villiers whispered as the front door slammed shut.

'She will have gone too. She has ballet or riding classes on Saturday mornings.'

Silently they emerged from the wardrobe, keeping a wary eye on the sleeping Mac.

The plan, starkly simple, had been conceived by Davies after studying Mac's medical report and a good deal of literature on the topic of epilepsy. Cling film applied to mouth and nostrils would cause

asphyxiation, and death would be attributed to a severe epileptic fit. Coroners, Davies knew, will seldom spend more time and energy than common sense dictates. If there is no reason to suspect foul play, why waste hours searching for signs of it? If the BBC World Service announcer Gyorgi Markov had not been Bulgarian or had not complained long and loud about an invisible umbrella jab in his leg, his coroner would never have initiated the blood tests that uncovered the rare toxin leaked into his bloodstream from an ampoule smaller than a pinhead.

Everyone, including his doctor, knew that Mac's condition was gradually worsening and death by asphyxiation following a fit would surprise no one. Davies set up the video camera on its light alloy tripod at the side of Mac's bed head and de Villiers silently mouthed his accusation from a prepared script. A gauze-filtered spotlight was affixed to the camera. The video showed the back of Mac's head on his pillow and de Villiers facing him from the far side of his bed. Later they would synchronize de Villiers's voice to his lip movements. The sheikh would receive enough visual evidence to satisfy him. He would not see Mac's face during the accusation sequence, but this would be rectified by what followed.

Davies moved the tripod in readiness for the next action. Mac's duvet was awry and his legs uncovered, but he remained in the deepest of sleeps because of the side-effects of his pills.

'What the hell?' Davies hissed in alarm. He had spotted the buzzer strapped to Mac's ankle.

'Don't worry,' de Villiers murmured, 'many patients have them to summon aid if in distress.'

'But why on his ankle?' Davies was definitely unhappy.

'Whatever the reason, remove it,' de Villiers snapped.

With everything ready for a hasty departure while the last dark vestiges of the winter dawn remained, Davies moved to the bed head and unpeeled the cling film. He nodded to de Villiers. In a single movement, they straddled Mac's body, de Villiers pinning down his legs and arms and Davies, with his knees over Mac's shoulders, applying the cling film to his mouth and nostrils.

The result was not as expected. Mac was not of a robust stature but he was tough and wiry. In normal circumstances he could never have unseated both men while starved of oxygen. But, within seconds of the interruption to his rhythmic breathing, Mac's limbs lashed out with superhuman power produced by a convulsive, myoclonic attack

triggered by brain disturbance. De Villiers was thrown to the floor but Davies managed to retain his position. De Villiers heard noises downstairs. He pulled at Davies and both men retired to the cupboard.

Lucia had decided to skip her ballet class. She was watching television in the sitting room when she heard a thud from her father's bedroom. She knew at once that he had fallen over, probably in a fit, and ran up to help him.

Lucia had dealt with Mac's fits for many years but nothing like the violent convulsive attack that she saw her father was now suffering. Sensibly, she rushed straight downstairs to call for assistance from the neighbours.

De Villiers and Davies heard Mac crash to the floor and Lucia leave the house. Every second counted. They climbed down to the lawn and reached the road several gardens away from Mac's house. Within two minutes of Lucia's sudden appearance, both men were well separated from the scene.

An ambulance, summoned at once by the neighbours, arrived within minutes but Mac was dead on arrival at the hospital. The cause of death was later to be confirmed by autopsy as asphyxia due to a fall and subsequent blockage of the air passage by the tongue.

At 8.30 Pauline got off the bus close by Chelsea Girl in Maylord Orchards Shopping Precinct, to be met by two policemen. They had been called by radio as soon as the ambulance crew sent news of Mac's death.

Hallett's watchman during the night of 12 December was a reliable man from Portsmouth who worked in a travel agency and had served some years before with D Squadron of the Territorial SAS. He remembered seeing two dinner-jacketed passers-by during the small hours but had certainly not noticed them go into Mac's garden. Nor had there been any other suspicious signs or sounds audible from his car until Lucia had burst from the front door and, soon afterwards, the ambulance had arrived.

The watchman, known to all but Spike as 'Wally', telephoned Hallett's hotel but could not make contact. He kept trying.

Hallett, unaware that the Tadnams watchers had withdrawn some days earlier on Davies's orders, had grown impatient with his own passive waiting role and decided to put himself into the mind of the Welshman. How would *he* learn more about Mac? Hallett knew from Spike that Mac received occasional check-ups from Professor

Hitchcock, a neurosurgeon in Harley Street, but was cared for on a general basis locally. He deduced that Mac's general practitioner, a Dr Wylie of the local Sarum House surgery, may well have received a visit from the Welshman, posing in all probability in some suitable role. Hallett arrived early at the surgery to avoid queuing patients, only to find that the place was shut. He drove slowly back to Salisbury Avenue and found Wally's car by the nearest phone box.

'What's up?' he asked.

'Mac's daughter rushed out of the house around 8.10 and, soon after, an ambulance came and they took Mac away. I was trying to call you.'

Hallett took the phone and called the hospital, saying he was a relative. He put the phone down and turned to Wally.

'He's dead.' He shook his head in consternation. 'If you saw no one enter the premises, he may well have died through natural causes connected with epilepsy.'

He called Spike, who thanked him and asked for a full report that he would collect that evening. Hallett and Wally, after calling Mason and one other Local with the sad news, retired to their Ross hotel, Wally to catch up on his sleep and Hallett to complete the report. That evening, soon after Spike had come and gone, a porter brought Hallett a message with a telephone number to call back.

A woman with a Welsh accent replied. She had just come off duty at the Green Dragon Hotel in Hereford. He might remember contacting her two weeks previously. Hallett did not, but he knew Mason had shown the Sumail photographs at the Green Dragon and left their hotel contact number plus the promise of a healthy tip should anyone resembling the men in the photographs turn up at the Dragon.

The woman, reassured by an eagerly affirmative response from Hallett, passed on the information that a man, very similar to the stockier of the three described, had booked a double room for the night just before she had gone off duty. Hallett took her address and promised her ten pounds for her troubles. Spike was *en route* and uncontactable but Hallett knew what to do. He went to wake Wally at once.

42

Davies felt unusually elated and relieved. A call from the Tadnams woman had confirmed that Mac was without question dead and there were no signs of undue police activity at his home indicating official suspicion of foul play. De Villiers had gently replaced the receiver, raised a hand to Davies's shoulder and exclaimed, 'You did well, very well indeed.' Unprecedented praise and it went with a rare if fleeting smile that quite unsettled Davies. 'I will contact you as usual, when I leave Dubai,' had been de Villiers's parting words.

Davies had determined to celebrate before returning to Cardiff. He had taken a room at the most expensive-looking hotel in the centre of Hereford, smartened himself up in gear that he considered decidedly trendy and driven to a local jeweller's. Then he had picked up a bored forty-year-old housewife in a singles bar and taken her to the Crystal Rooms disco, where they pretended they were back in the late sixties.

At 6 p.m. Hallett reserved two single rooms at the Green Dragon under false names. He and Wally booked in at 7.30, had supper, then split up. Hallett remained reading magazines within sight of Reception and Wally retired to his room.

The woman looked pretty good by candlelight. Only dedicated aerobics, Davies decided, could keep her in the shape that so provocatively beckoned from her tight teenage jeans and open-neck, frilly white shirt.

'Getting quite randy, aren't we,' she cooed as a Johnny Mathis ballad ended. They left the disco and, in his car, he gave her the pearl earrings just to make sure. Her left hand confirmed his expectations and he drove her back to the Green Dragon.

Davies and the woman arrived back at the hotel soon after 10 p.m.

'Thank you very much, sir.' The receptionist handed him his key and pocketed the ten-pound note. She made no comment, then or later, about Davies's companion. Davies had pre-paid for his room, as was his custom.

Hallett recognized Davies immediately and noted the number of

his room. The woman was a complication but Hallett's mind was made up.

Davies watched the woman undress with the mirror behind her. The champagne he had ordered that afternoon was ostentatiously expensive. She giggled as the cork eased silently free and he touched her glass against her nipple. They entwined arms as they toasted the night ahead of them. 'To your imagination,' Davies grinned and let her undress him.

'How will we get in?' Wally asked. 'Credit card?'

'Not with a modern hotel door, boyo.'

'But the Green Dragon's nine hundred years old.'

'So it is, so it is. But the door locks have changed with the times. Trusthouse Forte will have seen to that.'

Hallett took a ring of tools from his wash bag and silently opened the locked door of Wally's room from the outside.

'So long as the Welshman does not apply the chain, there will be no problem and I think he will have other matters on his mind just now.'

'Where did you learn how to use those things?' Wally asked.

Hallett replied by placing one finger along the side of his boxer's nose. From his wash bag he now withdrew a coil of thin wire, a simple poacher's snare, and placed it in the chest pocket of his windcheater. He again phoned Spike and this time made contact.

When he replaced the phone he told Wally, 'We are to go ahead but, I quote, "do him no harm". If we succeed we are to park your van by the Upleadon crossroads, east of Newent, where a Y-registration Volvo will collect our cargo.'

While Hallett held the attention of the receptionist, Wally took their bags out to his Bedford, an old van that had seen better days. Wally returned and asked Hallett, in front of the receptionist, where his colleague was. 'Must be upstairs still, the idle devil. Never mind, we'll go and get him. Pinch a drink on his room bill, then bring him down.'

They took the stairs to the second floor.

The door responded to Hallett's practised technique and the security chain was not in place. The bedside light was on but the bed was empty. There were unmistakable sounds from the far side of the room. The thick carpet ensured their approach was noiseless and Hallett elongated the rabbit snare's loop to fit over Davies's head.

The woman's eyes were closed and her mouth open. Her legs were

clasped around Davies's back as they rocked back and forth. Hallett changed his mind and, adjusting the size of the wire loop, bent down and pulled it tight around Davies's scrotum. The effect was immediate. Davies swore and withdrew from the woman. Further movement was strictly limited since Hallett kept the wire taut.

'Try to be clever and my friend will drill your stomach with .44 calibre lead.' Davies tugged ineffectively at the snare. 'But only after I have castrated you.' Wally, taking the hint, bulked out his jacket pocket with his right hand.

Hallett gave the naked woman a friendly smile and nodded towards the bed. She eased away from under Davies and, following Hallett's instructions, slit the rear seam of Davies's trousers from crutch to waistband with Wally's penknife.

'Get up and get dressed,' Hallett bade the Welshman, 'No, not the pants. My friend will take them.'

With difficulty, and wincing from the pain in his testicles, Davies put on his trousers, holding them in place with one hand. Then his shirt, jacket and raincoat. Finally his socks and shoes, an especially painful process.

'You are a lucky girl,' Hallett told the woman. 'This man has already cut the throats of two ladies. You will stay here and speak to nobody. Tomorrow morning you will leave as though nothing has happened. No further harm will come to you if you do exactly as I say. Understand?'

The woman cowered on the bed, clutching her breasts. She nodded vehemently. 'Thank you, thank you. I promise.' Hallett believed her but he tore the phone cable from its wall plug before they left.

Wally moved down the stairs beside Davies. Hallett stayed a step behind them, keeping taut the thin wire that disappeared into the rear vent of Davies's raincoat. As the three men passed the receptionist Wally handed in his and Hallett's keys. 'Back in a couple of hours,' he promised.

From the Bedford van, Wally produced a ball of orange twine with which he lashed the Welshman's thumbs and wrists together behind his back. The free end of the snare was then fastened to the wrist knot. Both men hauled Davies into the rear of the van and laid him face down among the garden tools and other odds and ends that Wally kept there.

They drove down Victoria Street and crossed the Wye by Greyfriars Bridge, heading south for the A49. Hallett turned to look back

through the mesh of the dog-grille between the driver's compartment and the rear of the van.

'You killed Mac, didn't you? And the others. You bastard! Who are you? Who pays you? My God, I hope you live to regret everything you've done.'

Davies squirmed some inches to the left and positioned his wrists against the blade of Wally's trenching shovel. Quietly he applied pressure in a see-saw motion until the twine was cut and his arms were free.

He waited for a steeply descending stretch of the road. Up ahead he saw approaching car lights and lurched for the rear doors of the van. Finding no inner handle, he kicked out with all his might at the central catch and, as Wally brought the van to a skidding halt, the right-hand rear door burst open and Davies rolled out into the road. His concentration was focused on the oncoming cars, to flag them down and, probably, plead abduction by thugs. He did not see the juggernaut that sped downhill behind them until it was too late.

The driver, tired and caught unawares by Wally's sudden halt, had decided his best answer was speed, to overtake the van and return to his side of the road before the arrival of the oncoming cars. From his point of view a sensible decision but, by the time he saw Davies, his momentum was unstoppable. The nearside corner of the lorry's bumper struck Davies and catapulted his body to the side of the road. The driver narrowly avoided colliding with the approaching traffic and thundered on his way without pausing.

The lorry's lights must have blinded the approaching car drivers so that none witnessed Davies's death. At any rate no one stopped.

'Quick.' Hallett did not hesitate. 'Get him.' They picked up the limp and shattered body. As they bundled it into the back of the van, the driver of a car coming up fast behind them from the north with dipped headlights, flicked on full beam and illuminated Hallett, Wally and the body. As he flashed by, the driver applied his horn in an angry peal.

'Did he see us?' Wally asked.

'Maybe,' said Hallett. 'We will have to assume that he did. He may have a car phone. We must get off this road as soon as we can.'

By a circuitous route they reached the agreed rendezvous. The Volvo driver, to whom Hallett handed his report, hastily updated, agreed to take Wally straight back to his home.

'If the police visit you,' Hallett instructed Wally, 'simply say your

van has been stolen. If nothing happens, I will tell you in a week or so where I have left it. Thanks for your help.'

They placed Davies's body in the back of the Volvo. Hallett assumed Spike would know what to do with it. He drove Wally's van to a free car park in Ross and then hitched a lift back to his car.

Hallett telephoned Spike from home and was thanked in a non-committal tone. He had no way of imagining the ructions that would be caused by Davies's death, since he, like all the Locals, knew nothing of the workings of the Committee, nor the identities of the members.

43

The meeting was held in the Wandsworth home of Bob Mantell. There was a full house despite the short notice.

Colonel Macpherson arrived early. He was expecting big trouble, and had seen it coming from the moment Spike had called with the news. He was angry with Spike yet, without admitting it openly, sympathetic to the thought processes that had led Spike into acting as he had, without authority.

There was nothing that could be done now about Mac except to add his name to the list of those the Feather Men had failed to protect. At least Spike had tried: Macpherson knew the Committee would have refused any request Spike might have made for an authorized Mac-watch. Nevertheless, Spike had unintentionally caused what Macpherson recognized to be conditions ripe for a showdown.

Spike had assured Macpherson that there was no longer any traceable evidence that the Welshman was dead, by whatever cause, but even so Macpherson had instructed him to send a full report on the accident to their in-house solicitor and to be ready for police enquiries at any time. Hallett and Wally were told to make no comment but to contact the solicitor at once if they received a visit from the police.

Tommy Macpherson sighed. If only the Founder had been well enough to attend the meeting and make his presence felt there might

yet be a sensible outcome. As it was, Bletchley would undoubtedly blow a gasket and do something foolish.

The Committee members were unusually silent as they awaited the start of the proceedings. Jane completed her vacuum-flask routine to a roll-call of 'thank you's' and Bletchley, whose personal hygiene and mannerisms had deteriorated so much that the Committee members no longer doubted that he was seriously ill, received his in an unbreakable mug. Unsubstantiated hints that he had some sexually transmitted disease were circulating but, when August Graves had openly asked him what was wrong following a particularly alarming attack of leg jerking and impaired speech, he had merely responded, 'Nothing's wrong. Nothing at all.'

Graves had approached Macpherson and most of the others individually and suggested that Bletchley be asked to resign. The majority view was that he should remain in the chair for as long as he wished. After all, his presence at meetings, although embarrassing owing to his impediments, did not in practice curtail their routine activities. So Bletchley had remained nominally at the helm alongside Macpherson. His hostility towards what he chose to see as 'increasingly irregular behaviour by certain elements of our movement' had grown to paranoiac proportions.

'Colonel Macpherson,' Bletchley salivated as he spoke, 'has called us together due to exceptional happenings.' He nodded curtly at Macpherson, who thanked him and, without undue preamble, broke the unwelcome news. He gave a resumé of the Dhofar-connection killings and explained why Spike had seen fit to act over the Mac affair without Committee approval.

Spike stared impassively at his lap under the hostile stares of the members. When Macpherson related the events leading to the death of Davies, there were shocked murmurs from the Grey Men and Panny, a strangulated grunt from Bletchley and an angry snarl from Mantell. Jane, the Don and August Graves remained outwardly impassive.

'I must stress,' said Macpherson, 'that our people did not murder Davies. Indeed they did no physical damage whatsoever to his person. They did not in any way precipitate his death but they were there and they did witness the event without reporting it to the police. They further compounded the problem by disposing of the body.' He paused and then spoke slowly and clearly. 'This may come to nothing. The police may never even learn of the event. Perhaps

no motorist contacted them or did so without having taken the number of the Bedford van. Nonetheless, if our driver is traced and, via him, Spike and the Committee, then *all* of us will have questions to answer.'

He looked at all those present in turn. 'I must also stress that the authorities *may*, through this incident, learn of our existence and, if they do, you will all, theoretically, be implicated as conspirators in events leading to a death; possibly presented as manslaughter. In order to prepare for the worst, I called you all together without delay to discuss and execute a suitable course of action.' He sat down.

For a moment there was stunned silence, then Bletchley stood up, his mouth gaping goldfish-like. Almost immediately his balance gave and he sat down again. His words came hissing out in a rush.

'Ruined. All these years. Ruined.' He glared at Spike. 'How *dare* you act without my authority? Do you realize you have irreparably damaged the very soul of our movement? And what of our personal reputations? Our integrity? If this gets out we will be drummed out of our clubs, our directorships, the City ... my God, it does not bear thinking about.'

He looked around wildly, his gaze settling with intensity on Mantell and Jane. 'There is but one course of action and we must take it firmly and at once. All the records, Jane, every file and every document, must be destroyed right away. Burnt. At once. And we must disband as of now. It must be as though we never existed, should the police come searching.'

He reached for his coffee and gulped at it greedily, spilling some down his shirt and over the table. For a while he could not talk and his head jerked sideways in a series of violent spasms. The condition slowly eased, although his shoulders continued to shake and beads of sweat trickled down his forehead. Nobody spoke.

Again a burst of indignation and anger. 'How *dare* you, Allen, follow your own private war, which this has undoubtedly become, and without reference to the Committee? You have caused untold harm. If this escalates, even our Founder's name will be besmirched. Everything I, many of us, have built up over so many years, all torn down by your stupidity. There is but one course now and that is damage limitation. The Committee must disappear from being and, I tell you now, I will personally consider what I shall do to protect my own reputation.'

Drained, Bletchley slumped like a dying spider. Jane watched him

with obvious concern but did nothing. Mantell filled the gap. 'I can only agree with our Chairman's decision. Extremely sad though it makes me, any course other than disbandment would be to court extreme unpleasantness for each and every one of us. I suggest a show of hands.' There was a general nodding of heads and the matter was put to an open vote.

Only Graves and Tommy abstained; the rest voted in favour of disbandment. Mantell telephoned the Founder and relayed his vote, which, to the unspoken surprise of most people present, was in favour of Bletchley's motion: immediate closure and destruction of all records. Existing business was to be curtailed as neatly and speedily as possible by Mantell working alongside Spike.

The Feather Men, it appeared, ceased to exist as from Monday 14 December 1987.

The following morning Macpherson took a further step since, with no further action from the Feather Men, he feared the possibility of an unchecked continuation of the Dhofar-connection killings. During his 1983–4 tenancy of the office of High Sheriff of Greater London he had made many police friends. Now he telephoned the most senior of them to ask for an immediate off-the-record meeting.

Later that day he told his friend that certain people with whom he had served in the past had uncovered the fact of, but not the motive behind, a series of murders of ex-Forces personnel. The most recent incident involved Mac in Hereford and there was reason to believe a man thought to have been killed two days previously in a road accident on the A49 was one of the killers. He knew no more and could say no more, but could the four cases be re-examined?

The police officer called Macpherson back three days later. There was no mention of any death on the A49. 'We have looked at the files on the deaths that occurred in the United Kingdom and we cannot see any grounds for reopening them unless some new motive and/or evidence is produced.'

Macpherson had expected this response, but felt he owed his action to those who had tried to protect the killers' targets. He received a worried call from Jane the following week and as a result met up with her and Spike at the London office of the Founder. Jane, torn between her loyalty to the movement as a whole and her personal devotion to Bletchley, owned up to an action she much regretted. At Bletchley's insistence and in the state of shock that followed disbandment, she had taken Bletchley a single clutch of files

before undertaking the soul-destroying business of burning all the records that she had lovingly prepared, collated and filed for so many years.

Only when she had delivered the files had Bletchley made clear his reason for wanting them. He had made up his mind to write a book and reveal how *his* movement had been derailed by Macpherson and others, how even the Founder himself had been hoodwinked into condoning the following of dangerous, unethical paths, how a magnificent and pure concept had been dragged into a mire of vigilantism and how he, Bletchley, disassociated himself from the unfortunate results. He had appeared terrified lest his zealously nurtured reputation be blemished by a police investigation and the resultant publicity owing to the Davies fiasco or, should that not materialize, some similar future indiscretion.

Jane had attempted to dissuade Bletchley from such a course but the man was delirious. He had refused to give Jane back the files.

'Which files?' Macpherson asked her.

'1977–87: The Dhofar-connection deaths,' she replied.

'Do you think he really intends to go to print?' Spike asked.

'If he was able to think clearly about the results of such a book,' Macpherson replied, 'no I don't. But the man is, in my opinion, no longer *compos mentis*. I am not worried for myself but we must not allow the Founder's good name or yours to be falsely tarnished by the warped and inaccurate version of events that Bletchley's deranged blatherings are likely to be. His revelations, in the hands of the wrong MP, caring nothing for the truth, could be immensely damaging and serve to blemish the Founder's enormous achievements for this country.'

'So what do we do?' asked Spike.

'I will privately approach the top libel lawyer, Peter Carter-Ruck, for advice. Maybe such a book could be stopped on some libel basis. I will let you know but there is something else that may make it impossible for Bletchley ever to write this or any book.' He passed Spike a single typed sheet of A4.

'Before you read that, let me tell you something of Bletchley's background. He was adopted when his parents were killed in a train crash in the 1920s. After Sandhurst he joined a rifle regiment in 1938 and saw action against the Italians in the western desert in the early forties. He was one of only a few officers with desert experience to be promoted to the Army Staff in Cairo and he did an excellent job

which greatly helped turn the tables on Rommel. At the end of the war he faced rank reduction from lieutenant-colonel to captain, so he left to become an accountant.'

'A far cry from his current City pre-eminence,' Spike commented.

'Quite so,' Macpherson agreed. 'But his timing was good and he "left the profession" at a time of post-war expansion to become Finance Director of an independent company. He never looked back and retired aged fifty-five in 1972 to a plethora of non-executive directorships and top charity appointments. Until his illness developed, everybody admired him. He was the perfect Chairman: respectable, pedantic and safe, undeniably clever and rich in influential friends.'

'What is his health problem?' Spike asked. 'Does anybody know?'

Macpherson nodded at the paper he had given Spike. 'Read it,' he said. 'If I am right, and all the symptoms seem to fit, then Bletchley was first affected, in character only, in the early seventies. The *physical* signs first became marked only last year. That précis was prepared for me by a friend in Edinburgh.'

Spike read the text aloud: 'In 1872 the American, George Huntington, first defined a disease, which is now named after him, as Hereditary Chorea (*chorea* means to dance). Huntington wrote, 'The disease is confined to few families and has been transmitted to them as an heirloom from generations way back in the dim past. It is spoken of by those in whose veins the seeds of the disease are known to exist with a kind of horror. The disease is now understood a great deal better and certain drugs can delay its dread progress although it is still classified as incurable. One in every twenty thousand people worldwide is affected.

'Twenty or even forty years may separate the first tiny mood changes that signal the onset, from the chronic mental and physical afflictions that lead to death, usually by asphyxiation whilst eating.

'The disease may strike at any time and, when the onset is first experienced only after fifty years of age, the victim can continue with intellectually demanding work for many years, providing the subject is familiar.

'If either or both parents have the disease then one or more of their children will sooner or later suffer from it. However, since they may remain apparently healthy until they are middle-aged or older, they are likely to marry and infect further generations.

'Once the disease decides to show itself, the deterioration, though

often imperceptible day by day, is inexorable. The victim may suffer no physical problems for some years but his or her character will undergo insidious change. Friends and family will be upset and hurt. Divorce may follow. Inevitably, sooner or later, certain muscles will spasm and this will gradually spread through the body until each and every voluntary muscle is shaken puppet-like.'

'Luckily,' Macpherson commented, 'Bletchley never married.'

'Poor devil,' said Spike. 'I would not wish such horrors on any man.'

'He may yet write a book,' Macpherson said. 'He *may* retain at least partial clarity for years to come.'

44

Nine years after de Villiers's last meeting with Sheikh Amr, he returned to Dubai in November 1987 to collect the final payment of two million dollars from his son Bakhait. The assignment had cost him the lives of both his Clinic colleagues. Tadnams checked thoroughly but no whisper ever surfaced as to Davies's fate. De Villiers did not waste time, nor grey hairs, on useless theories.

In a way the deaths of his colleagues, assuming Davies *was* dead, were a bonus. Not only would the Dubai payout remain all his but any threat in years to come from ghosts in his past was minimized.

Bakhait's younger brother, the junior partner in their retailing empire, welcomed de Villiers but showed no interest in the purpose of his visit. That whole matter was nothing to do with anyone but Bakhait, who was absent. 'He has been in Iran for seven months now. I have done all I can to have him released.'

'Released?' De Villiers did not understand.

'Yes. He is in the Gohar Dasht prison. The *Pasdari*, the Revolutionary Guards, arrested him on some pretext of spying for Iraq. It is, of course, untrue although he spent much time on business in both countries. It is a trumped-up charge to earn foreign currency.'

'How so?' de Villiers asked.

'They knew I would send money to obtain his release. Those mullahs are devils. Each time they make contact, it is a different man

and each time it is to say they need more money. To carry out an investigation into my brother's innocence is, they maintain, a very expensive business.'

'So when will he be free?'

The Dhofari shook his head, his normally friendly face creased with worry. 'All I get is promises. I dare not hope too much any more. I continue to send the money and to look after his family. *Insh' Allah* he does not suffer and will come back to us soon.'

De Villiers contained his feelings. There was no good to be had from venting his frustration. He was owed two million dollars and, once he was paid, he was freed of any further involvement. No more contracts. No more contact with the agencies. Only Anne and La Pergole. He could see that fate had placed him in an impasse with no course of action other than patience. Bakhait was the only signatory to the cheques and de Villiers was not about to bust Bakhait from an ayatollah's jail.

De Villiers left Dubai with the promise that, as soon as Bakhait was released and returned home, Bakhait's younger brother would call him. He retained the video taken in Mac's bedroom as well as the report on the Clinic's relevant actions and Mac's obituary in the *Evening News*, a local Hereford paper.

45

... In July 1990, on a cool and lovely day, they rode through the vineyards to the Vrede Huis ruins and enjoyed the sunset as they discussed the summer house they planned to build in the clearing.

Anne must have caught a cold, or so de Villiers thought at first. Flu followed with a bad cough and breathlessness.

The doctor came but Anne did not respond to antibiotics. De Villiers drove her to the hospital with full-blown pneumonia and an X-ray showed that her lungs were infected by pneumocystis. There being nothing else wrong with her health, the doctors began to suspect the AIDS virus and, two days later, informed de Villiers that Anne was HIV positive. The doctors agreed that the source was

likely to have been the blood transfusion she had received after the road accident four years before.

De Villiers was devastated. He felt personally to blame. Anne appeared to take the news calmly. 'God will look after me,' she murmured. 'Will you be able to visit me, my love?'

He vowed to stay with her. He telephoned hospitals and specialists in Europe and the United States. He wanted only the very best treatment for Anne and the most up-to-date drugs. They had no insurance to cover treatment for an incurable disease and, as full-time, unpaid foreman at La Pergole, he had earned no money for three years. Jan Fontaine had left many bad debts and although they had coped by eating into his invested capital and then by selling off parts of the estate, de Villiers knew he could not hope to pay for the top-class treatment he was determined Anne should receive. For the present they remained in South Africa and he visited her daily. He became an avid reader of medical journals on all AIDS-related topics, searching for mentions of hopeful-sounding breakthroughs.

In the long hours spent by her bedside he marvelled at the unshakeable confidence and serenity Anne obtained through her religious beliefs. He too, for the first time in his life, began to think and talk about God; sometimes even to believe. He prayed for her deliverance, for a miracle cure or at least a remission.

There was plenty of time to reflect on his own life. Slowly, painfully, he allowed himself to think back through its dark pages, to ask for forgiveness and purge himself, one by one, of the killings.

The day came when, for the first time, he willed back the long-dormant memories, so long and forcefully shut away, of the colour and the horror of the night in Vancouver when his family died.

The little blonde Anna, his youngest sister: they had never found her body. Try as he might he could not bring back the details of her features. He saw only the face of his sleeping Anne and, confused subconsciously by all his medical reading, the dreadful marks of Karposi's Sarcoma ravaging her skin.

On 22 August he received a call at La Pergole from the Tadnams office in Earls Court. The client in Dubai required contact.

De Villiers telephoned and, to his surprise, was answered by Bakhait.

He told Anne, as he said goodbye, that he would return just as soon as he could. He would not go but for the fact that it was his best chance of paying for her treatment in Washington or Los

Angeles, in a place where he could have a bed beside hers, and where they might even have a cure before very long ...

46

In August 1990 Saddam Hussein ordered his troops to pull out of territory they had won from the Iranians after years of bitter fighting and at a cost of many lives. Towns that to Iraqis in 1990 meant as much as Verdun and Passchendaele to Europeans in the 1920s were given up overnight. The pull-out from Meymak, Mehran and the Kalleh Qandi heights in Ilem province was accompanied by Saddam's announcement of the release of some fifty thousand prisoners of war.

President Rafsanjani was naturally delighted by this unexpected largesse from his arch-enemy, and on 18 August the first one thousand Iraqi prisoners were released by Tehran. Bakhait came out with a later batch on 21 August and vowed never to do business with either country again.

After an extravagant welcome-back feast in Dubai and an updating on the affairs of the business, Bakhait learnt that de Villiers had, two years since, completed the *thaa'r*.

De Villiers could see immediately that Bakhait had not enjoyed his time in Iran. He was thin and cadaverous, his hair had receded and he walked with a faint stoop. Certainly he looked far older than his thirty-one years and had lost his natural bonhomie. Nevertheless, he made de Villiers welcome and apologized for his earlier absence.

After the customary coffee and small talk Bakhait studied the Clinic's written report on the location and identification stages of the fourth operation. He looked at the photographs, the medical reports and the obituary, then slotted the video in place and watched Mac, apparently listening from his bed, being accused by de Villiers of killing Bakhait's brother Mahad.

The Dhofari, showing no sign of emotion, wrote out a cheque for one million dollars.

'As regards the final payment, for completing the entire assignment, I have a single query. Yesterday I forced myself to review the earlier films. As you know I did not agree with the pursuance of this whole

matter, but I am a man of my word and I pledged my father on his deathbed that I would see the family *thaa'r* through to its end and re-establish our good name in our homeland.'

De Villiers nodded, quite unaware of what was to come.

'The Kealy film and the Marman video raise no doubts in my mind, but the Milling film should have been queried when first you showed it to me. I was at the time eighteen years old and I made the mistake of accepting evidence which, I can see now, will not only prove inadequate but may raise doubts in the minds of the relevant Jarboatis in Dhofar as to the correct identification of the killers of my other three brothers.'

The original Milling Super 8 film footage had been transferred on to video and together they watched as de Villiers accused John Milling of killing Salim bin Amr. When the film ended Bakhait raised his arms.

'Can you not see the problem?'

'No,' said de Villiers. 'I have no problem with that.'

'But Inspector Milling clearly states that he did *not* kill my brother Salim. He even tells you that the officer responsible for the ambush openly admitted his role in a book.'

'That is true,' de Villiers agreed, 'but I have experienced such flights of the imagination from condemned men on other occasions. It is not uncommon. If Milling had really known of such a book, he would certainly have known its title and the name of its author. He would have revealed both key points then and there. Surely you can see that?'

'You assume that he had no honour.' Bakhait gave a small smile. 'I look at this man Milling's face and I see a strong personality. A soldier who would not have another man killed to save his own neck.'

'With all due respect,' said de Villiers, 'I cannot agree with you. We are talking of a European, not a Muslim.'

'You are very cynical about your own race,' Bakhait commented.

'I am not European but, yes, I have over the years noted a different set of priorities between the true followers of Islam and the majority of Western Christians.'

Bakhait stared straight at de Villiers. The Dhofari's face was set. 'I cannot accept the *thaa'r* as settled nor my pledge complete until this is thoroughly checked out. Did you search at all for a book such as Milling refers to?'

251

'We contacted main retailers in New York and London. There was no such book available.'

'Does that mean it does not exist?'

'Not at all, but the circumstances did not warrant an exhaustive search due to the rationale I have already explained. It is conceivable that some officer had printed a book privately rather than through a known publisher. Or there may have been such a book but, by the time of our enquiry, it might have gone out of print, become unavailable.'

'So a more detailed check would be needed to entirely eliminate the possibility that Milling's "book" exists or existed?'

De Villiers nodded.

Bakhait was a successful businessman. Ambitious and anxious to make up time wasted in the stinking Iranian jail, he wished above all to succeed in his own homeland. He had complete confidence that he could expand the business not just to Muscat and Salalah but throughout Oman. He could become a senior citizen, a minister. There was no end to the possibilities. He already shone in the Gulf States but, as he had grown older, the urge for recognition in his own land had become a grail of which he had often dreamt in the long Tehran nights.

The other side of the coin was the *thaa'r*. The family of his cousin Hamoud would not wish to see him back. Without exoneration and acceptance by the Jarboati elders, he could never be safe, nor could his young family, without constant vigilance. He did not wish to spend his life looking over his shoulder.

He addressed de Villiers as he would his accountant. 'I would like you to check thoroughly the assertion of Inspector Milling. All your expenses will be covered. If, as I personally expect, you find that an error has been made, then that is God's will; you will not be to blame. But my father's wishes, to which I am bound, were to avenge all four killers of his sons, my brothers. One of these killers *may* still be alive. The payment cannot therefore be made. Either we must have incontrovertible proof that there is no such book and never was one or we discover that the book and the author exist, in which case you still have work to do.'

Between 1977 and 1990 considerable progress was made by many libraries and retailers in the computerization of their books by title

and by author. This did not help de Villiers, who knew neither detail. He knew only the subject matter and, to within five or six years, the publication date.

Back in London he visited a number of shops, starting with Hatchards and Harrods, then branching out to lesser known but well-stocked shops dealing in second-hand books. When asked, as he often was, for the book's general classification, he guessed at War, History and Arabia.

After a frustrating week, he finally made progress on 17 September. Arthur Probsthain & Co's Oriental Bookshop was one of many shops that he telephoned. The receptionist who answered his call passed him to a Mrs Sheringham, whose accent sounded Germanic and who, according to the receptionist, knew everything about every book ever published.

'Good afternoon, my name is Lawrence. I am researching on Middle East matters and am looking for a book on the Dhofar war in Oman, Arabia. Do you have anything that deals with the late-sixties period of that conflict?' After a number of forays from her end of the phone, the redoubtable Mrs Sheringham finally established three possible titles and their publishers.

Thanking her and cursing to himself, for he had earnestly hoped for a negative outcome to his search, he called the publisher of the most likely of the three titles, Hodder & Stoughton of Bedford Square in London. The receptionist passed de Villiers to the publicity department, as was her wont with all enquiries about non-current titles.

'Kate Farquhar-Thompson. Publicity. Can I help?'

'I believe you have a book about the Dhofar war in 1969 written by an ex-Army officer.' De Villiers gave her the title. 'Do you have a copy please, or know where I can get one?'

After several minutes the girl returned sounding pleased with herself. 'We have no copies left. It went out of print in early 1977, was reprinted in '78 and no copies have been available for eleven years. Sorry.'

'Is there no way I can borrow or copy some sort of master-copy of the book?'

'Not with us but maybe a second-hand bookshop, you never know.'

De Villiers could see he had run out of options. He contacted Tadnams for the first time in months and was relieved to find one of

his old contacts. It was agreed they would 'do a drag' for the book as soon as staff was available.

In fact de Villiers found the book for himself in a run-down antique shop in Kilburn. The book was battered and dog-eared with various paragraphs heavily underlined, some pages removed and comments scribbled in the margins by, de Villiers deduced, an ultra-left-wing student in the seventies.

He was charged twenty-five pence for the book and went back to his hotel to read the key passages.

There was no doubt in his mind. They should not have killed Milling. He could see only too clearly why the error had been made. At the time the Clinic knew only that their target was the white officer in charge of Operation Snatch. They had learned from Brigadier Maxwell and others that there was only one army unit in the region of Operation Snatch and that the only officer from that unit involved in Operation Snatch was the then Captain John Milling ... QED.

The book, however, now revealed to de Villiers that the *adoo* had been deceived into making more or less the same false assumption as had the Clinic. The Sultan's Intelligence Officer, one Tom Greening, was a clever sod who had secretly ordered up a roving desert unit from the South Yemen border zone and sent them by night to execute the ambush many hours away from their normal patrol area. Had the real Operation Snatch officer not written this book, Milling's identification would never have been questioned.

As it was, in the light of this new information de Villiers had no option but to call Bakhait.

'You are quite sure this is the man?' Bakhait asked.

'A hundred percent,' de Villiers replied. 'I have it in black and white.'

'Is he alive?'

'I believe so.'

'If he is, go ahead.'

De Villiers telephoned Tadnams. They suggested he check the *Who's Who of International Writers*. 'It gives all authors' updated addresses,' he was told.

47

Darrell Hallett had time on his hands. He had recently passed his yearly relicensing exams and continued success could mean promotion to Area Manager. Life-assurance sales was a highly competitive business and Hallett was determined to do well. Right now, however, after the exertions of the exams, he had given himself a few days' rest. He took his rod and tackle down to the river and spent many happy hours with the latest Colin Thubron book in his lap and a straw in his mouth.

Next day, 5 October, the weather precluded fishing, so he decided to pursue his other great hobby, collecting travel books. His favourite topics were sailing, mountaineering and wild river journeys, but he also collected all books by certain travel authors and, where possible, had them signed.

Hallett telephoned a number of publishers including Hodder & Stoughton, whose book list included more travel subjects than most of their competitors. Hallett was put through to Kate Farquhar-Thompson in the publicity department and he asked for a copy of a book about a Canadian river journey entitled *Headless Valley*. She disappeared, presumably to a computer.

'Sorry about the delay,' she said cheerily. 'It's odd. Someone rang not long ago about the same author. He wanted his book on some Arab war. I'm afraid it's the same for you as it was for him. We have no copies left. *Headless Valley* is out of print. You will have to try the second-hand shops. You could make a start with Foyles ... OK?'

She was about to ring off. He could hear her other phone.

'Wait a second,' he said.

'Yes?'

He paused, not quite certain what was niggling him.

'Listen. Thanks very much for your advice ... Can you tell me who called you about the Arab war book?'

'No,' she replied after a pause. 'Sorry, but it was two or three weeks ago and I get a lot of enquiries. I think he was foreign. Maybe American ... I think he mentioned Amman or Oman.'

He thanked her, rang off and reached for a brown book on his top bookshelf. It was a long shot but Hallett believed in the saying 'Better safe than sorry'. He called Spike.

Three days after Hallett's call to Kate Farquhar-Thompson, Colonel Macpherson caught the 4.15 p.m. shuttle flight from Glasgow and reached his home in Archery Close at 6.30. Spike's Mini was parked further down the cobbled mews.

After a dram, Macpherson led Spike through to an inner room.

'So they are back again?' he asked.

'There is that possibility, Colonel. It is a very slim lead; certainly not enough to enable us to entice the police into providing protection.'

'But enough to raise your concern or you wouldn't have brought me south in a rush.'

Spike nodded. 'I would hate to ignore it.'

'Very well,' said Macpherson. 'There's nothing to be lost, providing we have no repetition of the A49 event. Strangely enough, I met your new "target" about twelve years ago on an export promotion committee on to which I was inveigled by Campbell Adamson.'

'I will check on his background right away and start to alert the Locals,' said Spike.

'How many?' asked Macpherson.

'That may depend on where the target lives but, in principle, I would like to give this high priority. Two teams of four if I can find them.'

'I agree,' said Macpherson. 'Give it all you've got. I had stopped hoping we would ever catch these people, but I would pay a high price to run them to earth. I blame the demise of the Committee largely on them.'

'If they are free, I thought Mason and Hallett could each lead a team since both have been involved in this since the beginning. Mason probably even knows, or knows of, the target. All those types who served in Oman met up at one time or another.'

Macpherson nodded.

'Anything new on Bletchley?' Spike asked.

'I was going to tell you. Jane phoned just before I went north last week. She says Bletchley sounds pretty offhand when she calls, so she doesn't press him with too many questions. One thing she did mention was a complaint he made about his fingers. She says he is finding it increasingly difficult to type and he may hire a secretary.'

'Couldn't Jane suggest herself for the job?'

'My thoughts precisely. I put it to her but you know how reserved the dear lady is. I left it that there would be great benefits to all concerned if she were to become his assistant. She understands.'

'What if he goes ahead with the book?'

'Since there are no libel grounds to prevent him, we will just have to grin and bear it. Most of the Locals will be safe, but Mason, Hallett and others, whose signed reports were passed to Bletchley by Jane as part of those files, might be in trouble. God knows what he intends to say.'

'So will we,' Spike said, 'if Jane gets the job.'

Part 5

48

On Monday 22 October I returned late from the most northerly of our tree plantations. It was a fine evening and, with the tractor lights to help, I completed the staking of the rabbit tubes. From the boundary gate, and for some twelve miles to the west, the high wilderness of Exmoor stretched unbroken along the coastline of North Devon. I loved the place and although we had only been there six years we had planted sixteen thousand, mostly deciduous, trees. My wife bred Aberdeen Angus cattle and St John waterdogs and my job as European representative of the well-known, nonagenarian oil magnate, Dr Armand Hammer, had helped us to turn the long-neglected land into a working smallholding.

I was worried, for Dr Hammer was not well and I could see the spectre of unemployment looming ahead. To avert the likelihood of no income in the near future, I had begun, in my spare time, to write a novel about Iran. It was close to completion. Another three months perhaps and I would approach a literary agent.

The tractor descended the steep cleeve and the lights of our house flickered through the trees. All electrical power was supplied by a twenty-two-year-old generator. All water for the house and for the cattle arrived by gravity along a hosepipe from a distant spring. There were no deliveries of milk or papers. In short, a pleasantly cut-off atmosphere.

I put the tractor in its garage. As I looked east over the Brendon Hills, the entire countryside was dark. Not a single light was to be seen for seven miles, for the Exmoor folk sensibly build their homes down in the valleys.

We lived at fourteen hundred feet above sea level and the winds that evening blew fresh over Hurdledown and Badgeworthy. My wife heard me removing my boots.

'What about the rubbish?' she shouted from the kitchen.

'What about supper?' I responded.

'It'll wait,' she assured me.

Every Monday evening, when in Exmoor, I take the week's accumulated rubbish in black bags to the stipulated roadside collection point a mile away. It is just about the only thing I ever do on a regular basis because my work in London, and lectures all over the place, run to no set schedule. The bags are best left out as late as possible before their early-morning collection by the council truck. The foxes attack the bags and strew the contents all over the place if given more than a few hours' notice of their presence.

At 8 p.m. I hitched the trailer, full of rubbish bags, to my wife's ancient Montego estate and drove up the long, narrow lane known as the Drift Road. A trio of long-horned Highland cattle blocked the lane and ignored my hooting. I eventually edged them on to the verge. Then, on rounding the last bend before the lane reaches the moor road, I found a car parked in the middle of the lane. With the support of the local Master of Foxhounds, Captain Ronnie Wallace, I had agreed with the Exmoor Park Department to erect a large sign saying 'Bridle Path Only' to keep cars out, so I was annoyed, to put it mildly.

Lovers, I presumed, hard at it in the back.

But the car, a black Volvo estate, was empty. I had no torch but I noticed an unusual modification to its front bumper, rather like an improvised steel snow-clearing blade.

I returned to the Montego intending to hoot loudly, since I presumed the occupants were nearby in the grass. Something, a noise or a brief flash of light, attracted my attention to the old barn on the far side of the hedge. My wife had rented this barn for some years for storing hay and had recently complained of missing bales. At £2.75 each this was serious, so I forgot the missing Volvo lovers and, fetching a tyre lever from the Montego, climbed the five-bar gate and quietly entered the barn.

As I moved between the two tiers of bales, a torch was switched on immediately ahead, blinding me. A voice from behind the light ordered, 'Drop it'.

As far as I could tell, four torches were being directed at me, and I was herded to the empty side of the barn.

'Sit down.'

I sat on a bale, totally bewildered. Perhaps these were anti-hunt saboteurs. Such people had recently been active in the area. Since neither of us had hunted for years this solution did not seem very

likely. Maybe they wanted to steal the Montego. They were welcome. It was battered and scarred.

My eyes began to accustom themselves to the torchlight. I saw one of the men set up a video camera on a tripod and another threw on to my lap a copy of a book I had written many years before entitled *Where Soldiers Fear to Tread*.

The hay smelled very good, very sweet. I was sweating and realized that I felt afraid.

One of the men began to address me, his accent not dissimilar to that of my American godmother from Connecticut.

'In that book, Captain Fiennes, you admit to shooting and killing a Dhofari named Salim bin Amr, on the morning of 18 October 1969. Is this true?'

I could not see the face of the speaker behind the torch. The man must be mad.

'If I wrote that in this book then, of course, it is true,' I replied.

'So you admit to the murder of that person?' His voice was level and humourless. Not the voice of a nutter or a crank. My confusion was turning to apprehension.

'Of course not.' I could hear the edge of fear in my voice and feel it in the pit of my stomach. 'I have never murdered anyone. Never. You are talking about military actions, not murder, and at least twenty years ago. This is absurd. What do you want?'

Unbidden, and in the space of mere seconds, my memory played back the long-ago events in Dhofar, twenty-one years ago almost to the day.

We sat in the centre of the wide wadi Habarut, halfway between the two whitewashed forts and exactly astride the unmarked border between Dhofar and South Yemen. My companion was the garrison commander of the communist forces, who was threatening retaliation for an incident provoked by a Dhofari tribesman. I offered him two hundred Rothmans cigarettes. He settled for four hundred.

My signaller called. A Priority Message from my boss, Colonel Peter Thwaites: Go at once to Thamrait. We drove east through the heat-shimmer of the gravel steppes and reached the base by noon.

Tom Greening, the Sultan's Intelligence Officer, was there with new orders. I was to go that night on to the *jebel* and, some fourteen miles into *adoo*-held territory, at the village of Qum, capture two communist leaders and bring them back to him alive. He introduced

to me a Mahra tribesman, a decidedly shifty-looking character who, he said, would be our guide. My men were appalled. This *jebali* was an *adoo* spy. We would be led into a trap. We would be cut off and killed to a man in the military heartland of the *adoo*.

I could see my men's point of view. Just one wounded man would put us in a potentially disastrous position. As twenty-six, fit and able soldiers, my platoon normally relied on speed, night travel and silence to survive. We would set out ambushes and then withdraw without delay back to the safety of the desert. Our greatest fear was to be cut off on the *jebel*. We had no stretchers, no mules, no helicopter assistance and, in the area Greening had indicated, no other army back-up to help us.

But orders were orders, so we drove south to the well of O'bet at dusk and climbed to the escarpment. After some miles we entered the foliated region of the *jebel* and behind us I saw flares fired into the air.

My sergeant whispered: 'We are cut off. We must return by a different route.'

But we marched on through the night with our heavy loads of ammunition and water. No compass could have guided us along the confusing route of camel paths that meandered up and down deep wadis where no Sultanate troops had previously been fool enough to wander.

Within the thick screen of thorn bush and creeper that crammed the defiles, there was no room to manoeuvre off the narrow paths. Mosquitoes attacked in whining clouds and a sticky heat emanated from the foliage. After ten hours we came to a place of skull-like stones that littered the fields of knee-high grass. We stumbled and fell. I began to fear that dawn would find us short of Qum.

Dark amorphous shapes blobbed the upper slopes of the surrounding hills: wild fig trees and cattle kraals of thorn. Twice we passed the acrid tang of burning dung. To the south-east a patch of spreading grey crept into the blue-black sky.

The guide raised his hand. The village, he indicated, was directly below us. I moved with speed to place the sections before first light. Four or five men to a group, each with a machine-gun, each hidden in clumps of thorn above and around the unseen houses. At last, with my own four-man section, we burrowed into a hollow-centred thicket with a floor of stones.

We slept for an hour with one man on watch. On waking I saw

hummingbirds hovering and darting in the chintz ceiling of our hide. Through a break in the thorns I looked south at the scattered huts below and the rolling green land all about us. Beyond the rim of the mountains the Plain of Salalah was edged by the distant blue of the Indian Ocean.

Four men in dark-brown uniforms moved from hut to hut below us. Through binoculars we counted some sixty or seventy armed men to the immediate south of the village, a mile or so away. They were preparing some sort of fortification.

Since waking I had felt sick with stomach pains; nothing new, for they had come frequently in the desert. Perhaps the water or the goat meat caused the trouble. Normally I could rush to some bush or rock and squat behind it for relief and to wait for the pains to pass. Then the sickness would abate, leaving me weak and sweating. But now there was nowhere to go but outside the thorn walls. To emerge even momentarily would put us all in great danger.

For an hour we had been forced to beckon passing villagers into our thicket at gunpoint for fear that, having spotted us, they might alert the *adoo*. The tiny hide was overcrowded. I built a parapet of rocks around my backside, between me and the others, and lowered my trousers just as my insides seemed to give way to an agonizing flood. At once the flies swarmed into the thicket. I used rocks instead of paper and collapsed the little 'cubicle' on to the results of my personal crisis. Not a moment too soon.

As I wiped the sweat from my eyes I sensed movement outside the hide. Quietly I slid my rifle towards me and released the safety-catch.

A narrow goat trail ran between our thicket and the top of a steep, grassy slope. Two tall men were approaching fast along it. I noticed their dark clothes and the glint of guns in their hands; also the polished red badge on the cap of the second man. It was not the tiny Mao button-badge worn by many of the *adoo* but the hexagonal red star of a political commissar.

These were our men. I was sure of it. There was no time to think. They were fifteen yards away; soon they would see us. The first man stopped abruptly, seeming to sniff the air. His face was scarred, his hair close shaven. I watched fascinated as the Kalashnikov, its ugly round magazine cradled in his elbow, swung around as the man turned to face us. A Kalashnikov is an unpleasant weapon; a touch of its trigger will squeeze off a long burst of hollow-nosed 7.62

bullets that tear bone apart and pass through a man's guts as they would through papier mâché.

Inch by inch I lifted my rifle. The sun was in the east behind the man, outlining him. Only his shadow falling on the thicket shielded my eyes, stinging with sweat, from the direct glare. He peered straight at me now. I remember thinking, 'He has seen us. He is weighing his chances.'

My voice seemed to come of its own volition. 'Drop your weapons or we will kill you.'

The big man moved with incredible speed, twisting at the knee and bringing the Kalashnikov to bear in a single, fluid movement. I squeezed the trigger automatically. The guerrilla was slammed backwards as though caught in the chest by a sledgehammer. His limbs spread like a puppet and he cartwheeled out of sight down the grassy slope.

Behind him the other man paused for a moment, unsure what to do. I became aware of his face beneath the jungle cap.

He looked sad and faintly surprised. His rifle, a Mark IV.303, was already pointed at my stomach when a flurry of shots rang out. Two of my section fired simultaneously.

The man's face crumpled into a bloody pulp: the nose and eyes smashed back into the brain. Bullets tore through his ribs and a pretty flowering thorn bush caught his body at the top of the grassy slope.

My signaller crawled on his belly from the thicket. There might be other *adoo* behind these two. Expertly he searched the corpse, bringing back rifle, ammunition and a large satchel stuffed with documents.

I glanced south: the bush was glinting with movement, dark forms scurrying towards us through the scrub. There was little time for making decisions; the other sections would be awaiting orders.

I flicked the national radio switch, no longer bothering to whisper. 'All stations! Five! Withdraw now ... over.'

Fatigue forgotten, the men needed no encouragement and broke from their hides to fan out in a long, straggling line. Speed was their only hope and they moved with the wings of fear. Shots sounded from behind but no intercepting group materialized in front of us and the *adoo* never quite caught up with our retreat.

Back in Thamrait the soldiers slept like dead men but I found sleep elusive. I had often shot at people hundreds of yards away, vague shapes behind rocks who were busy firing back; but never before had

I seen a man's soul in his eyes, sensed his vitality as a fellow human and then watched his body ripped apart at the pressure of my finger.

I tried to force away the image of his destruction but his scarred face stayed watching me from my subconscious. A part of me that was still young and uncynical had died with him and his comrade, the commissar, spread-eagled on a thorn bush.

The memory passed as quickly as it came. The man behind the torch spoke again. 'The need for justice is not eliminated by the passage of time. You will go now back to your car and drive to the point where you dispose of the bags every week on Monday evening. You will get out and unload the bags. No more, no less. Do nothing stupid, for we will have you covered at all times.'

One of the man's colleagues hissed for silence, whispering, 'I saw movement by the roadside.'

Two men went out to check. I could see little, my vision impaired by the torchlight.

It must have been a false alarm, for the men returned and I was prodded back to the Montego's driving seat, one man climbing into the seat beside me. My brain raced. I remembered the old army maxim taught during resistance to interrogation training: make your escape move as *soon* as possible after being caught. Desperately I tried to concoct a workable plan.

My passenger spoke. He had a hard, East London accent. 'Wait until the Volvo moves out. Then go. They will turn left out of the lane. You go right and down the hill as you normally do. Do not exceed fifteen miles per hour.' My brain continued to race, but in neutral. No plan of action materialized. I felt like a rabbit in the presence of snakes.

I counted four men climbing into the Volvo immediately ahead. As the fourth closed his door, it happened. From the lane's T-junction with the road some fifteen yards ahead, an intense white light beamed down the lane. My eyes hurt and I turned away, clutching at them and fearing I was blinded. I expected the sound of bullets and shrank back behind the steering wheel. But I heard only the noise of breaking glass and a quickly cut-off scream.

The passenger door of the Montego was flung open and the man beside me disappeared as though sucked from the car. The all-consuming light was switched off and the night was black as pitch, the silence punctured only by the sound of oaths and muffled violence.

This tailed away but for the scuff of rubber soles on tarmac. Then a car started up and someone climbed into the Montego. I felt a hand grip my shoulder and a friendly voice said, 'Cheer up. They've all gone. You're in no danger.'

My vision slowly began to return.

'Thank you, officer,' I said. 'Are you from Dulverton, or Minehead?' I found myself naming the two district police stations.

'Don't you worry where we're from. Just hang on right there a minute and I'll explain.'

Dimly I saw a vehicle reverse into the lane with only its side lights on; almost certainly a Range Rover, judging by its silhouette. On its roof an orange glow and the glinting parabola of a satellite dish, probably the light source. Doors slammed and the vehicle accelerated away. A large van then reversed towards us, similar to a standard high-roofed Transit laundry van. The back doors were opened and an interior roof light revealed an empty, cell-like cargo space lined with mattresses.

Four men approached the Montego, all with dark ski-goggles hanging loose round their necks and carrying what appeared to be police truncheons. Their faces were streaked with black lines and unrecognizable. The man beside me spoke rapidly and the others dispersed. Soon I watched as five figures, all with their hands on their heads, entered the rear of the van. The doors were closed and the vehicle drove off, heading north towards Porlock.

'Come back for a drink,' I said, trying to make out the features of my rescuer. 'I would like my wife to meet you. I really can't thank you enough. Who were those people?'

'Call me Spike,' he shook my hand. 'Don't be surprised but I am not from the police nor are my men. We are your friends and we have hunted those men for a long time. A very long time. Who were they? Well, that will take a wee while to explain.'

'Whoever you represent, Spike, I will forever be grateful, but come back to the house ...'

He lifted his hand. 'Do you trust me?' he asked quietly.

'Of course.'

'Listen. I have a great deal to do and very little time. I must ask you to speak to no one at all about all this. Your car is undamaged. No one has touched you. The police will think you have had a bad dream, to put it politely, if you tell them what happened. They will ask what has been stolen and they will look for motives.'

He paused but I said nothing. I could see the sense of his words.

'On Thursday you will be driving to London. Correct?'

'Why, yes. How do you know?' I asked.

'Never mind. Come to this address at 11.30 p.m.,' he said, scribbling on the back of a card and giving it to me, 'and I will personally explain everything. Until then tell no one, not even your wife. There's no point in upsetting her. Remember this, you are no longer in any danger. *All* those who wished you ill are accounted for. OK? Do you agree?'

I felt I could trust this man. His features were clearer to me now. He had a large, careworn face. His gravelly voice was North Country and steady.

'No problem,' I told him. 'I will see you on Thursday and talk to no one.'

He shook my hand again. 'You'd better dump the rubbish and get back home or your wife will think the Highland cows got you.' He smiled and left. His car must have been along the Porlock road.

I emptied the trailer and returned home. My wife seemed to notice nothing amiss. 'Your supper's in the oven,' she said.

49

On Thursday, 25 October 1990 I represented Dr Hammer at the annual dinner of the International Board of the United World Colleges. Many members from various countries, such as Sonny Ramphal, the Secretary General of the Commonwealth, had come to say farewell to their long-serving Director, who happened to be a personal friend of mine. I was very sorry indeed to see him go, but my mind was filled with curiosity and a certain degree of apprehension about my imminent visit to see the man called Spike.

From the dinner in Mecklenburgh Square I drove my American colleagues back to Claridges, then walked through Grosvenor Square, and reached the address in South Audley Street at 11.30 p.m.

Spike, respectable in a grey suit, ushered me into the hallway. The house appeared to be both office and home, well furnished but

functional, and we climbed the stairs to a sitting room, expensively decorated, where Spike introduced me to the 'Colonel', a fit-looking man, probably in his late sixties. I recognized him at once although at least ten years had passed since the days of the committee meetings in which we had both participated.

'You are surprised?' Colonel Macpherson smiled. 'Wondering perhaps how I could possibly be involved with such reprobates as Spike here? I will explain. Do sit down.'

He sat behind a fine, dark desk and, a master of economy with words, explained that he was part of a small group of people around the country who, for a dozen years and more, had hunted a band of contract killers in the pay of a Dubai merchant. These men sought to carry out revenge murders in return for the deaths of the merchant's four sons during the Dhofar fighting in the late sixties and early seventies.

I shook my head in amazement. Had such a tit-for-tat feud involved the IRA, I could easily have believed it, but all the Arabs I had ever known were gentle folk who believed in the will of Allah and seldom bore grudges. Nevertheless, the Colonel was deadly serious and I could certainly think of no other possible rationale for the events in the barn.

'May I ask what happened to the other men they were after?'

Macpherson shook his head sadly. 'Our people were not able to prevent their deaths. In your case we were in the right place at the right time. We had watched them watching you for the previous three weeks, but we were never sure where they would strike until one of our men pointed out that your only recurrent weekly activity was your dustbin removal. We predicted their strike and Spike was ready with eight others and suitable gear.'

'And the killers? Where are they now?'

Macpherson looked at me closely. 'Ranulph, I know something of your past. I know that your non-fiction books have sold well, that you were in the SAS and, of course, the Sultan's Armed Forces. Fate has brought you into contact with us, however briefly, and at the same time into contact with the contract killers.'

He paused, but I made no comment.

'After much soul-searching, we have reached a decision. This has been forced upon us and we do not take it lightly. It is the lesser of two evils. We have reason to believe that one of our past members, now an ill man, intends to publish a book about our existence and

our past activities. This book will be a sadly warped version of the truth.' He turned to Spike and nodded. 'Go ahead.'

'Rather than have this happen,' Spike said, 'we have concluded that we need the true story told.' I listened carefully, for his voice was low and expressionless. 'The other would-be author must find that he has been pre-empted and no publisher will reckon it commercially worthwhile to take on his vitriolic tale.'

'May I ask how you are so sure this other man's account will be as you describe it?'

'We have a lady friend,' Spike replied, 'who works as his secretary. About two weeks ago she saw the outline synopsis of his work – a tissue of distortion, as she described it – and was horrified.'

He tapped two folders that lay on his lap. She has copied a series of papers held by this man ... I will call him Bletchley ... and given them to us. They are the detailed reports by our field operators on their attempts to catch the contract killers. Bletchley intends to base his book very largely on these papers, so we must do the same. We always protect the names of our people, but some will, through these files, be known to Bletchley and we can, if you decide to write our book, make them available to you along with the contents of these files.'

'What other materials would I have?' I asked.

'The full and very detailed results of my debriefing of the senior contract killer. It amounts to his life story and, contrary to what you might expect, is not that of an archetypal villain. You will also be able to ask me whatever questions you feel appropriate and necessary to complete your account of the events.'

'Is the aim to produce a story of your group's history?'

'Negative. We can tell you only about our involvement in the long hunt for the people who planned to kill you on Monday.'

My head swam. I never sit on decisions. I believe in intuition. If I were to agree to this book, I would have to shelve my novel and many months of work on it. On the other hand, I could always publish the novel in a year or two, whereas this offer was on a 'now or never' basis. There was another issue too. I instinctively liked these people and felt a deep, personal gratitude to them.

'Spike, Colonel, I do not want to sound ungrateful but I must ask you three upfront queries. It may take me a long time to write your book, assuming I find a literary agent willing to take it on. I am expecting to lose my job with Armand Hammer in the near future

and I have a wife and farm to support. Will the revenue from the book be mine?'

'All of it,' Macpherson replied. 'We want only a widely-published work giving a fair and balanced picture of the events.'

'Secondly,' I pressed, 'since it is my name that will appear as author, any libel suits that may result will be directed at me, not you. I will, therefore, need to go and see anybody mentioned by name, even the next of kin of the dead men, to obtain their approval.'

Again Macpherson nodded. 'Obviously the next of kin will know nothing of the killers, but they will be able to tell you what they think happened to their husbands. So you will be able to cross-check what we tell you.'

'Good. My third point concerns my own safety. How will I know that the people in Dubai will not hire other men to kill me?'

Spike smiled. 'You have my personal assurance. One of our men will be in Dubai next week. You will never be troubled again.'

'I will write your book,' I told them, 'providing the facts tally and, of course, assuming I can find an agent and publisher.'

We shook hands. For the next three weeks, whenever my normal work allowed, I met Spike in the same room, and together we prepared a framework by which I could relate the events accurately but in a readable manner. For a while there were two areas of disagreement. I needed the real name of a real person within the Feather Men in order to authenticate the book.

'You have at least twenty real names already,' Spike had protested.

'I do not have yours or the Colonel's.'

'You do,' he replied with a smile. 'Simply check the names of your 1979 Export Committee.' He became serious. 'We had already identified the need for an indisputable means of authentication. Much as the Colonel dislikes the idea, there is no alternative. You will have his identity.'

'And yours?'

'That,' said Spike, 'will not be necessary.'

My second problem was an inability to explain to prospective readers, at an early stage of the book, the nature of the work of the Feather Men. I needed a single example, but Spike refused with persistence. Involvement with the killers, yes; any other operation, definitely not. In the end I made my point and was given an account of a 1976 action in Bristol involving two of Spike's men whose identities would anyway be revealed by the book.

On 6 November, Spike informed me that the man he had sent to Dubai, his Arab specialist, had just called him. He had seen the sheikh the previous day and shown him a photograph of de Villiers in captivity as well as the video taken in the Exmoor barn. Under threat of exposure to the Royal Oman Police and the British authorities, the sheikh had handed over the original films and video copies of the previous activities by the killers. He also promised, in the name of God, that he would cease all further involvement with his father's *thaa'r*. The aim of his father had been to reinstate his sons in Dhofar. That, he could see, was no longer an option.

During the winter of 1990 and the following spring I traced and visited twenty-six people who were still alive and, wittingly or unwittingly, had been involved with the events of Spike's story. Some aspects of his account initially struck me as implausible in the extreme but again and again I found that the facts and the figures tallied.

Since none of those I approached knew of, or even suspected, the contract killers' intentions, I had to present the series of events, especially the point where their own lives had been affected, as pure hypothesis. This was especially important in the case of the next of kin of the four men, whom I had no wish to alarm or distress.

After reading the field reports of Spike's Locals I met three of them and tried to get to grips with their personal motivations and memories of the events. As they were instinctively reticent I was not as successful as I would have wished, except in the case of David Mason, with whom I was at an advantage as I had known him in Oman, in Antarctica and in London. I had always thought of him as a rather cool and arrogant individual. But after three long interviews with him to discuss his reports in depth, I came away with a very different picture. He cared deeply for certain principles and people. His strength of character and the depth of his resolve were awesome. I would not have wanted him as an enemy.

I decided to include the SAS Headquarters in my list of people to visit, but Spike advised against it. 'They will kick you out of the door, Ran. Forget it. Any non-curricular activity is anathema to them. They know nothing about us nor have we ever involved any of their members, past or present.'

Spike was also reticent when pressed about the fate of the surviving contract killer and his cronies from the agency.

'Are they dead?' I asked.

'No,' he replied.

'Did you pass him to the police?'

'No.'

'Why not?'

'He would have walked free from any court. We had no proof. No evidence. His defence lawyer would have laughed our story right out of the Old Bailey and all the way back to Dhofar.'

'Do you believe what he told you?'

'Yes, strange as it may seem. But I do.'

'He need have told you nothing.'

'What he told me tallies with the events. Have you not found that in your recent research?'

I had to admit this was true. 'Where, if you have released him, is he now?'

'NTK,' said Spike. 'Neither you nor our book *needs to know.*'

I could see he would not budge. 'What happened to his girlfriend, or rather wife, Anne? I can hardly write a book leaving such items in mid-air. A reader would want to know.'

'Too bad,' said Spike.

I gave up asking. In the spring and summer of 1991 I described these events with complete attention to accuracy. Some of the dialogue and the emotions, the inner thoughts and the assumptions are, of course, mine. In fiction there is always a villain. But real life does not fit into neat themes. To my mind Sheikh Amr and his son Bakhait were honourable men. De Villiers was dealt the cruellest of blows in childhood. Evil, like good fortune, can arrive on the wind and out of the clouds, attributable merely to the whim of Fate.

As to my own chance involvement in these events, I am truly thankful that the Feather Men exist, or existed. Without them I suspect there would have been a hit-and-run accident on an October night on the Porlock Road. I am, I suspect, only one of many people in Britain who, over the past twenty years, have good reason to be grateful for their protective presence. Otherwise, my life has changed not at all except that I no longer take the rubbish out after dark. I leave the bags out during the daylight hours and to hell with the foxes.

EPILOGUE

Neither Colonel Macpherson nor Spike Allen ever divulged to me the identity of the Committee's Founder, but the week before I met them there was an Associated Press news release:

'David Stirling, Founder of Elite British Unit, Dies
LONDON – Colonel Sir David Stirling, 74, who in World War II founded the Special Air Service, an elite British special forces unit, died Sunday after a long illness, according to his biographer, Alan Hoe.

The Special Air Service, or SAS, with its motto 'Who Dares Wins', remained on active duty after the war and has kept its reputation for swift, clandestine and effective action.

Born Archibald David Stirling on November 15, 1915, the son of a Scottish brigadier general, he joined the Scots Guards at the outbreak of World War II. Six months later, he transferred to No. 3 Commando Group of the Brigade of Guards and went with them to the Middle East.

He persuaded military authorities that "an army within an army" was needed to make secret raids against the enemy. With six officers and sixty enlisted men, he became known as the "Phantom Major" among the troops of Field Marshal Erwin Rommel's Afrika Korps after destroying at least 250 enemy aircraft and scores of fuel and ammunition dumps in attacks behind German lines.

In 1943, Colonel Stirling was taken prisoner in Tunisia. He escaped, was recaptured and was transferred to Colditz Castle prison camp in Germany, where he remained a captive for the rest of the war . . .'

On the morning of Thursday 12 February 1991 an IRA action unit mortared the Gulf War Cabinet meeting of Prime Minister John Major at 10 Downing Street while, a few hundred yards away at the Wellington Barracks, a great assembly of SAS men, past and present, converged to pay their last respects to the Phantom Major.

Sir Fitzroy Maclean, giving tribute to the man whose name would always be synonymous with the Special Air Service, mentioned that, 'Even his closest friends seldom knew what he was up to.'

The keening notes of 'Flowers of the Forest' played by a single Scots piper reached out from the Guards Chapel to the deserted streets of Whitehall and across the frozen lakes of St James's Park.

Colonel Tommy Macpherson and Spike Allen knelt in different pews to the words of the Celtic Blessing:

> Deep peace of the running wave to you
> Deep peace of the flowing air to you
> Deep peace of the quiet earth to you
> Deep peace of the shining stars to you
> Deep peace of the Son of Peace to you ...

Outside the snowflakes settled, light as feathers, over Whitehall.

OMAN IN 1976

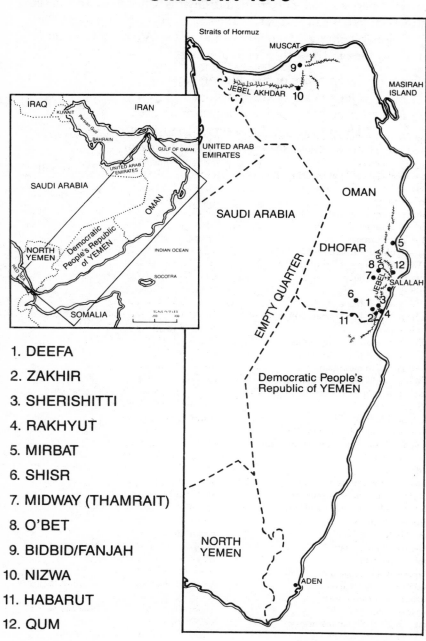

1. DEEFA

2. ZAKHIR

3. SHERISHITTI

4. RAKHYUT

5. MIRBAT

6. SHISR

7. MIDWAY (THAMRAIT)

8. O'BET

9. BIDBID/FANJAH

10. NIZWA

11. HABARUT

12. QUM

GLOSSARY

57-pattern – type of military body harness and belt used by infantry (lighter than carrying a rucksack)

abra – local type of boat used in Dubai creeks

adoo – enemy

arrondisement – district

ayeb – in disgrace

baht – Thai currency

bedu-ar-ruhhal – true desert bedouin

Bin Dhahaib unit – a PFLO regiment

brocanteur – antique dealer

cochin – pig

dhille – metal coffee-pot

dishdash – skirt-like wraparound garment worn in Oman

DMS – rubber-soled army boots

falaj – underground water canal

Fan – Pen y Fan mountain

fardh – a subdivision of the sharia

firqat – group of ex-communists fighting for the Sultan's forces

FST – Field Surgery Team

gatn – dry mountain zone in Dhofar

geh schnell, mach schnell, man – get a move on, man

ghadaf – palm

ghazu – inter-tribal raid

hadiyth – the Prophet's sayings

indee mushkila – I have a problem

Ingleezi – English

Insh' Allah – God willing

jebali – mountain man

jebel – mountain

jellaba – Arab female attire

khadim – slave, ex-slave

khareef – monsoon (mist)

khayma – tent

laqat – high-quality frankincense

LAW – anti-tank rocket

leaguer up – to make camp (usually temporary halt only)

loomee – lime

majlis – inner 'socializing' room

MAM – the headquarters complex of the Sultan's forces

MFO – Military Forwarding Organization

min fadlak – please

Muaskar al Murtafa'a *see* MAM

mughir – incense tree of a type to be found in arid gravel desert

muqanat – killers, falaj-diggers

murrim – compacted dirt

nejd – arid desert region

OG – green cotton uniform worn by British Army in jungle regions

PMN – Anti-Personnel Mine

qadhi – religious judge

qithit – blood-money

rashiyd – wise man

RMP – Royal Military Police

SAF – Sultan's Armed Forces

sanuk – Thai beverage

sharia – Islamic rules

shebeen – illegal drinks party

shemagh – headcloth

shimaal – dry desert wind from the north

sooq – market

sous-chef – underchef

tamimah – headman of local tribe

tapineuse – entrepreneur/freelance prostitute

thaa'r – blood feud/revenge killing

travelo – transvestite

tuk-tuk – Thai rickshaw

va te faire sauter ailleurs, conasse – rude comment

Wahidaat a Wasata wa Sharqeeya – a PFLO regiment

wizaar – Arab wraparound robe

Index

INDEX